DATE DUE

5-16-05			

LOEB CLASSICAL MONOGRAPHS

❧ ❧ ❧ ❧

In Memory of
JAMES C. LOEB

ANCIENT
RHETORICAL THEORIES
OF SIMILE
AND COMPARISON

Marsh H. McCall, Jr.

❧ ❧ ❧ ❧

HARVARD UNIVERSITY PRESS

CAMBRIDGE, MASSACHUSETTS · 1969

*The Loeb Classical Monographs are published with
assistance from the Loeb Classical Library Foundation.*

Distributed in Great Britain by Oxford University
Press, London

Library of Congress Catalog Card Number 71–88807

SBN 674–03430–9

Printed in the United States of America

To My Parents

PREFACE

The subject treated in this study evolved from a somewhat different plan of work. I had started an investigation of Vergil's similes, not so much their symbolic aspects as their formal and rhetorical construction and use. The first step was to trace pre-Vergilian views on simile that might have influenced Vergil's own approach. No great obstacles threatened. The modern English concept of simile is clear enough, and Western literature for many centuries has recognized the power and charm of Homeric and Vergilian similes, to mention only those two ancient authors in whom the use of simile is perhaps most prominent. In addition, modern scholarship is filled with references not only to actual similes in ancient literature but also to comments and discussion of simile by ancient literary critics and rhetoricians. It was a matter of considerable surprise, therefore, that, as the ancient testimony was examined, the assumption that simile was being discussed came repeatedly under suspicion. Increasingly the possibility suggested itself that in reality there was no true concept in ancient literary criticism of simile as a rhetorical figure separate from other forms of comparison or illustration. If this were indeed the case, it would be difficult to establish any pre-Vergilian ideas of simile.

At this point, it seemed prudent to abandon—for the time being, at least—the original Vergilian investigation and to pursue further the question of the presence or absence of an ancient concept of simile. The problem seemed, and seems, to be the following. The English term "simile" refers very specifically to a comparison stated by means of an introductory comparative word or phrase. An example might be from Wordsworth:

> I wandered lonely as a cloud
> That floats on high o'er vales and hills.

There appear to be two major types of simile. One, with equal development of subject and comparative parts, generally takes the form *just as . . . so. . . .* The other develops only the subject or the comparative part and generally takes either the form *subject, verb, like/as, comparative part developed,* as in the Wordsworth lines, or the form *subject part developed, like/as, a single noun,* as in two more lines from Wordsworth:

> The winds that will be howling at all hours,
> And are up-gathered now like sleeping flowers.

Such handbook definitions of simile as "a simile is always a comparison; but a comparison is by no means always, and still less often deserves to be called, a simile . . . the simile is known by its *as* or *like* or other announcement of conscious comparison" or "a simile declares that A is like B and uses the word *as* or *like*"[1] reenforce the common understanding of the term. The technical terminology of English literary criticism will not easily accept under the rubric "simile" such a conditional comparison as "if wolves care for their young, so also should we cherish children," or such a causative comparison as "since trees are seen to put forth buds after a long winter, so also should men expect an appearance of happiness after a time of bad fortune," or such an illustrative comparison as "the sea brings destruction upon towns not provided with a sea wall; war, my friends, will destroy those who are unprepared for defense." In each of these examples there is an element of comparison; none of them, however, is in form a simile.

The situation in English critical terminology, then, is relatively

---

[1] H. W. Fowler, *A Dictionary of Modern English Usage* (Oxford: Clarendon Press, 1927) 535–536; *Crowell's Dictionary of English Grammar*, ed. M. H. Weseen (New York: Thomas Y. Crowell, 1928) 582.

clear, and the problem becomes this: are there critical terms in Greek and Latin that are used to denote as specific and restricted a figure as the English simile. The principal Greek and Latin terms are the following: εἰκών, εἰκασία, ὁμοίωσις, παραβολή, *collatio*, *comparatio*, *imago*, *similitudo*. Each of these terms, either in general or as used in certain contexts, has repeatedly received the translation "simile." The very number of the terms creates an initial doubt. Granting that critical vocabulary is one of the more inconstant elements of a language, is it likely that four Greek and four Latin terms are all limited to the single idea of simile? Of course not, but the question is phrased incompletely. Almost all ancient technical terms were originally nontechnical in meaning, and the ones listed here are no exception. Thus, for example, before being used as a rhetorical term, εἰκών meant "statue" or "portrait" or "image." The question, therefore, should be put differently: in contexts of rhetoric and literary criticism, is there a regular use of any or all of the terms under consideration in a meaning of "simile" such as can lead to recognition of an ancient concept of simile. If not, then what can the use of these terms tell about ancient ideas of comparison in general? It has been indicated above that the answer to the first query is repeatedly a negative one, and the focus has become the second, larger question, which still easily includes a recurring glance at the former, more limited point. The present study, then, seeks through a detailed analysis of such terms of comparison as are listed above to arrive at the ancient understanding of the nature, scope, and purpose of comparison. Further, and more specifically, the ancient use of the terms is divided between contexts describing the general act or process of comparison and contexts in which a figure of comparison is present, and this study is concerned primarily with the latter.

The absence of a rhetorical concept of simile does not, of course, arise from any lack of similes in ancient literature. Nor should it be thought that ancient rhetoric, involved as it was chiefly with prose and oratory, would for that reason have avoided analysis of figures that belong frequently to poetry. Modern scholarship has pointed out often that to the ancients prose and poetry were closely inter-related, with the problems and standards of the one bearing intimately on the other.[2] Even if similes had appeared exclusively in poetry, which they do not, they would still have been a legitimate object of investigation for the ancient critics.

It is to be hoped that this study may, among other things, serve as a reminder against easy equation of the critical terminology of different languages, particularly when they are separated by significant intervals of time. Ancient terminology certainly forms the basis for that of all subsequent literary criticism. This does not mean, however, that because we continually speak, for instance, of "metaphor and simile" we should assume without hesitation that the ancients did the same. Such facile assumptions have led, at best, to lack of precision among modern scholars in their understanding of ancient terms of comparison and, at worst, to real inaccuracies and misinformation to which even careful scholars have fallen prey.[3] It has seemed worthwhile throughout to note a fair number of the mistranslations and misinterpretations of passages dealing with comparison.

Certain limits had to be imposed. My first plan was to pursue the use and understanding of terms of comparison to the very end of antiquity, including such medieval figures as Isidore and the Venerable Bede; but considerations of length have prompted de-

[2] E. Nordén, *Die antike Kunstprosa*[2] (Leipzig 1909) 52; M. T. Herrick, "The Place of Rhetoric in Poetic Theory," *Quarterly Journal of Speech* 34 (1948) 3; H. North, "The Use of Poetry in the Training of the Ancient Orator," *Traditio* 8 (1952) 2; G. A. Kennedy, *The Art of Persuasion in Greece* (Princeton 1963) 7-8.

[3] A typical, and double, mistake is made by W. D. Anderson, "Notes on the Simile in Homer and his Successors," *CJ* 53 (1957) 81, when he says that there are just two classical words for simile, εἰκών and *similitudo*. Not only do these two terms really mean something different from "simile," but, if they had meant "simile" to the ancients, so too would have παραβολή, εἰκασία, *imago*, and *collatio*.

ferment of discussion of the late technical treatises. In some respects a clear watershed can be observed in rhetorical tradition around the time of Quintilian, or a little later. Treatises on the early side of the second century A.D. generally have literary pretensions and broad literary relevance; treatises on the late side generally do not. In this sense, to close shortly after Quintilian is logical. On the other hand, incompleteness and chronological difficulties inevitably result. The late handbooks may be mere compilations of lists, but they accurately reflect the views of a nonliterary age toward the component parts of rhetoric, and in their confusingly varied use of examples, definitions, and terminology they are even perversely original. Secondly, if a terminal point is set slightly after Quintilian, namely with Plutarch and Fronto, it must be granted that Hermogenes and Aelius Aristides are only a bit later than Fronto, while Rufus of Perinthus is his contemporary. Nevertheless, each of them is sufficiently lacking in literary aims to be associated more naturally with the late technical writers than with Quintilian, Plutarch, and Fronto. There is also the work on tropes ascribed by the Suda to Trypho Grammaticus, who lived in the first century B.C.; however, Wendel[4] is surely right that, despite the Suda, this highly technical and dry handbook belongs somewhere in the third century A.D. with the treatises of Herodian and Polybius Sardianus to which it is very similar. In sum, the chronological limit of the present study is defensible, but it is important that a comparable study of the late treatises also be made.

Clearly such a technical work as this is aimed principally at professional classicists, and within this body even more directly at those interested in rhetorical matters. But in an effort to make the study at least available to students of the history of literary criticism, translations (only occasionally my own) or close paraphrases have been provided for all Greek and Latin quotations and for the first several instances of individual words. The only excep-

---

[4] C. Wendel, "Tryphon" no. 25, *RE* 7A (1939) 729–730.

tions to this procedure are a few passages of a wholly technical nature, for example, those involving textual problems.

Thanks for permission to quote from his dissertation go to Dr. Richard M. Gummere. Quotes from W. Rhys Roberts, *Rhetorica*, are by permission of the Clarendon Press, Oxford; quotes from W. Rhys Roberts, *Demetrius On Style*, are by permission of the Cambridge University Press. Reprinted by permission of the Loeb Classical Library and Harvard University Press are passages from: Cicero, *De Oratore*, Books I and II; Cicero, *De Inventione*, *De Optimo Genere Oratorum*, *Topica*; [*Cicero*] *Ad C. Herennium de Ratione Dicendi* (*Rhetorica ad Herennium*); *Marcus Cornelius Fronto*; *The Institutio Oratoria of Quintilian*; *Seneca, Moral Epistles*. My thanks go also to the *American Journal of Philology* for permission to quote from my article, "Cicero, de Oratore III.39.157."

The opportunity to acknowledge invaluable aid is always pleasant. Under Professor Zeph Stewart's direction this study passed through an earlier stage as a doctoral dissertation. His guidance and criticism have been indispensable. Mr. D. A. Russell, Professor George Kennedy, and Miss D. Innes read the dissertation with kindness, and their advice has been of marked benefit in its transformation into a monograph. Professor Harry Caplan improved the monograph typescript in many ways. Professor G. P. Goold has encouraged and counseled me throughout. On a less spiritual but equally remembered plane, the Harvard Department of the Classics generously alleviated the cost of preparing the manuscript. Mrs. Gae Gregor was a willing and expert typist. Mr. Dean Nicastro indefatigably and calligraphically wrote the Greek. Finally, through all, my wife has been an acute critic while making life cheerful and sane.

Marsh H. McCall, Jr.

The Center for Hellenic Studies
March 1969

CONTENTS

ANCIENT RHETORICAL THEORIES
OF SIMILE AND COMPARISON

ABBREVIATIONS

AJP	*American Journal of Philology*
CAF	*Comicorum Atticorum Fragmenta*, ed. Kock
CJ	*The Classical Journal*
CQ	*The Classical Quarterly*
CR	*The Classical Review*
LSJ	Liddell/Scott/Jones, *A Greek-English Lexicon*
OCT	Oxford Classical Text
RE	*Paulys Realencyclopädie der classischen Altertumswissenschaft*
REG	*Revue des Etudes Grecques*
RhM	*Rheinisches Museum für Philologie*
TAPA	*Transactions of the American Philological Association*
ThLL	*Thesaurus Linguae Latinae*

CHAPTER I

THE PRE-ARISTOTELIAN
TESTIMONY

The testimony before Aristotle regarding comparison is of two kinds: traces of discussion of comparison in works of rhetoric, and actual use of terms of comparison in fifth- and fourth-century writers. One is forced to rely almost completely on the second kind because of the paucity of the first, a paucity attributable in large measure to Aristotle himself. His own survey of earlier rhetorical treatises, the Συναγωγὴ τεχνῶν, undermined their claim for an independent existence and they fell into disuse. When at a later date Aristotle's survey in turn was lost, the destruction of the pre-Aristotelian treatises was almost total.[1] Radermacher has collected in a modern συναγωγή what little evidence remains.[2]

In most of the early teachers of rhetoric, there is simply no record of any discussion of comparison. Corax and Tisias are thought to have introduced the doctrine of εἰκός (probability) into forensic rhetoric; to Thrasymachus is attributed the development of ἔλεοι (appeals to pity) and much work on rhythm;

[1] Kennedy 13.

[2] L. Radermacher, *Artium Scriptores* (Vienna 1951), supplanting L. Spengel, Συναγωγὴ τεχνῶν *sive Artium Scriptores* (Stuttgart 1828). Radermacher's brief foreword, the thoughts of a man who had enriched scholarship for half a century and realized that this would be one of his last works, is deeply moving, as is Solmsen's appreciation of the work after Radermacher's death in his *Gnomon* review (1954) 213–219. Solmsen points out that Spengel and Radermacher were separated by only a single generation of scholarship, since Usener was a pupil of the one and a teacher of the other.

Prodicus concerned himself with the question of brevity or detail in speech; Hippias was interested in rhythm and harmony and stressed the importance of improvisation; Protagoras often discussed the relationship of φύσις (nature) and ἄσκησις (training).[3] The testimony regarding Gorgias is equally devoid of mention of comparison. References to his rhetorical doctrines inevitably stress two tendencies: an overriding interest in expressiveness of speech and faults of excess in execution of this interest. A comment by Diodorus shows how Gorgias both innovated and went astray in the development of an artistic prose: "He was the first to make use of figures of speech which were far-fetched and distinguished by artificiality: antithesis, isocolon, parison, homoeoteleuton, and others of that sort which then, because of the novelty of the devices, were thought worthy of praise, but now seem labored and ridiculous when used to excess."[4] Gorgias' reputation for the use of bold metaphors and generally ornate verbal adornments is often pointed out.[5] There is never mention of discussion or even special use of comparison; but it is tempting to think he may have touched on it, especially since comparison was frequently classified as an ornate element of prose style.[6]

The three fifth-century rhetoricians who are connected, if only tangentially, with discussion of terms of comparison are Theodorus, Polus, and Theramenes, shadowy figures all. The floruit of Theodorus of Byzantium can be placed in the last quarter of the fifth century; his doctrines are surmised only from reports and references.[7] The eleventh chapter of Book III of Aristotle's *Rhetoric* is concerned with τὰ ἀστεῖα (witty sayings), effected

---

[3] W. Kroll, "Rhetorik," *RE* supp. bd. 7 (1940) 1046–1047 for sketches of the early rhetoricians.

[4] Diodorus Siculus 12.53.4, as translated by Kennedy 64.

[5] Norden 63–71; Kroll 1045; North 7.

[6] In the scanty remains of Gorgias' works, the word εἰκόνας occurs at *Helen* 17 but in a nonrhetorical sense of "images" or "representations."

[7] F. Solmsen, "Theodoros" no. 38, *RE* 5A (1934) 1839–1847.

principally through metaphor but also by other means, one of which is attributed to Theodorus:

καὶ (ὃ λέγει Θεόδωρος) τὸ καινὰ λέγειν. γίγνεται δὲ ὅταν παρά-
δοξον ᾖ, καὶ μή, ὡς ἐκεῖνος λέγει, πρὸς τὴν ἔμπροσθεν δόξαν.[8]
(3.11.1412a26–28)

So with the 'novelties' of Theodorus. In these the thought is startling, and, as Theodorus puts it, does not fit in with the ideas you already have.[9]

The scholiast comments: ἀλλὰ καὶ ὁ Θεόδωρος (ῥήτωρ δὲ ἦν) λέγει τὸ τὰς εὐδοκιμούσας εἰκόνας λέγειν {καὶ} σημαίνειν καινὰ ἤτοι παράξενα, ἂν καὶ ἄλλο τι φαίνηται λέγειν κατὰ τὸ φαινόμενον οἷόν ἐστι τὸ "οἱ τέττιγες αὐτοῖς χαμόθεν ᾄσον-ται."[10] The sense is that according to Theodorus εἰκόνες (images/illustrations) that are successful or popular (εὐδοκιμοῦσαι) can also, just as metaphors and apophthegms and riddles can,[11] consist of novel turns of phrase (καινὰ ἤτοι παράξενα) by meaning something other than what they appear to mean, as in "the cicalas will sing to them from the ground."[12] The scholiast unfortunately tells no more than that Theodorus commented in some fashion on successful εἰκόνες, and no further hint is given of the nature of the εἰκόνες.

For Polus of Acragas, a pupil of Gorgias and the second interlocutor of Socrates in the *Gorgias*,[13] a floruit of perhaps a few

[8] Ross's OCT is used throughout.

[9] Translation by W. Rhys Roberts in vol. XI (1924) of the Oxford *Works of Aristotle Translated* (W. D. Ross, ed.). Roberts' translation is used throughout for the *Rhetoric*.

[10] Radermacher, *Artium Scriptores* 110.

[11] The last two are mentioned by Aristotle along with metaphor as contributing toward witty sayings.

[12] This saying, which Aristotle himself uses slightly earlier in chap. 11 and which, he states elsewhere, Stesichorus addressed to the Locrians (*Rhet.* 2.21.1395a1–2), is taken to mean that the land of the Locrians will be destroyed, the trees cut down, and the cicalas forced to do their chirping on the ground.

[13] W. Rhys Roberts, *Greek Rhetoric and Literary Criticism* (New York 1928) 4,

years later than Theodorus may be assumed. Again none of his works survives.[14] The two passages that connect him with a term of comparison occur in the *Phaedrus*. In the technical part of the dialogue, which reviews the doctrines of various rhetoricians, Socrates mentions Thrasymachus, Theodorus, Evenus of Paros, Tisias, Gorgias, Prodicus, and Hippias, and then continues:

Τὰ δὲ Πώλου πῶς φράσωμεν αὖ μουσεῖα λόγων—ὡς δι-
πλασιολογίαν καὶ γνωμολογίαν καὶ εἰκονολογίαν—ὀνομάτων τε
Λικυμνίων ἃ ἐκείνῳ ἐδωρήσατο πρὸς ποίησιν εὐεπείας;[15]

(*Phaedrus* 267b10–c3)

And what shall we say of Polus and his shrines of learned speech, such as duplication and sententiousness and figurativeness, and what of the names with which Licymnius presented him to effect beautiful diction?[16]

A little later, in criticizing a purely technical approach to rhetoric as an ignorant substitute for dialectic, Socrates refers back with irony to one of Polus' terms: ... ὧν νυνδὴ ἡμεῖς διῆμεν τῶν παγκάλων τεχνημάτων—βραχυλογιῶν τε καὶ εἰκονολογιῶν καὶ ὅσα ἄλλα διελθόντες ὑπ' αὐγὰς ἔφαμεν εἶναι σκεπτέα—... (269a6–8). No examples of Polus' impressive terms are given in either passage, but by being literal one may be able to approach their meaning a little more closely than do Fowler's somewhat vague Loeb translations: speech with reduplications (διπλασιο-λογία), speech with maxims (γνωμολογία), and speech with images (εἰκονολογία).[17] Hackforth is restrictive when he translates the last term "similes"[18] and Thompson incautious when

---

describes Polus' demeanor in the *Gorgias* as that of a pupil "who in studied elegance of style outvies his master."

14 W. Nestle, "Polos" no. 3, *RE* 21 (1952) 1424–1425.

15 Burnet's OCT is used for all passages from Plato.

16 The Loeb Library translations are used throughout for passages from Plato.

17 B. Jowett, *The Dialogues of Plato*³ (Oxford 1892) I 476, merely transliterates: "diplasiology, and gnomology, and eikonology."

18 R. Hackforth, *Plato's Phaedrus* (Cambridge, Eng., 1952) 139. His translation

he comments that "εἰκονολογία may denote the free use of metaphor or simile, as when Gorgias called vultures 'living tombs.'"[19] Nothing in the context narrows εἰκονολογία to any specific form of likeness, let alone equates it with metaphor (μεταφορά), for which the simple term εἰκών is never a synonym.

The information regarding the third figure, Theramenes, comes from two entries in the Suda and is at once the most tantalizing and the most debatable. The first entry reads:

Θηραμένης ᾿Αθηναῖος, ῥήτωρ, μαθητὴς Προδίκου τοῦ Κείου, ὃς ἐπεκαλεῖτο Κόθορνος· Μελέτας ῥητορικὰς καὶ ἄλλα τινά.

Theramenes of Athens, orator, student of Prodicus of Ceos, who was called Cothornus; [he wrote] rhetorical *Exercises* and some other things.

The second, following immediately, reads:

Θηραμένης Κεῖος, σοφιστής. Μελετῶν βιβλία γ΄, περὶ ὁμοιώσεως λόγου, περὶ εἰκόνων ἤτοι παραβολῶν, περὶ σχημάτων.[20]

Theramenes of Ceos, sophist. [He wrote] three books of *Exercises*, *On Likeness in Speech*, *On Illustrations* or *Comparisons*, *On Figures*.

Radermacher and Stegmann[21] differ sharply in interpreting these two entries. Radermacher points out that much of the Suda's information seems to derive from the scholiasts to Aristophanes' *Frogs* 541,[22] who speak of more than one Theramenes. Deceived

---

of εἰκονολογιῶν in the second passage as "imageries" is much more accurate.

[19] W. H. Thompson, *The Phaedrus of Plato* (London 1868) 115. Kennedy 56 also sidesteps with Jowett's "eikonology." J. Ernesti, *Lexicon Technologiae Graecorum Rhetoricae* (Leipzig 1795) 94, regards the term as general in nature and equal to the Latin *figura*.

[20] These two entries are taken from Radermacher, *Artium Scriptores* 114–115. The Suda lists a total of four persons named Theramenes (A. Adler, *Suidae Lexicon* [Leipzig 1931] II 715).

[21] W. Stegemann, "Theramenes" no. 2, *RE* 5A (1934) 2320.

[22] Radermacher, *Artium Scriptores* 116. See also the statement of the Ravenna scholiast alone in W. G. Rutherford, *Scholia Aristophanica* (London 1896) I 338.

by the scholiasts, the Suda has made two Therameneses out of
one, the statesman-orator of the latter part of the fifth century.
In support of his view, Radermacher quotes passages from
Cicero[23] and pseudo-Plutarch[24] that mention a rhetorician
Theramenes contemporary with figures of the late fifth century.
He also relies on an article by Wilhelm Süss,[25] who takes another
part of the Aristophanic passage,

$$\mu\hat{a}\lambda\lambda o\nu\ \hat{\eta}\ \gamma\epsilon\gamma\rho\alpha\mu\mu\acute{\epsilon}\nu\eta\nu$$
$$\epsilon\grave{\iota}\kappa\acute{o}\nu'\ \acute{\epsilon}\sigma\tau\acute{a}\nu\alpha\iota\ \lambda\alpha\beta\acute{o}\nu\theta'\ \acute{\epsilon}\nu$$
$$\sigma\chi\hat{\eta}\mu\alpha, \qquad\qquad (Frogs\ 537\text{-}538)$$

Not like a pictured block to be,
Standing always in one position. . . .[26]

and links the words $\epsilon\grave{\iota}\kappa\acute{o}\nu'$ and $\sigma\chi\hat{\eta}\mu\alpha$, which are here pictorial
("pictured block" or "statue," and "position"), to the rhetorical
terminology of the time. Süss concludes that, because the passage
refers to the statesman-orator Theramenes, the rhetorician
Theramenes must be the same man, who will have been parti-
cularly concerned with rhetorical $\epsilon\grave{\iota}\kappa\acute{o}\nu\epsilon\varsigma$ (illustrations) and
$\sigma\chi\acute{\eta}\mu\alpha\tau\alpha$ (figures). This man, therefore, was the author of the
several works, including $\pi\epsilon\rho\grave{\iota}\ \epsilon\grave{\iota}\kappa\acute{o}\nu\omega\nu$ and $\pi\epsilon\rho\grave{\iota}\ \sigma\chi\eta\mu\acute{a}\tau\omega\nu$, assigned by the Suda to the Cean Theramenes. In addition, Süss
argues for the fifth-century currency of the terms $\acute{o}\mu o\acute{\iota}\omega\sigma\iota\varsigma$ and
$\pi\alpha\rho\alpha\beta o\lambda\acute{\eta}$ by citing the appearance of $\pi\alpha\rho o\mu o\acute{\iota}\omega\sigma\iota\varsigma$ and $\acute{o}\mu o\iota\acute{o}$-
$\tau\eta\varsigma$ in the *Rhetorica ad Alexandrum* and the easy use of $\pi\alpha\rho\alpha\beta o\lambda\acute{\eta}$
in Aristotle's *Rhetoric*.

Stegemann takes quite another approach. He stresses the fact
that the Ciceronian passage mentioned above (*de Oratore* 2.22.93)

[23] *De Oratore* 2.22.93.

[24] *Lives of the Ten Orators* 836f.

[25] W. Süss, "Theramenes der Rhetor und Verwandtes," *RhM* 66 (1911) 183–189.

[26] The Rogers translations in the Loeb Library are used throughout for
Aristophanes.

suggests that the fifth-century rhetorician Theramenes did no actual writing. He accepts identification of Theramenes the statesman with the rhetorician but argues that the works ascribed by the Suda to the Athenian Theramenes, μελέτας ῥητορικὰς καὶ ἄλλα τινά, are the same as those by the Cean Theramenes and appear in the earlier entry through a confusion. Stegmann further emphasizes that the works assigned to the Cean Theramenes deal with precisely the same narrow rhetorical concerns as do the works of such late technical writers as Polybius Sardianus, Cocondrius, Herodian, and Trypho. He therefore disengages the Suda's second Theramenes from any connection with the fifth-century Athenian statesman and rhetorician and declares that he is a Cean sophist of unknown date, closely allied, as the title of one of his works shows, to those late rhetoricians who used εἰκών and παραβολή almost synonymously.[27]

Stegemann is certainly right. Not only is the fifth-century Theramenes' reputed lack of literary activity evidence against ascription of several treatises to him; but, too, Süss's arguments are not without weaknesses. To claim currency of rhetorical terms from use of these or related terms almost a century later is not convincing. Both παραβολή and ὁμοίωσις, as will be seen,[28] do occur in fourth-century literature closer in date to Theramenes than any instances mentioned by Süss, but they occur in general, nonrhetorical (or only semirhetorical) contexts. Furthermore, Süss cannot point to any parallel fifth-century treatises dealing exclusively with σχήματα,[29] let alone subdivisions of σχήματα. It is true that Gorgias very probably concerned himself with σχήματα, that Theodorus talked of the effects of εὐδοκιμοῦσαι

[27] Stegemann refers here to R. Volkmann, *Die Rhetorik der Griechen und Römer*[2] (Leipzig 1885) 445, who makes the same point regarding the late rhetorical treatises.

[28] See below, p. 18.

[29] Indeed, Kroll 1109 feels that σχῆμα as a rhetorical term meaning "figure" appears only after Theophrastus, the word having meant only "form" in general until then.

εἰκόνες (successful images/illustrations), that Polus made use of εἰκονολογία (speech with images/illustrations). But any treatises by these or other rhetoricians of the time dealt with the art of persuasion in general. When Aristotle added to his *Rhetoric* a third book on λέξις (style)—the rhetorical category under which would properly appear a treatment of σχήματα[30]—it was an innovation. The book does not imply earlier studies of the stylistic topics it considers. Theophrastus' independent treatise περὶ λέξεως (*On Style*) was equally innovative. Treatises that further divided the category of style and dealt solely with σχήματα or its subdivisions did not appear until later. Stegemann correctly refuses to introduce such works into the fifth century, and the possibility evaporates that under the name of the fifth-century Theramenes the Suda has an accurate entry referring to works on terms of comparison.

Consideration of the early rhetoricians, then, produces little evidence regarding concepts of comparison. General pre-Aristotelian literature is more helpful. To be observed most widely in this period is the development of εἰκών as a standard term meaning "comparison" (as well as "image," "illustration," or "likeness") and its rather infrequent use to refer specifically to simile. Not all instances of εἰκών and other terms in passages of a rhetorical nature need be adduced; representative passages and any that depart from normal usage will be chosen. The great majority are from prose, but the first rhetorical appearance of a term of comparison is in Aristophanes.[31]

Apart from the nonrhetorical instance of εἰκών already mentioned (*Frogs* 538), the word appears twice elsewhere in Aristophanes.[32] In the *Clouds*, near the end of the parabasis proper, after Aristophanes has been defending himself and vilifying his

---

[30] Kennedy 11–12.

[31] The whole corpus of earlier poetry and drama produces not a single example. In Herodotus, εἰκών occurs eleven times but always in the meaning of "statue," "picture" (J. E. Powell, *A Lexicon to Herodotus* [Cambridge, Eng., 1938]).

[32] O. J. Todd, *Index Aristophaneus* (Cambridge, Mass., 1932).

8

competitors, he adds that they even imitate his εἰκούς, and he refers to his picture of eels in the *Knights* 864ff:

> εἶθ᾽ Ἕρμιππος αὖθις ἐποίησεν εἰς Ὑπέρβολον,
> ἄλλοι τ᾽ ἤδη πάντες ἐρείδουσιν εἰς Ὑπέρβολον,
> τὰς εἰκοὺς τῶν ἐγχέλεων τὰς ἐμὰς μιμούμενοι.
> ὅστις οὖν τούτοισι γελᾷ, τοῖς ἐμοῖς μὴ χαιρέτω.

> (*Clouds* 557–560)

Then Hermippus on the caitiff opened all his little skill,
And the rest upon the caitiff are their wit exhausting still;
And my simile to pilfer "of the Eels" they all combine.
Whoso laughs at their productions, let him not delight in mine.

The passage in the *Knights* to which he refers is spoken by the sausage-seller. Cleon boasts of ferreting out conspiracies against the state and sounding the alarm, and the sausage-seller retorts:

> ὅπερ γὰρ οἱ τὰς ἐγχέλεις θηρώμενοι πέπονθας.
> ὅταν μὲν ἡ λίμνη καταστῇ, λαμβάνουσιν οὐδέν·
> ἐὰν δ᾽ ἄνω τε καὶ κάτω βόρβορον κυκῶσιν,
> αἱροῦσι· καὶ σὺ λαμβάνεις, ἢν τὴν πόλιν ταράττῃς.

> (*Knights* 864–867)

O ay, you're like the fisher-folk, the men who hunt for eels,
Who when the mere is still and clear catch nothing for their
    creels,
But when they rout the mud about and stir it up and down,
'Tis then they do; and so do you, when you perturb the town.

The form of this first rhetorical instance of εἰκών in a literary context is that of a simile, though not a very straightforward one: *you do just what they do* . . . (conditional description) . . . *you likewise* . . . is not quite the same as *just as they* . . . *so you.* . . .[33]

---

[33] It should be noted that the normal introductory term of comparison, ὥσπερ, could have replaced ὅπερ metrically if Aristophanes had so wished.

The second rhetorical use of εἰκών is in the *Frogs,* where it has no explicit referent. It occurs at the beginning of the contest between Aeschylus and Euripides. Dionysus urges them:

> ἀλλ’ ὡς τάχιστα χρὴ λέγειν· οὕτω δ’ ὅπως ἐρεῖτον
> ἀστεῖα καὶ μήτ’ εἰκόνας μήθ’ οἷ’ ἂν ἄλλος εἴποι.

(Frogs 905–906)

Now then, commence your arguments, and mind you both display
True wit, not images,[34] nor things which any fool could say.

The two contestants obey his request and refrain from using figures of comparison of any kind in the ensuing contest. Interestingly, the same collocation of ἀστεῖα (witty sayings) and εἰκόνες occurs here as in the scholium on Aristotle's *Rhetoric* mentioning Theodorus.[35] In this passage, however, Dionysus encourages ἀστεῖα and discourages use of εἰκόνες.

In Xenophon εἰκών occurs once in a rhetorical context, in the *Oeconomicus,* and twice elsewhere with the meaning "statue."[36] In chapter 17 of the *Oeconomicus* Socrates and Ischomachus have been talking of sowing, and they move on to various related subjects such as weeds. Ischomachus asks what should be done with weeds that are choking and robbing the corn, and he draws a simile at the end of his question:

> ὥσπερ οἱ κηφῆνες διαρπάζουσιν ἄχρηστοι ὄντες τῶν μελιττῶν
> ἃ ἂν ἐκεῖναι ἐργασάμεναι τροφὴν καταθῶνται;   (17.14)

[What if weeds are springing up] . . . much as useless drones rob bees of the food they have laid in store by their industry?[37]

---

[34] I substitute "images" for Rogers’ "metaphors," an inaccurate translation of εἰκόνας.

[35] Scholium to *Rhet.* 3.11.1412a25.

[36] F. W. Sturz, *Lexicon Xenophonteum* (Leipzig 1801).

[37] The translations are those of Marchant in the Loeb Library.

Socrates' answer also contains a simile:

Ἐκκόπτειν ἂν νὴ Δία δέοι τὴν ὕλην, ἔφην ἐγώ, ὥσπερ τοὺς
κηφῆνας ἐκ τῶν σμηνῶν ἀφαιρεῖν.   (17.14)

The weeds must be cut, of course, just as the drones must be re-
moved from the hive.

Ischomachus asks if there is not good reason, then, for assigning
men to hoe, and Socrates replies:

Πάνυ γε. ἀτὰρ ἐνθυμοῦμαι, ἔφην ἐγώ, ὦ Ἰσχόμαχε, οἷόν ἐστι τὸ
εὖ τὰς εἰκόνας ἐπάγεσθαι. πάνυ γὰρ σύ με ἐξώργισας πρὸς τὴν
ὕλην τοὺς κηφῆνας εἰπών, πολὺ μᾶλλον ἢ ὅτε περὶ αὐτῆς τῆς
ὕλης ἔλεγες.   (17.15)

No doubt; but I am reflecting, Ischomachus, on the advantage of
bringing in an apt simile. For you roused my wrath against the
weeds by mentioning the drones, much more than when you
spoke of mere weeds.

The two comparisons used in these passages are certainly in the
form of similes, and yet it may be said that form is not the point
at issue here. Socrates' phrase τὰς εἰκόνας does not refer particularly to either simile, but rather to illustrations generally as an
inductive means of argument. The plural and the article suggest
this; even more, τοὺς κηφῆνας εἰπών ("by mentioning the
drones") indicates that the illustrative subject matter of drones is
Socrates' concern, not the form in which the illustration is
phrased. "Apt illustrations" would be closer to the meaning of
τὰς εἰκόνας than Marchant's "apt simile."[38]

Reasonably enough, Plato is the pre-Aristotelian (if the master
may be subordinated to the pupil) who furnishes most copiously
instances of terms of comparison. For the first time, terms other

[38] H. G. Dakyns, *The Works of Xenophon* (London: Macmillan, 1897) III i 272,
has almost caught this in his translation, ". . . how grand a thing it is to introduce
a simile or such like figure well and aptly."

than εἰκών are used, but they appear in insignificant proportion to the plentiful cases of εἰκών. More than sixty passages containing εἰκών are listed in Ast;[39] over twenty are in rhetorical contexts. Of these only three may be said certainly and a fourth possibly to refer narrowly to simile. The three certain references are all in earlier dialogues. Thus, if any movement can be traced it would be one increasingly away from specific referents for the term. All the instances of εἰκών when it refers to simile (which, it must be remembered, are but a small minority) will be presented, and a representative selection of the instances when it does not. The passages will be mentioned in an approximately chronological order.[40]

As an instance from a relatively early dialogue,[41] at *Gorgias* 493d Socrates has just finished his picture of the sieve and leaky jar as an illustration of the foolish soul. Callicles is unimpressed, and Socrates says:

> Φέρε δή, ἄλλην σοι εἰκόνα λέγω ἐκ τοῦ αὐτοῦ γυμνασίου τῇ
> νῦν. . . .   (493d5–6)

Come now, let me tell you another parable from the same school as that I have just told. . . .

He proceeds to compare temperate and licentious lives through a picture of sound and leaky jars. There is no question but that general comparative illustrations are being brought forward here.[42]

Next may be mentioned the three instances in which εἰκών certainly refers to simile. The first occurs in the *Meno*. Socrates

---

[39] D. F. Ast, *Lexicon Platonicum* (Berlin 1908).

[40] R. Simeterre, "La chronologie des oeuvres de Platon," *REG* 58 (1945) 146–162; E. R. Dodds, *Plato, Gorgias* (Oxford 1959) 18ff.

[41] There are no rhetorical uses of εἰκών, with or without a restricted referent, in the very earliest dialogues.

[42] Another instance in the *Gorgias* of εἰκών in the same sense occurs at 517d6.

has thoroughly perplexed Meno over the subject of ἀρετή (virtue), and Meno declares:

καὶ δοκεῖς μοι παντελῶς, εἰ δεῖ τι καὶ σκῶψαι, ὁμοιότατος εἶναι
τό τε εἶδος καὶ τἆλλα ταύτῃ τῇ πλατείᾳ νάρκῃ τῇ θαλαττίᾳ·
καὶ γὰρ αὕτη τὸν ἀεὶ πλησιάζοντα καὶ ἁπτόμενον ναρκᾶν ποιεῖ.

(80a4–7)

And if I am indeed to have my jest, I consider that both in your appearance and in other respects you are extremely like the flat torpedo sea-fish; for it benumbs anyone who approaches and touches it.

Socrates pleasantly retorts that Meno is hoping, but in vain, for an answering comparison:

ἐγὼ δὲ τοῦτο οἶδα περὶ πάντων τῶν καλῶν, ὅτι χαίρουσιν
εἰκαζόμενοι—λυσιτελεῖ γὰρ αὐτοῖς· καλαὶ γὰρ οἶμαι τῶν
καλῶν καὶ αἱ εἰκόνες—ἀλλ᾽ οὐκ ἀντεικάσομαί σε.   (80c3–6)

One thing I know about all handsome people is this—they delight in being compared to something. They do well over it, since fine features, I suppose, must have fine similes. But I am not for playing your game.[43]

Meno has drawn a simile, and Socrates refers to it with the phrase αἱ εἰκόνες, but as in the Xenophon passage the plural, referring to a single simile, and the word καλαὶ (fine) suggest that Socrates is thinking principally of the *type* of comparison that handsome

---

[43] It should be noted that this passage and several others dealt with in this chapter not only illustrate pre-Aristotelian rhetorical ideas of comparison but are also examples of the popular Athenian game of εἰκάζειν-ἀντεικάζειν, in which one party asks, "Do you know what someone is very much like?" and then supplies his own answer, to which the second party makes a comparison in reply. Socrates refers openly here to this Athenian pastime in his final sentence. Other passages that have been or will be mentioned and that seem to illustrate or refer to the game are: *Frogs* 905–906; *Phaedo* 87b; *Symposium* 215a; *Republic* 488a; [Demosthenes] *Eroticus* 10–11. See E. Fraenkel, *Elementi Plautini in Plauto* (Florence 1960) 163ff, and the same author's commentary on vv.1629ff in his *Aeschylus, Agamemnon* (Oxford: Clarendon Press, 1950) III 773.

men hope to hear in answer to their own comparisons. Because Socrates adheres to his refusal to draw one, what form it would have taken is left unknown.[44]

The case is somewhat different in *Phaedo* 87b, where a singular εἰκών refers both to a general comparison and to a simile. Cebes and Simmias are discussing with Socrates the nature of the soul. Simmias has pointed out what he feels are the weaknesses in Socrates' argument, and Socrates turns to Cebes for additional comments. Cebes makes a few opening remarks and then prefaces his main thought with this statement:

πρὸς δὴ τοῦτο τόδε ἐπίσκεψαι, εἴ τι λέγω· εἰκόνος γάρ τινος,
ὡς ἔοικεν, κἀγὼ ὥσπερ Σιμμίας δέομαι.   (87b2–3)

Now see if my reply to this has any sense. I think I may, like Simmias, best express myself in a figure.

The εἰκών of Simmias to which Cebes refers is an extended comparison that Simmias has just drawn between the soul and the body on the one hand and harmony and a lyre on the other.[45] The εἰκών used by Cebes himself, however, is in form a simile of several lines comparing a weaver and the soul.[46] This passage illustrates well a broad use of εἰκών and also the fact that within this larger meaning of the term lies simile, undifferentiated.

The third certain reference of εἰκών to simile comes in the *Symposium*. Alcibiades, at the very beginning of his praise of Socrates, says:

Σωκράτη δ' ἐγὼ ἐπαινεῖν, ὦ ἄνδρες, οὕτως ἐπιχειρήσω, δι'
εἰκόνων. οὗτος μὲν οὖν ἴσως οἰήσεται ἐπὶ τὰ γελοιότερα, ἔσται
δ' ἡ εἰκὼν τοῦ ἀληθοῦς ἕνεκα, οὐ τοῦ γελοίου.   (215a4–6)

[44] For εἰκών with an unambiguous meaning of "image" or "illustration" in the *Meno* see 72a8.

[45] *Phaedo* 85e3ff. There is a short simile earlier in Simmias' speech at 85d1, but it is of little importance to his argument and cannot be the object of Cebes' reference.

[46] *Phaedo* 87b4–c5.

of comparison other than εἰκών, namely, ὁμοίωσις and παραβολή. Three instances of ὁμοίωσις are listed by Ast. At *Republic*
454c9 the term means "likeness," "resemblance" as opposed to
ἀλλοίωσις (difference). At *Theaetetus* 176b1, it again means "likeness," "resemblance" and is nearly synonymous with the simple
adjective ὅμοιος (like, resembling). In the probably spurious
Epinomis, at 990d3, it means a "likening" or "comparing" of
numbers as part of a definition of geometry. In none of these passages does Plato use ὁμοίωσις as a technical term in a rhetorical
context.

Ast lists two occurrences of παραβολή, one in a rhetorical, the
other in a nonrhetorical context. The nonrhetorical instance
comes at *Timaeus* 40c4, where the word is in the plural and denotes the meetings of the stars. The rhetorical instance occurs in
the *Philebus*. Socrates has drawn a lengthy comparison between
different kinds of lives and refers to the comparison with the
phrase:

> Ἐρρήθη γάρ που τότε ἐν τῇ παραβολῇ τῶν βίων. . . . (33b2)

> Yes, for it was said, you know, in our comparison of the
> lives. . . .

There is little difference between this use of παραβολή and a good
many of the instances of εἰκών; indeed, Plato's employment of
παραβολή and ὁμοίωσις really tells us only that the terms have
now made a first appearance.[53]

Such is the evidence for terms of comparison in Plato. The remaining pre-Aristotelian testimony can be surveyed in rapid

[53] Since παραβολή first occurs in the two contemporary passages from the
Timaeus and the *Philebus*, it is hard to know which sense of the term was current
earlier. LSJ gives as the primary meanings "juxtaposition" and "comparison"
and refers to the *Philebus* passage; only under IV is the *Timaeus* passage listed. It
may rather be the case that the concrete and physical sense "location, juxtaposition of stars" is at least as early as the technical rhetorical meaning "comparison,"
and that therefore the *Timaeus* passage should be regarded as illustrating παραβολή in a sense as primary as that which occurs in the *Philebus*.

The way I shall take, gentlemen, in my praise of Socrates, is by
similitudes. Probably he will think I do this for derision; but I
choose my similitude for the sake of truth, not of ridicule.

He then describes Socrates in two similes:

> φημὶ γὰρ δὴ ὁμοιότατον αὐτὸν εἶναι τοῖς σιληνοῖς τούτοις . . .
>   (215a6–7)

For I say he is likest to the Silenus-figures that . . .

and:

> καὶ φημὶ αὖ ἐοικέναι αὐτὸν τῷ σατύρῳ τῷ Μαρσύᾳ. (215b3–4)

And I further suggest that he resembles the satyr Marsyas.

The greatest number of instances in which εἰκών refers broadly
to general illustrations or comparisons occur in the *Republic*. A
well-known passage near the beginning of Book VI is representative. Adeimantus asks Socrates to explain why philosophers
should be rulers when Socrates himself has admitted the truth of
the popular belief that philosophers seem useless. Socrates replies:

> Ἐρωτᾷς, ἦν δ' ἐγώ, ἐρώτημα δεόμενον ἀποκρίσεως δι'
> εἰκόνος λεγομένης.   (487e4–5)

> Your question, I said, requires an answer expressed in a com-
> parison or parable.

A few lines later he adds this sentence:

> ἄκουε δ' οὖν τῆς εἰκόνος, ἵν' ἔτι μᾶλλον ἴδῃς ὡς γλίσχρως
> εἰκάζω.   (488a1–2)

But, all the same, hear my comparison so that you may still better
see how I strain after imagery.

The εἰκών that follows is the lengthy illustration or parable of the
sailors who do not appreciate their pilot, cast him aside, and turn

the voyage into drunken revelry. After finishing the illustration, Socrates twice more refers to it as an εἰκών.[47]

One more instance may be taken from the *Republic*. In Book VII, in the discussion of the study of harmony, Glaucon outlines the absurdities of those who approach harmony purely empirically. Socrates begins his answer, "You, said I, are speaking of the worthies (τοὺς χρηστούς) who vex and torture the strings and rack them on the pegs" (531b2–4); he then continues

ἵνα δὲ μὴ μακροτέρα ἡ εἰκὼν γίγνηται πλήκτρῳ τε πληγῶν γιγνομένων καὶ κατηγορίας πέρι καὶ ἐξαρνήσεως καὶ ἀλαζονείας χορδῶν, παύομαι τῆς εἰκόνος καὶ οὔ φημι τούτους λέγειν.
(531b4–7)

but—not to draw out the comparison[48] with strokes of the plectrum and the musician's complaints of too responsive and too reluctant strings—I drop the figure, and tell you that I do not mean these people.

Here εἰκών refers to the torture imagery that has been applied to the approach of the "worthies" to harmony, and Socrates refuses to continue the strained and unattractive figure.[49]

There is one passage from a later dialogue, the *Politicus*, in which εἰκών refers in part to simile. Near the end of the dialogue, the stranger states that the education to be supervised by the kingly art (ἡ βασιλική)[50] will take different natures and weave them together. This process will include

τούτων τὰς μὲν ἐπὶ τὴν ἀνδρείαν μᾶλλον συντεινούσας, οἷον στημονοφυὲς νομίσασ' αὐτῶν εἶναι τὸ στερεὸν ἦθος, (309b2–4)

[both] those natures which tend more towards courage, considering that their character is sturdier, like the warp in weaving,

and other natures that incline toward mildness and order a continuing the εἰκών, are thick and soft and may be likened the woof: τὰς δὲ ἐπὶ τὸ κόσμιον πίονί τε καὶ μαλακῷ καὶ κ τὴν εἰκόνα κροκώδει διανήματι προσχρωμένας (309b4–6). κ τὴν εἰκόνα refers to the weaving image being developed. form this image takes at first, οἷον στημονοφυές ("like the w in weaving"), is that of a simile; its form when comparing souls to the woof is not. The concern of the passage clearly s not to be the particular form of the image.[51]

A concluding example of a completely general use of εἰκ in the *Laws*. Toward the end of Book I the Athenian says he restate more clearly his earlier point that men are good if the capable of ruling themselves, bad if not. He continues:

καί μοι δι' εἰκόνος ἀποδέξασθε ἐάν πως δυνατὸς ὑμῖν γένω δηλῶσαι τὸ τοιοῦτον.   (644c

With your permission, I will make use of an illustration in hope of explaining the matter.

And his εἰκών is a picture of human beings as puppets gods.[52]

The total impression of Plato's concept of εἰκών is ha doubt. Of the four instances in which the term refers at part to simile, all but one (the *Symposium* passage) allow considerable latitude of meaning. More than a dozen ot stances show εἰκών in an unambiguous sense of "illustr "image," or "comparison." This is certainly Plato's unde ing of the term.

It has been mentioned that Plato is the first writer to us

---

[47] 489a5; 489a10.

[48] Jowett III 234 translates carelessly with "metaphor."

[49] For other passages in the *Republic* in which εἰκών bears a similarly general meaning, see 375d5 and 538c5. It should also be remembered that εἰκών is used in the famous cave image at the beginning of Book VII, e.g., 515a4 and 517a8.

[50] *Politicus* 308e4.

[51] Another passage in the *Politicus* in which εἰκών refers only to illustrative comparison occurs at 297e8.

[52] A similar use of εἰκών in the *Laws* is at 10.906e8.

order. Isocrates has only one passage of relevance. εἰκών occurs four times, but always in its nonrhetorical meaning of "portrait," "image," "picture"; ὁμοίωσις does not occur; παραβολή is used once.[54] Toward the end of the *Panathenaicus*, the orator includes in his praise of Athens and abuse of Sparta the statement that the Spartans illustrate an evil type of concord—concord among themselves for the purpose of destroying others—and he compares their concord to that of brigands and pirates.[55] He then adds:

εἰ δέ τισι δοκῶ τὴν παραβολὴν ἀπρεπῆ πεποιῆσθαι πρὸς τὴν
ἐκείνων δόξαν, ταύτην μὲν ἐῶ, λέγω δὲ Τριβαλλούς, οὓς
ἅπαντές φασιν ὁμονοεῖν μὲν ὡς οὐδένας ἄλλους ἀνθρώπους,
ἀπολλύναι δ' οὐ μόνον τοὺς ὁμόρους καὶ τοὺς πλησίον οἰκοῦντας
ἀλλὰ καὶ τοὺς ἄλλους, ὅσων ἂν ἐφικέσθαι δυνηθῶσιν.[56]   (227)

But if I appear to some to use a comparison which is not in keeping with the reputation of the Spartans, I discard this and instance the Triballians, who, according to what all men say, are of one mind as are no other people on earth, but are bent on destroying not only those who border upon their territory and those who live in their neighbourhood but also all others whom they are able to reach.[57]

Both the παραβολή comparing Spartans to pirates and the subsequent description of the Triballians are general illustrations without particular form, and, as was the case with Plato's single rhetorical use of παραβολή, this Isocratean instance of the term appears to be virtually synonymous in application with the common use of εἰκών in Plato.

In Demosthenes παραβολή and ὁμοίωσις do not occur. εἰκών appears eight times, all but once in the pictorial sense of "image,"

---

[54] S. Preuss, *Index Isocrateus* (Leipzig 1904).
[55] *Panathenaicus* 226.
[56] Benseler/Blass Teubner text.
[57] Norlin's Loeb Library translation.

"statue."[58] The exception is in the *Eroticus*, generally thought to be falsely ascribed to Demosthenes but perhaps belonging to the same period and thus a valid illustration of usage of terms in the second half of the fourth century. In section 10 the speaker begins his praise of Epicrates and says, referring to his beauty:

ᾧ τίν' ἁρμόττουσαν εἰκόν' ἐνέγκω σκοπῶν οὐχ ὁρῶ, ἀλλὰ παρίσταταί μοι δεῖσθαι τῶν ἀναγνόντων τόνδε τὸν λόγον σὲ θεωρῆσαι καὶ ἰδεῖν, ἵνα συγγνώμης τύχω μηδὲν ὅμοιον ἔχων εἰπεῖν.[59]

Wondering what fitting comparison for this I may offer, I find none, but it is my privilege to request those who read this essay to see you and contemplate you, so that I may be pardoned for declaring that I have no suitable simile.[60]

The next sentence begins:

τῷ γὰρ ἂν εἰκάσειέ τις. . . .   (11)

For to what could anyone liken. . . .

A long series of sentences follows exclaiming on the absolute perfection of every feature and trait of Epicrates, each exclamation containing the unspoken conclusion "therefore, no εἰκών can be found for this instance of perfection." No part of the passage indicates that any more limited figure than "resemblance," "comparison" is being discussed.[61]

Demosthenes concludes the pre-Aristotelian testimony except for the curious and unique *Rhetorica ad Alexandrum*. Though this work was at one time thought part of the Aristotelian corpus, its author and date are unknown. Many scholars have ascribed

[58] S. Preuss, *Index Demosthenicus* (Leipzig 1892). No rhetorical uses of any of these terms occur in Aeschines (S. Preuss, *Index Aeschineus* [Leipzig 1926]).

[59] Rennie's OCT is used.

[60] The Loeb translation by N. W. and N. J. DeWitt.

[61] This is in opposition, therefore, to the Loeb use of "simile."

authorship to Anaximenes,[62] and a date in the fourth century is almost certain, a date before Aristotle's *Rhetoric* quite possible.[63] As an extant rhetorical treatise close to Aristotle in date of composition, its testimony differs in kind from the lost fifth-century treatises of Theodorus and Polus.

The relevant section of the *Rhetorica ad Alexandrum* is as unique as the work in general. It presents a term of comparison, παρο-μοίωσις, that is used nowhere else as such, although it does appear as a technical term of rhetoric with quite a different meaning. In all other rhetorical passages in which it occurs the term carries the meaning "assimilation of sounds" and refers particularly to assonance in the closing syllables of successive clauses. It is closely associated with ἀντίθεσις (antithesis) and παρίσωσις (even balancing of clauses). The three appear in conjunction in Aristotle's *Rhetoric* 3.9.1410a24–25 and in Dionysius of Halicarnassus *Lysias* 14 and *Isocrates* 2. In the *Rhetorica ad Alexandrum*, however, the term appears to bear the meaning "parallel" and refers to two similes. Chapters 7–13 of the treatise deal with direct proofs such as probabilities, examples, tokens, enthymemes, maxims, signs, and refutations. Maxims (γνῶμαι) are drawn from the peculiar nature of a case (ἐκ τῆς ἰδίας φύσεως), from hyperbole (ἐξ ὑπερβολῆς), or ἐκ παρομοιώσεως.[64] After illustrating the first two the author continues:

> αἱ δ' ἐκ παρομοιώσεως τοιαίδε εἰσίν· ὁμοιότατόν μοι δοκοῦσιν
> οἱ τὰ χρήματα ἀποστεροῦντες τοῖς τὰς πόλεις προδιδοῦσι
> ποιεῖν· πιστευθέντες γὰρ ἀμφότεροι τοὺς πιστεύσαντας

[62] Such as Wendland, Spengel, Hammer, and Spalding. See also Kroll 1052–1053.

[63] See E. M. Cope, *An Introduction to Aristotle's Rhetoric* (London 1867) 402ff, for a treatment of this problem. The author of the *Rhet. ad Alex.* appears wholly unaware of Aristotle's *Rhetoric* and quite dependent on Isocrates' τέχνη. It seems doubtful that Aristotle could have been ignored to such an extent if the *Rhetoric* had already been written. Cope also accepts, with some reservations, ascription of the work to Anaximenes.

[64] *Rhet. ad Alex.* 11.1430b10.

ἀδικοῦσιν. ἑτέρα δέ· παραπλήσιόν μοι δοκοῦσι ποιεῖν οἱ ἀντίδικοι τοῖς τυράννοις· ἐκεῖνοί τε γάρ. . . .⁶⁵   (11.1430b20ff)

The following are maxims based on parallels: "Those who appropriate money seem to me to act very like those who betray cities; for both are trusted and wrong those who have trusted them"; or again, "My opponents seem to me to act very like tyrants: for tyrants. . . ."⁶⁶

"Parallel" is a sound translation of παρομοίωσις,⁶⁷ so far as one can judge from the two examples. Each example compares one action with another and shows by detailing both actions how the particulars of one correspond to the particulars of the other. Since these are the only examples of παρομοίωσις and are in the form of similes, the possibility exists that the author intended the term to *mean* exclusively "simile." But the rest of the pre-Aristotelian evidence makes it unlikely that such a restricted sense should be understood.⁶⁸

The conclusions to be drawn from consideration of the pre-

---

⁶⁵ The text used is L. Spengel/C. Hammer, *Rhetores Graeci* (Leipzig 1894) I ii.

⁶⁶ The translation is that of E. S. Forster in *Works of Aristotle Translated*, ed. Ross (Oxford 1924) XI. Forster believes the author must be considered an anonymous Peripatetic writing about 300 B.C.

⁶⁷ It is also the translation of H. Rackham in the Loeb Library.

⁶⁸ Although the latest critical edition, M. Fuhrmann, *Anaximenis Ars Rhetorica* (Leipzig 1966), indicates no disquiet at the manuscript reading, the unique nature of παρομοίωσις as a term of comparison is curious enough to suggest the possibility of an error in the text. An original ὁμοιώσεως seems called for rather than the strangely used compound. In general the terminology of the *Rhet. ad Alex.* is regular for the late fourth century. Cope, *Introduction* 401ff, discusses the verbal and stylistic features of the work. He lists only one word, καθυποπτευθέν- των, as occurring uniquely, although there are other words that do not appear again until considerably later. If παρ' ὁμοιώσεως were the true reading, the insertion of ἐκ could be explained easily by a scribal desire to make the phrase parallel in expression to the other sources of maxims, i.e., ἐκ τῆς ἰδίας φύσεως and ἐξ ὑπερβολῆς. The use of παρά is, however, difficult. Again, an original reading ἐξ ὁμοιώσεως would give an easy and parallel construction but does not lead readily to the present text. Nevertheless, the suspicion remains that ἐκ παρομοιώσεως may not be correct.

Aristotelian testimony are few and clear. At least two words, εἰκών and παραβολή, are current as technical terms of comparison before Aristotle. A third, ὁμοίωσις, is used in Plato only in semirhetorical contexts in the sense of "likeness," "resemblance." A fourth, παρομοίωσις, appears as a technical term of comparison but will not be seen again as such. εἰκών far exceeds the others in frequency of use. The sense most consistently fitting the contexts of these terms is perhaps "illustrative comparison" or "comparative illustration," the emphasis shifting from passage to passage. Although the terms refer at times to simile, none of them should be thought to mean primarily "simile."

CHAPTER II

ARISTOTLE

Aristotle is as central a figure for ancient theories of comparison as he is for the whole field of rhetoric. His work presents a good deal of doctrine not appearing in earlier testimony that, whether followed or rejected, had a lasting effect on subsequent treatises. παραβολή and εἰκών are his two essential terms of comparison.[1]

Two of the several appearances of παραβολή occur in important and similar contexts. Of these the longer and more detailed, and therefore the more significant, is in Book II of the *Rhetoric*. The first two books of the *Rhetoric* are concerned with subject matter (εὕρεσις), more particularly with argument and proof. Chapter 19 of Book II lays down some general lines of argument (κοινοὶ τόποι), and chapter 20 moves on to general means of persuasion (κοιναὶ πίστεις):[2]

[1] ὁμοίωσις occurs once in the Aristotelian corpus (H. Bonitz, *Index Aristotelicus* [Berlin 1870]), but the passage is in the spurious *de Plantis* 2.6.826b34, in the sense of a plant not of the same "likeness" as another. This is similar to Aristotle's use of the terms ὁμοίωμα and ὁμοιότης, both of which carry the meaning "quality of resemblance" or "quality of likeness." See *Rhet.* 1.2.1356a31 for ὁμοίωμα; *Topica* 6.2.140a12 and *de Sophisticis Elenchis* 15.174a38–39 for ὁμοιότης. ὁμοίωσις, therefore, does not really develop into a technical term of comparison until some point after Aristotle.

[2] F. Solmsen, "The Aristotelian Tradition in Ancient Rhetoric," *AJP* 62 (1941) 39, considers the κοιναὶ πίστεις as one of Aristotle's innovations in ancient rhetoric. He suggests that Aristotle's theory of rhetorical argument is based on his logic, the rhetorical term παράδειγμα (example), for instance, corresponding to the logical term ἐπαγωγή (induction). Kennedy 84–85 mentions the *Prior Analytics* as the work on logic from which the rhetorical enthymeme and example were developed. Kennedy also feels that the discussion of τόποι in this section of Book II represents one of the earliest layers in the *Rhetoric*, whereas the theory of the enthymeme and example was added somewhat later.

εἰσὶ δ' αἱ κοιναὶ πίστεις δύο τῷ γένει, παράδειγμα καὶ ἐνθύμημα.   (2.20.1393a24–25)

These [the κοιναὶ πίστεις] are of two main kinds, "Example" and
"Enthymeme".[3]

Aristotle treats παράδειγμα first and finds that it has two divisions, the actual or historical example and the manufactured example. Of the latter there are again two subdivisions, παραβολή
and λόγοι (fables; for example, those of Aesop): παραδειγμάτων
δὲ εἴδη δύο. ἕν μὲν γάρ ἐστιν παραδείγματος εἶδος τὸ λέγειν
πράγματα προγενομένα, ἕν δὲ τὸ αὐτὸν ποιεῖν. τούτου δὲ ἕν
μὲν παραβολή ἕν δὲ λόγοι, οἶον οἱ Αἰσώπειοι . . . (2.20.1393a28–
31). An instance of the historical example follows; then Aristotle
illustrates παραβολή:

παραβολὴ δὲ τὰ Σωκρατικά, οἶον εἴ τις λέγοι ὅτι οὐ δεῖ κλη-
ρωτοὺς ἄρχειν· ὅμοιον γὰρ ὥσπερ ἂν εἴ τις τοὺς ἀθλητὰς
κληροίη μὴ οἳ δύνανται[4] ἀγωνίζεσθαι ἀλλ' οἳ ἂν λάχωσιν, ἢ
τῶν πλωτήρων ὅντινα δεῖ κυβερνᾶν κληρώσειεν, ὡς δέον τὸν
λαχόντα ἀλλὰ μὴ τὸν ἐπιστάμενον.   (2.20.1393b4–8)

The illustrative parallel is the sort of argument Socrates used:[5]
e.g. "Public officials ought not to be selected by lot. That is like
using the lot to select athletes, instead of choosing those who are
fit for the contest; or using the lot to select a steersman from
among a ship's crew, as if we ought to take the man on whom the
lot falls, and not the man who knows most about it."

The importance of the passage lies in the collocation of

[3] Roberts' Oxford translation (ed. Ross) is used throughout for the *Rhetoric*.
LSJ gives as a definition of ἐνθύμημα in Aristotle's logic "rhetorical syllogism
drawn from probable premises."
[4] μὴ οἳ δύνανται is Spengel's emendation, accepted by Ross, for the manuscript οἳ μὴ δύνανται ΑΓ or μὴ οἳ ἂν δύνωνται ΘΠ.
[5] Cope, *Introduction* 254, remarks on this prefatory phrase that τὰ Σωκρατικά
refers to Socrates' frequent argumentative analogies from Greek political and
social life. Aristotle does not mean that παραβολή will be found only in the
Socratic sayings but rather that the sayings offer many examples of παραβολή.

historical example and fictional comparison as closely related forms of persuasion or proof. In Theodorus[6] a term of comparison, εἰκών, was associated with metaphor, and this connection recurs frequently in Aristotle and elsewhere. Probably the most common association of comparison in ancient rhetoric, however, is with historical example, and the first moderately full statement is in the present passage. The collocation receives only limited emphasis from Aristotle when compared to the repeated pairing of εἰκών and metaphor in Book III; but in subsequent works such as the *Rhetorica ad Herennium*, Cicero's *de Inventione*, Quintilian's *Institutio Oratoria*, and the late technical treatises historical example and fictional comparison are coupled in a fixed rhetorical canon, while metaphor and comparison are connected less frequently. This section in the *Rhetoric* is not the only instance in Aristotle in which historical example and παραβολή are joined. In the *Topica* the same collocation is expressed, but briefly and without elaboration:

Εἰς δὲ σαφήνειαν παραδείγματα καὶ παραβολὰς οἰστέον.[7]

(8.1.157a14–15)

For clearness, examples and comparisons should be adduced.[8]

It is slightly confusing that παράδειγμα is the regular term for "historical example" as well as for "example" in general. In the passage from the *Rhetoric*, Aristotle employs a periphrasis for "historical example" because he has just used παράδειγμα for "example" and seems to wish to avoid confusion. But it will be seen that Quintilian uses the Latin equivalent of παράδειγμα, *exemplum*, in successive lines to mean first "example" and then "historical example."[9]

---

[6] Actually in a scholium on Aristotle referring to Theodorus; see above, p. 3.
[7] Ross's OCT.
[8] W. A. Pickard-Cambridge's Oxford translation, ed. Ross, is used for the *Topica*.
[9] See below, p. 188f.

The identifying features of παραβολή do not, in Aristotle's mind, seem to include a particular form. This is indicated both by the careless phrasing of the illustration of παραβολή and by the similar form given to the surrounding illustrations of historical example and fable (λόγοι). Translated literally, the illustration of παραβολή would begin: "Those selected by lot must not rule, for that is like just as if. . . ." A series of comparative words (ὅμοιον γὰρ ὥσπερ ἂν εἴ) is used, making the illustration in form partly a simile and partly conditional. Aristotle is simply imprecise in choice of words here—a fault he would probably avoid if form were crucial. The instance of historical example is phrased "we must do thus-and-such, because. . . ." The form is of the same persuasive character as the opening words of the παραβολή: "Thus-and-such must not occur, for. . . ." The two instances given of fable state the fable, then follow it with "so also . . ." (οὕτω δὲ . . .)[10] or "in the same way . . ." (ἀτὰρ καὶ . . .).[11] These resemble the παραβολή in being similarly comparative. Form, therefore, is a relatively interchangeable feature of historical example, παραβολή, and fable: all serve as means of persuasion and differ not so much in form as in content.

Thus one arrives at some such sense for παραβολή as Roberts' "illustrative parallel" or Pickard-Cambridge's "comparison." The remaining occurrences of the term fit this meaning, as two passages will illustrate. In the *Topica*, shortly before the sentence pairing παράδειγμα and παραβολή, Aristotle gives counsel on how to conceal an intended conclusion. One should raise an objection against oneself; one should not be too insistent; furthermore,

> καὶ τὸ ὡς ἐν παραβολῇ προτείνειν· τὸ γὰρ δι' ἄλλο προτει-
> νόμενον καὶ μὴ δι' αὐτὸ χρήσιμον τιθέασι μᾶλλον.
>
> (8.1.156b25–27)

[10] *Rhet.* 2.20.1393b18.
[11] *Ibid.*, 1393b31.

formulate your premiss [sic] as though it were a mere illustration: for people admit the more readily a proposition made to serve some other purpose, and not required on its own account.[12]

An instance from a nonrhetorical work occurs in the second book of the *Politics*. Aristotle is discussing, and criticizing, Plato's ideal state. On the issue of men and women following common pursuits, he says:

$$\mathring{\alpha}τοπον \ \delta\grave{\epsilon} \ κα\grave{\iota} \ τ\grave{o} \ \mathring{\epsilon}κ \ τ\mathring{\omega}ν \ θηρίων \ ποιε\mathring{\iota}σθαι \ τ\grave{η}ν \ παραβολήν, \ \mathring{o}τι$$
$$δε\mathring{\iota} \ τ\grave{α} \ α\mathring{υ}τ\grave{α} \ \mathring{\epsilon}πιτηδεύειν \ τ\grave{α}ς \ γυνα\mathring{\iota}κας \ το\mathring{\iota}ς \ \mathring{α}νδράσιν, \ ο\mathring{\iota}ς$$
$$ο\mathring{\iota}κονομίας \ ο\mathring{υ}δ\grave{\epsilon}ν \ μέτεστιν.^{13} \qquad (2.5.1264b4-6)$$

It is absurd to argue, from the analogy of the animals, that men and women should follow the same pursuits, for animals have not to manage a household.[14]

The *Republic* passage to which Aristotle refers is 451d4ff, where Socrates poses a series of questions to Glaucon in order to force an admission that no dissimilarity should exist between the lives of lower animals and human beings. Again, therefore, παραβολή carries the sense of "illustrative comparison" (or Jowett's "analogy"), its purpose being to persuade or prove, and this is Aristotle's regular understanding of the term.[15]

A final point in connection with παραβολή is Aristotle's use of the term ἀντιπαραβολή; it occurs three times in the third book of the *Rhetoric* and almost nowhere else in the ancient testimony.[16]

[12] Other parallel instances in the *Topica* of παραβολή occur at 1.10.104a28 and 8.14.164a15. See also *de Soph. Elench.* 17.176a33.

[13] Ross's OCT.

[14] Jowett's translation (vol. X of *The Works of Aristotle Translated*, ed. W. D. Ross [Oxford: Clarendon Press, 1921]).

[15] Other relevant passages are *Metaphysics* H.11.1036b24; *Eudemian Ethics* 7.12.1244b23 and 1245b13; *Magna Moralia* 1.9.1187a23 (that is, if the work is not actually post-Aristotelian).

[16] LSJ cites one appearance in Plutarch, one in a fragment of Longinus, and one in the medical writer Rufus (second century A.D.) as reported by the fourth-century medical writer Oribasius.

In sense it is closely related to παραβολή, and the two terms appear in proximity on the last page of the *Rhetoric*. Aristotle suggests that the epilogue of a speech be concluded by a review of the case; the speaker must state what has been said and why. One method of doing this is by ἀντιπαραβολή with the opponent's case: λέγεται δὲ ἐξ ἀντιπαραβολῆς τοῦ ἐναντίου (3.19.1419b34). There are two ways to make the ἀντιπαραβολή, either directly, as in "my opponent said thus-and-such; I said thus-and-such," or indirectly, as in ironic statements and questions. In conclusion,

> ἢ δὴ οὕτως [ἢ] ἐκ παραβολῆς ἢ κατὰ φύσιν ὡς ἐλέχθη, οὕτως
> τὰ αὑτοῦ, καὶ πάλιν, ἐὰν βούλῃ χωρὶς τὰ τοῦ ἐναντίου λόγου.
>
> (3.19.1420a4–6)

You may proceed, then, either in this way by setting point against point, or by following the natural order of the arguments as spoken, first giving your own, and then separately, if you wish, those of your opponent.

Both ἐξ ἀντιπαραβολῆς and ἐκ παραβολῆς refer to the same thing, comparison of one's own case with the opponent's, but ἀντιπαραβολή may better be regarded as a subspecies of παραβολή than as synonymous with it. παραβολή denotes more than mere comparison of *opposite* viewpoints; ἀντιπαραβολή is restricted to this one sphere.[17]

Aristotle's most extensive and intricate discussion of comparison comes in his treatment of εἰκών in Book III of the *Rhetoric*. To look for anything wholly straightforward and consistent in this book is fruitless. Like the rest of the *Rhetoric*, it probably was formed from lectures.[18] Furthermore, although there is

[17] The two other instances of ἀντιπαραβολή occur in a single passage at 3.13.1414b2 and b10. In both cases, the term carries a sense of "comparison of opposing arguments." At 1414b11, it is said to be μέρος τι τῶν πίστεων ("a part of the arguments"), recalling the inclusion of παραβολή in *Rhet.* 2.20 as part of the κοιναὶ πίστεις.

[18] Kroll 1058 emphasizes that Aristotle had already written a Περὶ ῥητορικῆς (*On Rhetoric*) ca. 362 and that therefore his rhetorical views developed over a long space of time.

no longer doubt that the book is actually Aristotelian,[19] it does seem to have been a later addition to the unit formed by Books I and II.[20] Its construction from notes results in difficulties of expression and arrangement; moreover, the lecture notes seem in part to have been compiled after Aristotle's death, and contradictions result. There are also inaccuracies of citation and reference.[21] Cope sums up the obstacles with a certain degree of understatement: "This book, by the extreme brevity of expression which characterizes it, leaving even more than usual to the reader's ingenuity to supply, by the consequent difficulty of translation, and the obscurity of many of the allusions, offers at least as many impediments and stumblingblocks to the embarrassed commentator as either of the two preceding."[22]

Book II of the *Rhetoric* concludes exhaustive treatment of subject matter, and Book III moves on to λέξις (style) and τάξις (arrangement). The first twelve chapters deal with style: chapter 1 is introductory, chapters 2–4 treat single words, chapters 5–12 treat the combination of words into longer units. There is definition and discussion of εἰκών in chapters 4, 10, and 11. The most recurrent motif in Aristotle's analysis of the word is that it is a subordinate and less desirable form of metaphor, and every mention of it arises from a larger context of metaphor. Aristotle's remarks on the term will be seen at times to reflect the nature of Book III as a whole in their elusiveness.

Metaphor, as a basic aid toward excellence of style, occupies Aristotle as early as chapter 2 of the book. A good style in both poetry and prose, he states, employs striking diction at appro-

---

[19] Kroll 1062 mentions the views of Diels, Rabe, and Usener, all of whom thought the book a post-Aristotelian addition.

[20] Kennedy 103 remarks: "The book gives something of the impression of an afterthought and may well have been originally a separate treatise which Aristotle subsequently united to his discussion of invention."

[21] See Kroll 1062–1063 and Kennedy 84 for these and other characteristics.

[22] E. M. Cope, *The Rhetoric of Aristotle*, rev. ed. by J. E. Sandys (Cambridge 1877) III 1.

priate times, and metaphor is perhaps the best way to achieve this. Poetry can bear figures even stronger than metaphor, but prose must be more contained; in prose, therefore, metaphor is certainly the most important feature of striking diction.[23] Having stressed the close relation of good metaphor to good style, Aristotle turns in chapter 3 to stylistic faults, including the bad use of metaphor. Then, in chapter 4, he concludes his treatment of single words by discussing the chief subdivision of metaphor, εἰκών.

It is noteworthy, though difficult to evaluate, that in all of Aristotle εἰκών is used as a rhetorical term only in these chapters from Book III of the *Rhetoric*.[24] In pre-Aristotelian literature εἰκών is by far the most general term of comparison, but Aristotle appears to think instead of παραβολή as a general term and to avoid the use of εἰκών. The frequent, but sudden and isolated, use of the term in this section of the *Rhetoric* may indicate reliance on a different source from that (or those) employed for the remainder of the work. Or, possibly, Aristotle himself is innovating in his own terminology and is seeking a different, though certainly not new, term for his discussion of comparison as a feature of style. It is difficult to conclude more than that the most common term of comparison has been neglected, consciously it seems, and then has been applied for a single, specific purpose.[25]

[23] This chapter is one of several examples in the *Rhetoric* of the duality of Aristotle's view toward prose and poetry as one and the same in many respects and yet as requiring sharp differentiation. See North 7 where cross-references between the *Rhetoric* and the *Poetics* are pointed out.

[24] Bonitz 219. There are other instances of the word in the meaning of "image," "statue" (two of them in the earlier books of the *Rhetoric*), but no other rhetorical instances. See *Rhet.* 1.5.1361a36; 2.23.1397b32; *Top.* 6.2.140a7ff; *Meta.* A.9.991b1; M.5.1079b35. In the last two passages εἰκών is coupled with παράδειγμα, but its meaning is "copy," "image," and there is no connection between this coupling and that of παραβολή and παράδειγμα. εἰκών also occurs several times in the sense of "pictorial image" in *de Memoria* 450b21–451a15.

[25] On the amount of originality in Aristotle's categories of style in Book III,

Chapter 4 opens with a definition of εἰκών in terms of its relation to metaphor. Aristotle's language is forceful and fairly brief:

> Ἔστιν δὲ καὶ ἡ εἰκὼν μεταφορά· διαφέρει γὰρ μικρόν· ὅταν
> μὲν γὰρ εἴπῃ [τὸν Ἀχιλλέα]²⁶ "ὡς δὲ λέων ἐπόρουσεν",
> εἰκών ἐστιν, ὅταν δὲ "λέων ἐπόρουσε", μεταφορά· διὰ γὰρ τὸ
> ἄμφω ἀνδρείους εἶναι, προσηγόρευσεν μετενέγκας λέοντα τὸν
> Ἀχιλλέα. χρήσιμον δὲ ἡ εἰκὼν καὶ ἐν λόγῳ, ὀλιγάκις δέ·
> ποιητικὸν γάρ. οἰστέαι δὲ ὥσπερ αἱ μεταφοραί· μεταφοραὶ γάρ
> εἰσι, διαφέρουσαι τῷ εἰρημένῳ.   (3.4.1406b20–26)

The Simile is also a metaphor; the difference is but slight. When the poet says of Achilles that he
>   Leapt on the foe as a lion,
this is a simile; when he says of him "the lion leapt", it is a metaphor—here, since both are courageous, he has transferred to Achilles the name of "lion". Similes are useful in prose as well as in verse; but not often, since they are of the nature of poetry. They are to be employed just as metaphors are employed, since they are really the same thing except for the difference mentioned.

It would appear that a straightforward definition of simile has been made. The difference between εἰκών and metaphor is illustrated specifically by means of the comparative particle/conjunction ὡς (as, like). This implies not just that ὡς is an integral part of an εἰκών but, even more, that the label εἰκών can only be applied to the phrase ὡς δὲ λέων ἐπόρουσεν ("leapt on the foe as

---

Solmsen, *AJP* 62 (1941) 44, is cautious: "Yet we are not in a position to define the degree of his originality here; and, as we lack material for a comparison, any attempt to detect new departures in his theory of the metaphor or other phases of the rhetorical ornament would necessarily lead to guesswork." Kennedy 108, however, suggests a fair amount of originality in Aristotle's approach to metaphor (and, therefore, perhaps to εἰκών) when he says that Aristotle's theory of metaphor is "a topic which is conspicuously lacking in the *Rhetorica ad Alexandrum* and, indeed, was surely not to be found in any sophistic handbook."

²⁶ Ross's brackets.

a lion") as long as ὡς or some other introductory word of comparison is present. The example of εἰκών is thought[27] to be a
faulty reproduction of *Iliad* 20.164, ὦρτο λέων ὥς (he sprang
forth like a lion). The phrase might just as well have derived from
Iliad 10.485, 11.129, or 12.293, however, all of which are equally
close to (or distant from) Aristotle's words. Cope ascribes the lack
of accuracy to a lapse in memory, and such a lapse is, as has been
noted, not unique in Book III.[28] The short statement that εἰκών
is useful, but rarely, in prose because of its poetic coloring will be
examined together with Aristotle's evaluation of the moral and
instructive aspects of εἰκών.[29]

Immediately after the above passage a long paragraph begins
that casts interesting light on Aristotle's understanding of εἰκών
and particularly on the question of whether he intends to mean
"simile" by it.[30] He opens with the phrase:

εἰσὶν δ' εἰκόνες οἷον. . . .   (3.4.1406b27)

The following are examples of similes. . . .

Almost a dozen illustrative passages follow from fifth- and fourth-
century orators and prose writers: Androtion, Theodamas, Plato,
Pericles, Demosthenes (the fifth-century Athenian general),
Democrates, and Antisthenes. Many of the examples, unfortunately, are reported indirectly, and of these none of the original
passages from which they are taken is extant: "Theodamas compared (εἴκαζεν) Archidamus to an Euxenus . . ." (3.4.1406b30ff);
"Pericles compared (ἐοικέναι) the Samians to children . . ."
(1407a2ff); "Democrates compared (εἴκασεν) the political orators

---

[27] By Cope, Sandys, Roberts, Stanford, Freese, e.g.

[28] It is also possible that Aristotle's words came from some lost part of the Epic
Cycle, much of which was considered by the ancients to be Homeric, in which
case the citation may be wholly accurate.

[29] See below, p. 41f.

[30] All translators and commentators have rendered εἰκών "simile," indicating
a general belief in a positive answer.

to nurses . . ." (1407a8ff); "Antisthenes compared (εἴκασεν) the lean Cephisodotus to frankincense . . ." (1407a10ff). Others are reported more directly, but again the original words do not exist as a check on their exact form: "Androtion said of Idrieus that he was like (ὅμοιος) a terrier let off the chain . . ." (1406b27ff); "Pericles said that the Boeotians were like (ὅμοιοι) holm-oaks . . ." (1407a4ff); "Demosthenes said that the Athenian people were like (ὅμοιος) sea-sick men . . ." (1407a6ff). Only in three of Aristotle's ten examples of εἰκών can his actual source be referred to: Plato's *Republic*. What emerges when these passages are examined scarcely fits the common conviction that Aristotle is here discussing simile only. Of the three Platonic passages, two contain no introductory word of comparison and are simply general illustrative comparisons. The first example from Plato is reported:

καὶ τὸ ἐν τῇ Πολιτείᾳ τῇ Πλάτωνος, ὅτι οἱ τοὺς τεθνεῶτας σκυλεύοντες ἐοίκασι τοῖς κυνιδίοις ἃ τοὺς λίθους δάκνει, τοῦ βάλλοντος οὐχ ἁπτόμενα.   (3.4.1406b32–34)

In Plato's *Republic* those who strip the dead are compared to curs which bite the stones thrown at them but do not touch the thrower.

Aristotle's version of the Platonic passage contains a verb of comparison (ἐοίκασι), but the original words in the *Republic*, Book V, do not:

ἢ οἴει τι διάφορον δρᾶν τοὺς τοῦτο ποιοῦντας τῶν κυνῶν, αἱ τοῖς λίθοις οἷς ἂν βληθῶσι χαλεπαίνουσι, τοῦ βάλλοντος οὐχ ἁπτόμεναι;   (*Rep.* 469d9–e2)

Do you see any difference between such conduct and that of the dogs who snarl at the stones that hit them but don't touch the thrower?[31]

31 It is true, however, that to ask "do you see any difference between . . ." is a negative form of "don't you think they do just as. . . ." Thus this type of comparison is certainly not unrelated to simile.

Aristotle's second Platonic example of εἰκών,

καὶ ἡ εἰς τὸν δῆμον, ὅτι ὅμοιος ναυκλήρῳ ἰσχυρῷ μὲν ὑποκώφῳ δέ, *(Rhet.* 3.4.1406b34–36)

and there is the simile about the Athenian people, who are compared to a ship's captain who is strong but a little deaf,

is drawn from the famous illustration[32] of the perils of democracy in Book VI of the *Republic*, which has already been discussed in connection with Plato's use of εἰκών.[33] Plato's actual opening words in the lengthy illustration are:

νόησον γὰρ τοιουτονὶ γενόμενον εἴτε πολλῶν νεῶν πέρι εἴτε μιᾶς· ναύκληρον μεγέθει μὲν καὶ ῥώμῃ ὑπὲρ τοὺς ἐν τῇ νηὶ πάντας, ὑπόκωφον δὲ καὶ ὁρῶντα ὡσαύτως βραχύ τι καὶ γιγνώσκοντα περὶ ναυτικῶν ἕτερα τοιαῦτα. . . . *(Rep.* 488a7–b3)

Conceive this sort of thing happening either on many ships or on one: Picture a shipmaster in height and strength surpassing all others on the ship, but who is slightly deaf and of similarly impaired vision, and whose knowledge of navigation is on a par with his sight and hearing. . . .

Once again, Aristotle's word of comparison (ὅμοιος) is absent from the original passage. Only the final example from Plato contains an introductory word of comparison, ἔοικεν, the same comparative verb in fact that Aristotle uses in his adaptation:

καὶ ἡ εἰς τὰ μέτρα τῶν ποιητῶν, ὅτι ἔοικε τοῖς ἄνευ κάλλους ὡραίοις· οἱ μὲν γὰρ ἀπανθήσαντες, τὰ δὲ διαλυθέντα οὐχ ὅμοια φαίνεται. *(Rhet.* 3.4.1406b36–1407a2)

And the one about poets' verses, which are likened to persons who lack beauty but possess youthful freshness—when the freshness has faded the charm perishes, and so with verses when broken up into prose.

[32] Not "simile," as in Roberts' Oxford translation.
[33] See above, p. 15.

The original passage from the *Republic*, Book X, runs thus:

Οὐκοῦν, ἦν δ' ἐγώ, ἔοικεν τοῖς τῶν ὡραίων προσώποις, καλῶν
δὲ μή, οἷα γίγνεται ἰδεῖν ὅταν αὐτὰ τὸ ἄνθος προλίπῃ;

(*Rep.* 601b6–7)

Do they [poet's verses] not, said I, resemble the faces of ado-
lescents, young but not really beautiful, when the bloom of youth
abandons them?

Aristotle's discussion of εἰκών now appears in a somewhat different light. His opening paragraph certainly seemed to define
simile, but the examples of εἰκών for which the original wording
can be checked suggest that not merely simile but stylistic comparisons in general are Aristotle's subject. The inexactness of his
citations indicates that he did not have a text of the *Republic* in
front of him; therefore it is possible to argue that through faulty
memory he may have thought each of the Platonic examples to
be, like the Homeric passage, a simile in form. It seems more
plausible that Aristotle was well aware of the varying form of his
Platonic examples, and that a similar variety would be found in
the other examples were their original contexts available. The
apparent limitation of εἰκών to simile in his opening statement is
due to the Homeric example. Similes are the regular form for
Homeric comparisons, and in turning to Homer for an initial
example Aristotle not only of necessity adduces a simile but is
also thereby somewhat constrained to discuss εἰκών in terms of
simile. A definite advantage accrues for his aim of differentiating
metaphor and εἰκών, since he is able to light on the introductory
comparative word of a simile as the key. To describe the comparative element of a general illustration would be more involved
and less well suited to his immediate purpose, but as a corrective
Aristotle shows in his ensuing list of examples that an overall element of comparison, just as much as the specific introductory
word of a simile, is the mark of an εἰκών.

Both the Homeric simile, then, and the more general comparative form of at least two of the prose examples of εἰκών can fit within a single concept of stylistic comparison. A second discrepancy between the Homeric and the prose examples of εἰκών is less troublesome. The Homeric simile ὡς δὲ λέων ἐπόρουσεν ("leapt on the foe as a lion") contains an introductory word and a substantive; it is the briefest possible comparison. All the prose εἰκόνες, on the other hand, contain several words and would comprise two or more verses of poetry. Aristotle might be distinguishing two different kinds of εἰκών on the basis of length, but almost certainly he is not. Whether "leapt on the foe as a lion" refers to *Iliad* 20.164 or to another Homeric source, the reference is surely to the whole of the original passage. In the case of *Iliad* 20.164 this turns out to be a simile of nine verses. Among the prose examples, the relatively brief reference to Plato's comparison of democracy with a shipmaster certainly refers to all of the lengthy illustration, not just to the approximately corresponding opening words. Thus, it seems accurate to say that Aristotle's concept of εἰκών is not concerned with length or brevity.[34] He can refer to a long comparison by means of a short one, and each is an εἰκών. In this area he does not make the distinction of some subsequent treatises.[35]

The list of prose examples of εἰκών is followed by a short passage of summation commenting on the examples and obscurely restating Aristotle's view of εἰκών as a subdivision of metaphor:

πάσας δὲ ταύτας καὶ ὡς εἰκόνας καὶ ὡς μεταφορὰς ἔξεστι λέγειν,
ὥστε ὅσαι ἂν εὐδοκιμῶσιν ὡς μεταφοραὶ λεχθεῖσαι, δῆλον ὅτι
αὗται καὶ εἰκόνες ἔσονται, καὶ αἱ εἰκόνες μεταφοραὶ λόγου
δεόμεναι.   (3.4.1407a11–15)

---

34 See D. M. Schenkeveld, *Studies in Demetrius On Style* (Amsterdam 1964) 99, for a similar conclusion.

35 In particular the *Rhetorica ad Herennium* and [Demetrius] *On Style*. G. M. A. Grube, *A Greek Critic: Demetrius On Style* (Toronto 1961) 37, is therefore off the mark when he says that Aristotle, though using a short simile, has the longer type in mind. Length is not a major concern to Aristotle, nor indeed is he discussing simile exclusively.

All these ideas may be expressed either as similes or as metaphors; those which succeed as metaphors will obviously do well also as similes, and similes, with the explanation omitted, will appear as metaphors.

All but the last phrase is clear enough. Aristotle says that any of the examples of εἰκών could also be expressed as metaphor, *mutatis mutandis*, and that any fine metaphor can be changed into an εἰκών. The latter point is probably not original. Interest in εὐδοκιμοῦσαι μεταφοραί (successful metaphors) will reappear, and the scholiast's comment in chapter 11 that Theodorus connected fine metaphors and εἰκών has already been remarked.[36] The final phrase, however, is puzzling, the difficulty lying specifically in the last two words. Two different meanings have been assigned by commentators to λόγου, "explanation"[37] or "development" and "(single) word." λόγος carries neither meaning easily, and the text is probably corrupt. A possible remedy is to take λόγου in the sense of "prose," a sense used by Aristotle in the opening part of the chapter ("similes are useful in prose, ἐν λόγῳ, as well as in verse; but not often, since they are of the nature of poetry"[38]), and to emend δεόμεναι so that the phrase will bear the meaning "and similes will appear as metaphors, but not normally/easily in prose." The text should perhaps be καὶ αἱ εἰκόνες μεταφοραὶ λόγου δὲ οὐκ οἰκεῖαι, or λόγῳ δὲ οὐ πρέπουσαι.[39]

This difficult passage and a short additional remark on metaphor (to be referred to in connection with chapter 11[40]) conclude chapter 4. Chapter 5 initiates a series of chapters dealing with λέξις (style) in groups of words. Such features of style as purity (τὸ Ἑλληνίζειν), grandeur (ὄγκος), propriety (τὸ πρέπον),

[36] See above, p. 3
[37] As in Roberts' translation.
[38] *Rhet.* 3.4.1406b24–25.
[39] For a full discussion of this textual difficulty, see M. McCall, "Aristotle, *Rhetoric* III.4.1407a15 and 11.1413a5," *RhM* 111 (1968) 159–163.
[40] See below, p. 45.

Aristotle

rhythm, and periodic structure are discussed in chapters 5–9. Chapter 10 turns to two kinds of sayings, τὰ ἀστεῖα καὶ τὰ εὐδοκιμοῦντα⁴¹ (lively and popular expressions), concentrating especially on τὸ ἀστεῖον (liveliness or vivacity). Again metaphor is lauded for conveying this quality in the highest degree, and εἰκών is also found praiseworthy in that it closely resembles metaphor. Metaphor, we are told, possesses the quality of liveliness because it is the stylistic figure that is most instructive for the reader. The theory that a feature of style is worthy of praise insofar as it is instructive is an important one to Aristotle, and it appears prominently in this chapter and the next in connection with discussion of metaphor and εἰκών.⁴² Indeed, it is the particular fact that εἰκών is closely related to metaphor, can therefore be instructive, and can thus possess the quality of τὸ ἀστεῖον that causes it to be mentioned in the present chapter:

τὸ γὰρ μανθάνειν ῥᾳδίως ἡδὺ φύσει πᾶσιν ἐστί . . . ἡ δὲ μεταφορὰ ποιεῖ τοῦτο μάλιστα. . . . ποιοῦσιν μὲν οὖν καὶ αἱ τῶν ποιητῶν εἰκόνες τὸ αὐτό· διόπερ ἂν εὖ, ἀστεῖον φαίνεται. ἔστιν γὰρ ἡ εἰκών, καθάπερ εἴρηται πρότερον, μεταφορὰ διαφέρουσα προθέσει·⁴³ διὸ ἧττον ἡδύ, ὅτι μακροτέρως· καὶ οὐ λέγει ὡς τοῦτο ἐκεῖνο· οὐκοῦν οὐδὲ ζητεῖ τοῦτο ἡ ψυχή.
(3.10.1410b10–11,13,15–20)

⁴¹ Rhet. 3.10.1410b6–7.

⁴² Kennedy 111 remarks: "Chapters ten and eleven are devoted to what would later be called figures of speech, all of which Aristotle treats as metaphors. This is a part of the theory of style which was destined for enormous amplification in the following centuries, but none of the later Greek or Roman accounts seem to share Aristotle's philosophical concern with the psychological bases of figures of speech. All four kinds of metaphor teach us something and as a result produce pleasure."

⁴³ There is a manuscript choice here between προθέσει and προσθέσει. Both make sense in the context, προθέσει meaning "differing in the way it is put, in statement," and προσθέσει meaning "differing in application." There is not much ground for a preference except that διαφέρουσα προθέσει is somewhat analogous to Aristotle's earlier phrase at 1406b26, διαφέρουσαι τῷ εἰρημένῳ. προσθέσει, on the other hand, may be supported by a phrase in [Demetrius] On Style; see below, chap. V n. 51.

We all naturally find it agreeable to get hold of new ideas easily . . . it is from metaphor that we can best get hold of something fresh. . . . The similes of the poets do the same, and therefore, if they are good similes, give an effect of brilliance (ἀστεῖον). The simile, as has been said before, is a metaphor, differing from it only in the way it is put; and just because it is longer it is less attractive. Besides, it does not say outright that "this" *is* "that," and therefore the hearer is less interested in the idea.

Several points deserve comment, all of them bearing on the relative degree of instructiveness of metaphor and εἰκών. It has been noted that in chapter 2 metaphor is called the most important aid toward an effective, distinctive prose style, if it is employed appropriately:

καὶ τὸ σαφὲς καὶ τὸ ἡδὺ καὶ τὸ ξενικὸν ἔχει μάλιστα ἡ μεταφορά. . . . δεῖ δὲ καὶ τὰ ἐπίθετα καὶ τὰς μεταφορὰς ἁρμοττού-
σας λέγειν.   (3.2.1405a8–9,10–11)

Metaphor, moreover, gives style clearness, charm, and distinction as nothing else can. . . . Metaphors, like epithets, must be fitting.

But in chapter 3, as has also been mentioned, an inappropriate metaphor is said to contribute to what Aristotle calls frigid style (τὸ ψυχρόν). The inappropriateness arises when a metaphor smacks too much of comic or tragic poetry: it becomes too poetical and loses its power to persuade.[44] Because instruction is a form of persuasion, the passage in chapter 3 can be connected with the passage on instructiveness in chapter 10. It may be surmised that Aristotle would have said that if a metaphor loses its power to persuade it also loses its power to instruct, and that this joint blow to its faculties of persuasion and instruction occurs when it becomes too poetical.

This connection will help, in turn, to explain one of the phrases regarding εἰκών in chapter 4 that was mentioned earlier only in

[44] *Rhet.* 3.3.1406b5–15.

passing:[45] "Similes are useful in prose as well as in verse; but not often, since they are of the nature of poetry" (3.4.1406b24–25). The phrase can now be allied with Aristotle's evaluation of the instructive potential of εἰκών in chapter 10. The train of argument is much the same as with metaphor: εἰκών will be used only occasionally in prose because it is poetical, which reduces its power to persuade. This is the expanded meaning of the phrase above from chapter 4 (analogous to Aristotle's criticism of the poetical metaphor in chapter 3). In chapter 10, εἰκών is said to be able to instruct, just as metaphor does, but to be less pleasant or attractive (ἡδύ) than metaphor because it is more extended. The exact sense of ἡδύ in this context is made clear earlier in the passage. Pleasure (τὸ ἡδύ) results from something learned easily, and when Aristotle states that εἰκών is less pleasant than metaphor because it is longer he is also saying that εἰκών instructs less readily than metaphor. Two reasons, then, are given in separate passages why εἰκών is less instructive than metaphor: it is poetical (chapter 4) and it is longer (chapter 10). Neither passage states the conclusion baldly, but the implications seem clear.

It is possible that Aristotle wanted these two deficiencies linked in a single process: because εἰκών is longer it is poetical and therefore instructs less well. More probably the two should remain distinct. The brief explanation of why the length of an εἰκών decreases its instructive value does not appear immediately related to the presence or absence of a poetical shading: "Besides (καί),[46] it does not say outright that 'this' *is* 'that', and therefore the hearer is less interested in the idea" (3.10.1410b19–20). The true instructive value of metaphor lies in the sense of direct correspondence between the subject and the predicate gained by the hearer from the form "this *is* that."[47] In an εἰκών, on the other

[45] See above, p. 33.

[46] The force of the καί is to introduce a different and independent thought from anything said previously.

[47] C. S. Baldwin, *Ancient Rhetoric and Poetic* (New York 1924) 31, discusses more fully this theme of intellectual suggestion.

hand, the hearer encounters an extended form in which subject and predicate are merely said to be similar in some way.[48] He does not perceive the two parts as corresponding directly, and this diluted character of the εἰκών makes the thought less readily instructive.

The final discussion of εἰκών comes in chapter 11. Between the appearances of εἰκών in chapters 10 and 11, however, two passages occur that stress Aristotle's lack of interest in the exact form of stylistic figures. Both deal with metaphor. The first is part of a treatment of proportional metaphor (ἡ μεταφορὰ κατ' ἀναλογίαν), about which more will be said in connection with the discussion of εἰκών in chapter 11. The second half of chapter 10 presents a long list of proportional metaphors, the opening example of which is a reported comment of Pericles. The metaphor is introduced by a comparative word, ὥσπερ:

Περικλῆς ἔφη τὴν νεότητα τὴν ἀπολομένην ἐν τῷ πολέμῳ οὕτως ἠφανίσθαι ἐκ τῆς πόλεως ὥσπερ εἴ τις τὸ ἔαρ ἐκ τοῦ ἐνιαυτοῦ ἐξέλοι. (3.10.1411a2–4)

Thus Pericles, for instance, said that the vanishing from their country of the young men who had fallen in the war was "as if the spring were taken out of the year".

The second passage is at the beginning of chapter 11, where Aristotle shifts from the proportional metaphor to metaphors that are graphic and active. After an example of one that is not graphic and active he quotes two metaphors from Isocrates' *Philippus* that are:

ἀλλὰ τὸ "ἀνθοῦσαν ἔχοντος τὴν ἀκμήν"[49] ἐνέργεια, καὶ τὸ "σὲ δ' ὥσπερ ἄφετον"[50] ἐνέργεια. (3.11.1411b27–29)

---

[48] Something that will be true whether the εἰκών is a simile or a more general comparison.

[49] Isocrates, *Philippus* 10.

[50] *Ibid.*, 127.

On the other hand, in the expression "with his vigour in full bloom" there is a notion of activity; and so in "But you must roam as free as a sacred victim."

The second of these graphic metaphors again contains an introductory word of comparison, ὥσπερ. There is no indication that Aristotle intends by "metaphor" something greatly different from our understanding of the term, and so the strange form— that of a simile—of these two Aristotelian metaphors is explicable only by supposing that he does not dwell on the particular form of his metaphors so long as they achieve the desired stylistic end, for example, proportionality or activity. Imprecision in form, observed already in the analysis of εἰκών in chapter 4, is now paralleled in Aristotle's approach to metaphor.

Chapter 11 continues to give examples, almost all from Homer, of metaphors that possess activity (ἐνέργεια) in that they endow inanimate objects with lifelike qualities. At the end of the list, Aristotle mentions εἰκών in a manner that is by now predictable, namely, that fine εἰκόνες can have the same desirable effect as metaphor. He refers specifically to Homer:

ποιεῖ δὲ καὶ ἐν ταῖς εὐδοκιμούσαις εἰκόσιν ἐπὶ τῶν ἀψύχων ταυτά·

"κυρτά, φαληριόωντα· πρὸ μέν τ᾽ ἄλλ᾽, αὐτὰρ ἐπ᾽ ἄλλα" ·51
κινούμενα γὰρ καὶ ζῶντα ποιεῖ πάντα, ἡ δ᾽ ἐνέργεια κίνησις.
(3.11.1412a7–10)

In his famous similes, too, he [Homer] treats inanimate things in the same way:

Curving and crested with white, host following host without ceasing.

Here he represents everything as moving and living; and activity is movement.

Possibly this example of activity in an εἰκών could be used to

51 *Iliad* 13.799.

suggest further that for Aristotle the form of an εἰκών is variable. The Homeric verse contains two images and a brief description; it might better be termed a metaphor than a type of comparison.[52] In fact, however, Aristotle's phrase is ἐν ταῖς εὐδοκιμούσαις εἰκόσιν, "in (or *within*) his famous εἰκόνες." He does not mean that the verse he quotes *is* an εἰκών, but only part of one—the part in which an inanimate object, in this case "waves" (κύματα),[53] is endowed with lifelike qualities, κυρτά and φαληριόωντα ("curving and crested with white").[54] The Homeric verse is part of a rather extended simile,[55] and the whole simile is the true referent of εἰκόσιν, not merely the single verse quoted.

A more extended passage on εἰκών comes near the end of chapter 11. Aristotle's general topic is still the several means of achieving liveliness (τὸ ἀστεῖον), and he now emphasizes the importance of antithesis and balanced clauses (ἀντίθεσις καὶ παρίσωσις) as aids.[56] As usual, metaphor is said to have the greatest potential for these virtues of style; εἰκών can make good use of them, too, because of its relation to metaphor. In this final Aristotelian passage on εἰκών, however, there is a subtle change in approach. Chapters 10 and 11 have stressed repeatedly that the finest metaphor is proportional (ἡ μεταφορὰ κατ᾽ ἀναλογίαν); the present passage in chapter 11 makes it clear that this is the kind of metaphor most nearly equivalent to εἰκών. So, while metaphor remains very much the major and εἰκών the subordinate figure, it now appears that the previous absolute supremacy of metaphor over εἰκών in value and desirability has been modified.

[52] Indeed, this is precisely what one ancient critic does term the verse; see below, p. 145, on [Demetrius] *On Style* 81.

[53] *Iliad* 13.798.

[54] Translators and LSJ render φαληριόωντα by some such passive phrase as Roberts' "crested with white." It seems more likely that Aristotle thought of the word as active in order for it to contain an animating quality: thus "whitening" or "cresting with foam" may be preferable.

[55] *Iliad* 13.795–799.

[56] *Rhet.* 3.11.1412b33.

Exactly what Aristotle means by proportional metaphor and in what way it resembles εἰκών can be seen from the text:

εἰσὶν δὲ καὶ αἱ εἰκόνες, ὥσπερ εἴρηται καὶ ἐν τοῖς ἄνω, αἱ εὐδοκιμοῦσαι τρόπον τινὰ μεταφοραί· ἀεὶ γὰρ ἐκ δυοῖν λέγονται, ὥσπερ ἡ ἀνάλογον μεταφορά, οἷον "ἡ ἀσπίς", φαμέν, "ἐστι φιάλη Ἄρεως",⁵⁷ καὶ "τὸ τόξον φόρμιγξ ἄχορδος".⁵⁸ οὕτω μὲν οὖν λέγουσιν οὐχ ἁπλοῦν, τὸ δ' εἰπεῖν τὸ τόξον φόρμιγγα ἢ τὴν ἀσπίδα φιάλην ἁπλοῦν. (3.11.1412b34–1413a3)

Successful similes also, as has been said above, are in a sense metaphors, since they always involve two relations like the proportional metaphor. Thus: a shield, we say, is the "drinking-bowl of Ares", and a bow is the "chordless lyre". This way of putting a metaphor is not "simple", as it would be if we called the bow a lyre or the shield a drinking-bowl.

Both εἰκών and proportional metaphor "involve two relations."⁵⁹ The examples given are proportional because of the reciprocity of their two parts, a quality absent in a metaphor like "they boiled with anger." Reciprocity is explained in an earlier remark on proportional metaphor at the end of chapter 4, about which comment was postponed at the time.⁶⁰ There the example of proportional metaphor is the same as the first example of the present passage. Aristotle presents the metaphor in two ways, one a reversal of the other, and states that the reciprocity makes the metaphor proportional:

ἀεὶ δὲ δεῖ τὴν μεταφορὰν τὴν ἐκ τοῦ ἀνάλογον ἀνταποδιδόναι καὶ ἐπὶ θάτερα τῶν ὁμογενῶν, οἷον εἰ ἡ φιάλη ἀσπὶς Διονύσου, καὶ τὴν ἀσπίδα ἁρμόττει λέγεσθαι φιάλην Ἄρεως.

(3.4.1407a15–18)

---

⁵⁷ Timotheus, frag. 21 (ed. Page).
⁵⁸ Attributed to Theognis, probably Theognis Tragicus, in [Demetrius] *On Style* 85.
⁵⁹ Or, as Cope, *Rhetoric* III 137, translates, "are composed of (or, expressed in) two terms."
⁶⁰ See above, p. 38.

But the proportional metaphor must always apply reciprocally to either of its co-ordinate terms. For instance, if a drinking-bowl is the shield of Dionysus, a shield may fittingly be called the drinking-bowl of Ares.

If a reversal of terms were not possible, there would be no proportional metaphor.

So much is clear. Some obscurity, however, surrounds the meaning of the last sentence of the passage from chapter 11. The literal sense is not difficult: "In this case, then, they are not speaking simply, but to say the bow is a lyre or the shield is a bowl is to speak simply." In question is the significance of οὐχ ἁπλοῦν, "not simple," and ἁπλοῦν, "simple." There is agreement that οὐχ ἁπλοῦν refers back to the proportional metaphors, while ἁπλοῦν denotes simpler metaphors that are not proportional (since there is no third stated term and no fourth understood term to complete the potential for reciprocity). Views differ, however, on the further nature of what is stated οὐχ ἁπλοῦν or ἁπλοῦν. Cope's interpretation is added to his translation: "'When thus expressed, the phrase is not single' (or simple; it has *both* terms expressed, the two terms viz. that are brought into comparison; and is therefore a simile); 'whereas to call the bow a harp or the shield a goblet is single' (and therefore only a metaphor)."[61] This must be erroneous. The text gives no indication at all that a proportional οὐχ ἁπλοῦν metaphor *is* a simile whereas a nonproportional ἁπλοῦν metaphor is just a metaphor. Indeed, the very next sentence in chapter 11 states, with examples, that there are also εἰκόνες that are ἁπλαῖ (simple). In addition, it is patently inaccurate to designate as a simile "a shield is Ares' bowl." What Aristotle does mean (and what the text says) is that the οὐχ

---

[61] Cope, *Rhetoric* III 137. The Loeb translator, Freese, concurs in his note: "These additions [Freese refers to "of Ares" and "chordless" in the two proportional metaphors], besides involving greater detail (a characteristic of the simile), distinctly bring out the contrast of the two terms and make a simile, whereas the metaphor simply transfers the meaning."

ἁπλοῦν and ἁπλοῦν metaphors are merely different types of metaphor, and that successful (εὐδοκιμοῦσαι) εἰκόνες are those containing the same characteristic of reciprocal terms as οὐχ ἁπλοῦν proportional metaphors. Roberts' careful translation of the whole passage, though it does not express in detail the above view, clearly differentiates between proportional metaphors and εἰκόνες and thus correctly departs from Cope.[62]

It is successful εἰκόνες that are constructed in similar fashion to proportional metaphors; but, as has been mentioned, Aristotle's next remark indicates that εἰκόνες also exist that resemble simple (ἁπλαῖ) metaphors. Two examples of such εἰκόνες are presented. Aristotle then seems to repeat for emphasis that the successful εἰκόνες are those resembling in construction proportional metaphors, and he appends three examples. But the language of his emphatic repetition is so abrupt that the text is again suspect:

> καὶ εἰκάζουσιν δὲ οὕτως, οἷον πιθήκῳ αὐλητήν, λύχνῳ ψακαζο-
> μένῳ μύωπα· ἄμφω γὰρ συνάγεται. τὸ δὲ εὖ ἐστιν ὅταν
> μεταφορὰ ᾖ· ἔστιν γὰρ εἰκάσαι τὴν ἀσπίδα φιάλῃ "Αρεως καὶ
> τὸ ἐρείπιον ῥάκει οἰκίας, καὶ τὸ τὸν Νικήρατον φάναι Φιλοκ-
> τήτην εἶναι δεδηγμένον ὑπὸ Πράτυος.... (3.11.1413a3–8)

There are "simple" similes also: we may say that a flute-player is like a monkey, or that a short-sighted man's eyes are like a lamp-flame with water dropping on it, since both eyes and flame keep winking. A simile succeeds best when it is a converted metaphor, for it is possible to say that a shield is like the drinking-bowl of Ares, or that a ruin is like a house in rags, and to say that Niceratus is like a Philoctetes stung by Pratys....

The opening phrase may be translated literally "and they also make εἰκόνες thus...." The two examples that follow are

---

[62] Jebb's translation (R. C. Jebb, *The Rhetoric of Aristotle*, ed. J. E. Sandys [Cambridge 1909] 175), "thus stated, it is not a *simple* metaphor; it would be a *simple* metaphor to say that the bow is a lyre, or the shield a goblet," also observes a division.

εἰκόνες, which, if expressed as metaphors, would be simple ones. In the next phrase:

τὸ δὲ εὖ ἐστὶν ὅταν μεταφορὰ ᾖ,

A simile succeeds best when it is a converted metaphor,

εἰκάζειν (to make an εἰκών) is easily understood with τὸ δὲ εὖ (fine, successful), and there is an immediate implied contrast between "to make εἰκόνες in a fine way" and the previous "to make (simple) εἰκόνες." The exact character of the fine εἰκόνες is disputed, however. Roberts speaks for the majority of commentators when he simply connects fine εἰκόνες with metaphor in general. Similarly, Cope translates: "Excellence is attained in them when they contain (involve) metaphor."[63] This interpretation creates two difficulties. The first is that Aristotle's statement would be pointless if he means no more than that *fine* εἰκόνες are those which derive from metaphor, since the preceding sentence has just stated that εἰκόνες *in general* can be formed that derive from metaphor. Second, the first of the three examples of τὸ δὲ εὖ (εἰκάζειν), "fine εἰκόνες," is formed from the familiar proportional metaphor "the shield is the drinking-bowl of Ares."

It would seem that "proportional" must be understood with "metaphor" (μεταφορά) in the phrase ὅταν μεταφορά ᾖ. A few commentators have realized this: Jebb, for instance, translates, "the happy simile is when there is 'proportional' metaphor."[64] But the text should probably be corrected to say what Aristotle means, and conceivably the words ἡ κατ' ἀναλογίαν (proportional) have been dropped. The whole original phrase, then, would be τὸ δὲ εὖ ἐστὶν ὅταν μεταφορὰ ἡ κατ' ἀναλογίαν ᾖ (successful εἰκόνες occur when they involve proportional metaphor).[65]

[63] Cope, *Rhetoric* III 139.
[64] Jebb 175.
[65] For fuller discussion of this difficulty, see M. McCall, *RhM* III (1968) 164–165.

The remainder of this final Aristotelian analysis of εἰκών is straightforward. After the three examples of εἰκόνες that are successful (εὖ), Aristotle repeats once again his theme that this type of εἰκών, which is akin to proportional metaphor, will be popular and successful. He gives two more examples, then concludes with a final declaration that εἰκών is really part of metaphor:

ἐν οἷς μάλιστά τ' ἐκπίπτουσιν οἱ ποιηταὶ ἐὰν μὴ εὖ, καὶ ἐὰν εὖ, εὐδοκιμοῦσιν· λέγω δ' ὅταν ἀποδιδῶσιν⁶⁶
　　"ὥσπερ σέλινον οὖλα τὰ σκέλη φορεῖ".⁶⁷
　　"ὥσπερ Φιλάμμων ζυγομαχῶν τῷ κωρύκῳ."⁶⁸
καὶ τὰ τοιαῦτα πάντ' εἰκόνες εἰσίν. αἱ δ' εἰκόνες ὅτι μεταφοραί,
εἴρηται πολλάκις.　　　　　　　　　(3.11.1413a10–16)

It is in these respects that poets fail worst when they fail, and succeed best when they succeed, i.e. when they give the resemblance pat, as in

　　　　Those legs of his curl just like parsley leaves;
and
　　　　Just like Philammon struggling with his punch-ball.

These are all similes; and that similes are metaphors has been stated often already.

A curious omission on Aristotle's part may be mentioned here. It has been noted that εἰκών is relegated mainly to the sphere of poetry, prompting a look at the *Poetics* for some discussion of the term. The result is disappointing: no discussion occurs and, indeed,

---

⁶⁶ It is not only the words εὖ and εὐδοκιμοῦσιν that indicate that Aristotle is discussing εἰκόνες deriving from proportional metaphor; ἀποδιδῶσιν recalls ἀνταποδιδόναι in the passage on proportional metaphor in chapter 4. Roberts' "give the resemblance pat" does not really catch this; Cope's "when they make (the two members) correspond" is better.

⁶⁷ Kock, *CAF* III 448 (fragmenta adespota 207).

⁶⁸ *Ibid.* (fr. adesp. 208). Interestingly, both of these examples are used in the next part of chapter 11 (1413a24ff) as instances of hyperbole. In other words, their simile form does not prevent them from fulfilling the purpose of, and therefore becoming, a second kind of figure.

there is not even a single mention of εἰκών.[69] Style (λέξις) is treated in the latter part of the *Poetics* and, as in the *Rhetoric*, metaphor is praised lavishly. In discussing the use of words and phrases, for instance, Aristotle says that the finest skill of all is command of metaphor:

πολὺ δὲ μέγιστον τὸ μεταφορικὸν εἶναι. μόνον γὰρ τοῦτο οὔτε παρ' ἄλλου ἔστι λαβεῖν εὐφυΐας τε σημεῖόν ἐστι· τὸ γὰρ εὖ μεταφέρειν τὸ τὸ ὅμοιον θεωρεῖν ἐστιν.[70] (*Poetics* 22.1459a5–8)

But the greatest thing by far is to be a master of metaphor. It is the one thing that cannot be learnt from others; and it is also a sign of genius, since a good metaphor implies an intuitive perception of the similarity in dissimilars.[71]

There is, however, no accompanying treatment of εἰκών. A lacuna occurs slightly earlier in the text, just after a discussion of various kinds of metaphor, and one might speculate that some mention of εἰκών filled the lacuna, but this is unlikely. The lacuna is brief, and there is a clear indication of what it contained. Aristotle has stated:

ἅπαν δὲ ὄνομά ἐστιν ἢ κύριον ἢ γλῶττα ἢ μεταφορὰ ἢ κόσμος ἢ πεποιημένον ἢ ἐπεκτεταμένον ἢ ὑφῃρημένον ἢ ἐξηλλαγμένον.
(*Poetics* 21.1457b1–3)

A noun must always be either (1) the ordinary word for the thing, or (2) a strange word, or (3) a metaphor, or (4) an ornamental word, or (5) a coined word, or (6) a word lengthened out, or (7) curtailed, or (8) altered in form.

He proceeds to define the first three of these and, under metaphor,

---

[69] W. B. Stanford, *Greek Metaphor* (Oxford 1936) 27, also remarks on the omission.

[70] Kassel's OCT.

[71] Bywater's translation (vol. XI of *The Works of Aristotle Translated*, ed. W. D. Ross [Oxford: Clarendon Press, 1924]).

particularly proportional metaphor.[72] Then at 1457b34 comes a short lacuna and immediately thereafter a definition of ὄνομα πεποιημένον ("a coined word"). The lacuna, therefore, undoubtedly defined κόσμος ("an ornamental word").[73] The absence of any mention of εἰκών in the *Poetics* might be explicable if one could assume that the *Rhetoric* was prior in composition: views expressed in the earlier *Rhetoric* on εἰκών as a part of metaphor could then apply to any discussion of metaphor in the later *Poetics*. References in the *Rhetoric* to the *Poetics* eliminate this possibility.[74] Similarly, if the *Poetics* preceded the *Rhetoric*, it might be argued that Aristotle's theories on εἰκών had not yet evolved—but here references in the *Poetics* to the *Rhetoric* stand in the way.[75] Neither work can be proved to precede the other; almost certainly both were revised and supplemented from time to time. The odd absence of εἰκών from the *Poetics* must be left unresolved.

Despite this puzzle, Aristotle's overall understanding of εἰκών is clear enough, and a summary is possible. Most obvious is the fact, continually stressed, that εἰκών is a subordinate part of metaphor. This basic relationship is stated six times in the three chapters that discuss εἰκών.[76] It is Aristotle's fundamental position on εἰκών and is the more interesting because, much as he is the *fons et origo* of so much ancient rhetorical theory, this particularly intense belief of his was followed only in a limited way and was disregarded by the many later rhetoricians and critics who separated metaphor and comparison, and reversed by those who made metaphor a subordinate part of comparison. Aristotle assigns several other characteristics to εἰκών: it is better fitted for poetry

[72] Including use of the standard example "the shield is the drinking-bowl of Ares."

[73] Kassel's critical note points this out.

[74] Such as at *Rhet.* 3.1.1404a37–39.

[75] Such as at *Poetics* 19.1456a33–36.

[76] *Rhet.* 3.4.1406b20; 3.4.1406b25–26; 3.4.1407a14–15; 3.10.1410b17–18; 3.11.1412b34–35; 3.11.1413a15–16.

than for prose; it will always be more extended than metaphor; its instructive potential, for reasons of length and poetic nature, is diluted, rendering it less valuable as a stylistic figure than metaphor.[77] One may infer, both from the varied length of his examples and from his silence on the matter, that Aristotle would make no distinction between a brief and a long stylistic comparison; one is as much an εἰκών as the other. A decisive line, however, is drawn between comparison as an element of proof (παραβολή) and comparison as a purely literary feature of style (εἰκών). Neither term appears in any connection with the other,[78] and it seems not to have occurred to Aristotle that the natures of a comparison of proof and a comparison of style might be in some ways similar, or even equivalent. In one sense his attitude is typical of ancient critics, in that almost never does a writer use one term of comparison for all contexts. But the different facets of comparison are rarely divided in the same manner from one critic to the next, and Aristotle's classification of παραβολή as a comparison of proof and εἰκών as a stylistic comparison never became standard. Finally, while readily acknowledging that the three εἰκόνες reported directly[79] in chapter 11 are similes, one may still maintain that the freedom of form belonging to εἰκών in chapter 4 remains in force for Aristotle's entire analysis of the word. The εἰκόνες he discusses in chapter 11 are only one particular kind, εὐδοκιμοῦσα (fine, popular, successful). The salient feature of this type of εἰκών is that it is the closest of all to proportional metaphor. If, then, it is to have a structure of reciprocal terms and be as much akin as possible to proportional metaphor,

[77] This unusual approach to the relative value of the elements of style is put nicely by Cope, *Rhetoric* III 130, when he speaks of "the theory which had become habitual with Aristotle, that all intellectual pleasure is due to the natural desire of learning." The disappearance in later rhetoric of this view of style helps explain why Aristotle's apotheosis of metaphor was not followed more often.

[78] Except that both are used, for different reasons, in collocation with παράδειγμα; see above, n. 24.

[79] Five others are reported indirectly.

it will undergo the minimal change from the form of a metaphor, namely by the lone addition of a comparative word. It would seem, therefore, that Aristotle constructs εὐδοκιμοῦσαι εἰκόνες as similes rather than as general comparisons or illustrations in order to effect the least possible change from metaphor and that, accordingly, similes are to Aristotle the finest kind of εἰκών, since to approach metaphor is to move upward on the scale of the ἀρεταὶ λέξεως (virtues of style). In Aristotle's system, it can be concluded, εἰκών comprises all types of stylistic comparison, but a partially distinct concept of simile as the most praiseworthy is in evidence.

A vast gap in the ancient testimony occurs between Aristotle and the subject of the next chapter, the *Rhetorica ad Herennium*. During this time virtually all the doctrines to appear in Latin and later Greek rhetorical writings evolved and solidified in their final form;[80] nevertheless, of this period of development extending from Aristotle's death to the first century B.C., almost nothing is known except what is stated in or can be inferred from later treatises. The first figure of the gap, Theophrastus, was active in rhetoric, but his theories are only partially reconstructible. His work περὶ λέξεως (*On Style*), famous in antiquity but now lost, was probably the first treatise to deal with style as a subject independent of rhetoric in general. It is reasonable to assume that it was based on Aristotle's own approach to style in the *Rhetoric*.[81] Whether Theophrastus specifically discussed terms of comparison cannot easily be said. A brief passage in *On the Sublime* suggests that comparison, indeed simile, at least was mentioned by

[80] Among the rhetorical doctrines that underwent change during this period were: the three parts of rhetoric increased to five by the addition of delivery and memory; the four parts of an oration increased to six by the addition of partition and refutation. See Kennedy 265ff on these and other changes. Kroll 1101 is of the opinion, however, that changes from the fourth to the first centuries were more of arrangement and emphasis than of basic theory.

[81] Kroll 1071.

Theophrastus, but it is more likely that the passage points to something quite different. In speaking of metaphor, the author of *On the Sublime* says that a metaphor, or even a string of them, is never too strong a figure if used at times of high emotion and real sublimity; but when emotion is at a lower key it is sometimes better to soften the intensity of the metaphor. The author then describes how Aristotle and Theophrastus advocated accomplishing this, namely by prefacing the metaphor with certain words and phrases:

διόπερ ὁ μὲν ᾿Αριστοτέλης καὶ ὁ Θεόφραστος μειλίγματά φασί τινα τῶν θρασειῶν εἶναι ταῦτα μεταφορῶν, τὸ "ὡσπερεὶ" φάναι καὶ "οἱονεὶ" καὶ "εἰ χρὴ τοῦτον εἰπεῖν τὸν τρόπον" καὶ "εἰ δεῖ παρακινδυνευτικώτερον λέξαι."[82]

(*On the Sublime* 32.3)

In the same spirit, Aristotle and Theophrastus point out that the following phrases serve to soften bold metaphors—"as if," and "as it were," and "if one may say so," and "if one may venture such an expression."[83]

It is tempting to take the first two of these μειλίγματα (softenings) as introductory words of comparison; the passage would then attribute to Aristotle and Theophrastus the view, not encountered until now, that comparisons—or perhaps just similes—are to be used when metaphors seem too bold. But because ὡσπερεί and οἱονεί, both by themselves and especially in collocation with the two longer phrases, seem surely to carry more a parenthetical than a comparative sense the temptation is illusory. The author of *On the Sublime* apparently is assigning to Aristotle and Theophrastus only the view that bold metaphors can be softened by various phrases; his next sentence supplies confirmation:[84]

[82] Russell's OCT.

[83] The translation by W. Rhys Roberts, *Longinus On the Sublime* (Cambridge, Eng., 1907), is used.

[84] Despite this negative yield of direct evidence, it is still arguable that Theophrastus did discuss terms of comparison. Kennedy 277 points out that Theophras-

ἡ γὰρ ὑποτίμησις, φασίν, ἰᾶται τὰ τολμηρά.   (32.3)

for the qualifying words mitigate, they say, the audacity of expression.

From the rest of the Hellenistic period not even a hint of discussion of comparison exists.[85] Hermagoras is probably the single author of these centuries whose loss is the most serious blow to a better understanding of all aspects of Hellenistic rhetorical theory.[86] The later Greek προγυμνάσματα (preliminary exercises), which originated in the Hellenistic period, often mention comparison; it is particularly regrettable that no early representatives of this genre have survived. Any belief in the total loss of Hellenistic rhetorical literature would, of course, be vitiated if

---

tus is known to have granted a separate section of his Περὶ λέξεως to σχήματα (figures), into which comparison may well have fitted. Kennedy adds, referring to the σχήματα: "Heretofore they had been treated almost incidentally, but from now on they play an increasingly important role in the theory of style. Theophrastus is probably responsible for elevating the subject to a level equal to diction and thus encouraging the process of identification of figures which led to the almost interminable lists in later rhetorical handbooks." See also below, p. 146 for the possibility that a passage in [Demetrius] *On Style* suggests treatment of comparison by Theophrastus. On the other hand, Schenkeveld 133 feels that Theophrastus probably discussed just the Gorgianic figures, such as antithesis and isocolon, and that a regular system of figures of thought developed only after him.

[85] An isolated instance of εἰκών occurs in the poet Menander, perhaps Theophrastus' student and at least very much under Peripatetic influence. In frag. 656 (Körte), a young lover addresses the audience thus: "By Athena, gentlemen, I am not able to come upon an εἰκόν' exactly like the real situation." He then proceeds in vain to seek a good analogy to his own predicament. As Fraenkel (*Elementi Plautini in Plauto* 164) shows, this is probably another case of the Athenian game of εἰκάζειν-ἀντεικάζειν; cf. above, chap. I n. 43.

[86] Kennedy 318 says of Hermagoras: "With him the rhetorical handbook and the traditional system of ancient rhetoric achieved almost its full development." He adds, however, that the most incomplete part of Hermagoras' system seems to have been his theories of style. The fragments and testimonia (D. Matthes, *Hermagoras Fragmenta* [Leipzig 1962]) reveal no mention of comparison, although the Suda lists as one of Hermagoras' works Περὶ σχημάτων (*On Figures*).

the third century B.C. date assigned by some recent writers to [Demetrius] *On Style* were acceptable.[87] It is not: a lacuna exists from Aristotle to the first century B.C., and the treatises that mark the reappearance of rhetorical literature are, geographically, not products of the Greek world but of Rome.

[87] Kroll 1079; Grube, *Demetrius On Style* 56. For fuller discussion of this question, see chap. V.

CHAPTER III

RHETORICA AD HERENNIUM

The *Rhetorica ad Herennium* is the first complete extant Latin rhetorical treatise. Its immediate background and importance are well stated in the introduction to Caplan's excellent Loeb edition: "The Greek art of rhetoric was first naturalized at Rome in the time of the younger Scipio, and Latin treatises on the subject were in circulation from the time of the Gracchi. But the books by Cato, Antonius, and other Roman writers have not come down to us, and it is from the second decade of the first century B.C. that we have, in the treatise addressed to Gaius Herennius, the oldest Latin Art preserved entire."[1] Although it is probable that Cicero's incomplete *de Inventione* precedes the *ad Herennium* by a few years,[2] it is more natural to discuss *de Inventione* with the other rhetorical works of Cicero. The two works appear not at all interdependent but rather mutually dependent upon an earlier Hellenistic source or sources,[3] and to treat *ad Herennium* first is not to discuss a derivative work before discussing its source.

The *ad Herennium* must be ascribed to an *auctor incertus*. For more than a millenium, beginning before St. Jerome, the treatise was imputed to Cicero, a contributing factor in its survival and popularity through the Middle Ages, but Ciceronian authorship

[1] H. Caplan, [*Cicero*] *Ad C. Herennium de Ratione Dicendi* (*Rhetorica ad Herennium*) (Cambridge, Mass., 1954) vii. The present chapter is much indebted to Caplan's work, and his text and translation are used throughout.

[2] Caplan xxvi.

[3] *Ibid.*, vii. Both Caplan xxii and Kroll 1100 characterize the Hellenistic source as a rhetorician interested also in philosophy.

has not been approved since the Renaissance.[4] More recent attempts to credit authorship to Cornificius have also foundered as he lived just before the time of Quintilian,[5] while *ad Herennium*, on internal evidence, should probably be dated to the period 86–82 B.C.[6]

Book IV of *ad Herennium* is devoted to systematic investigation of style (*elocutio*), and it is here that the chief discussion of comparison occurs. There are scattered appearances in the first three books, however, of different terms of comparison,[7] and their usage may be cited as an indication of the author's overall approach to comparison. Several terms—*similitudo, simile, comparatio, collatio*—occur, but none with frequency.

The first instance of a term of comparison comes early in Book I,[8] during a discussion of introduction by subtle approach[9] (*insinuatio*). One goal of this type of introduction is relief for an audience fatigued by previous speakers; the opening words

---

[4] Caplan viii. This is certainly the general case (e.g., Erasmus denied Ciceronian authorship), but as late as 1612 Thomas Heywood ascribed the treatise to Cicero. See D. L. Clark, *Rhetoric and Poetry in the Renaissance* (New York 1922) 64.

[5] See Caplan xiv for a brief survey. The problem has been revived by G. Calboli, *Cornificiana, 2: l'autore e la tendenza politica della Rhetorica ad Herennium* (Bologna 1965), who maintains that *some* Cornificius was the author, with political sympathies more Marian than Sullan.

[6] Caplan xxvi. An important dissent from the majority view has been made by A. E. Douglas. See his review of Caplan, *CR* 6 (1956) 132ff; his article "*Clausulae* in the *Rhetorica ad Herennium* as Evidence of its Date," *CQ* 10 (1960) 65–78; and his review of Calboli, *CR* 17 (1967) 105f. Douglas feels that the date 86–82 has been settled upon too much through the methodology of the last datable event mentioned (for the *ad Her.*, several references to the Social War). His own analysis of the prose rhythms leads him to a date well on, if not late, in the Ciceronian period. Nevertheless, on balance the earlier date is still to be preferred.

[7] These words make their first appearance as technical terms of comparison in explicitly rhetorical works, namely *ad Herennium* and *de Inventione*. Thus there is no problem in Latin, as there was in Greek, of tracing the history of terms of comparison before they first appear in rhetorical works.

[8] 1.6.10.

[9] Here, as in most passages, Caplan's renderings of the technical terminology are used.

should, then, provoke laughter. No fewer than eighteen possible methods for achieving this are listed, one by means of *similitudo*, which Caplan translates "comparison." Further on in Book I,[10] *comparatio* is listed as one of the four assumptive causes of proof and refutation in a juridical cause. Its sense is "comparison with an alternative course of action," and its aim is to prove that the better of two possible acts has been chosen.[11] *Collatio* appears in Book II[12] in the detailed analysis of the conjectural issue in a juridical cause. There are six divisions of this type of issue: *collatio* is one, and exists when the prosecutor maintains that the defendant is more suited to the crime than anyone else. Caplan again reasonably translates the word "comparison."

Thus far, the author of *ad Herennium* has been referring to a broad and nonfigurative kind of comparison with each of his terms. Something more specific, in Caplan's view, presents itself near the end of Book II.[13] The second half of Book II deals with the artistic development (*tractatio*) of an argument. Five parts of a complete argument are defined: the proposition (*propositio*), the reason (*ratio*), proof of the reason (*rationis confirmatio*), embellishment (*exornatio*), and summation (*complexio*).[14] After these parts are briefly illustrated in a model argument,[15] possible flaws in each are listed in some detail. Under the category of embellishment, the author first gives its components:

> Quoniam exornatio constat ex similibus et exemplis et amplificationibus et rebus iudicatis et ceteris rebus quae pertinent ad exaugendam et conlocupletandam argumentationem, quae sint his rebus vitia consideremus. (2.29.46)

---

[10] 1.15.25.

[11] *Comparatio* occurs again in the same context at 2.14.21. Its use in these two passages is quite similar to Aristotle's use of ἀντιπαραβολή in the *Rhetoric*; see above, p. 28.

[12] 2.4.6.

[13] 2.29.46.

[14] 2.18.28.

[15] 2.19.28–30.

Since Embellishment consists of similes, examples, amplifications, previous judgements, and the other means which serve to expand and enrich the argument, let us consider the faults which attach to these.

Then he notes the faults of the first component, *simile*:

Simile vitiosum est quod ex aliqua parte dissimile est nec habet parem rationem conparationis aut sibi ipsi obest qui adfert.
(2.29.46)

A Simile is defective if it is inexact in any aspect, and lacks a proper ground for the comparison, or is prejudicial to him who presents it.

The author gives no examples of *simile* in the immediate context, but the earlier model argument contains an indication that Caplan's "simile" is too restrictive. There, as mentioned above, the five parts of a complete argument are illustrated. The paragraph which deals with *exornatio* (embellishment) draws a general comparison between Ulysses' desire to kill Ajax (the subject of the model argument) and the desire of wild beasts to destroy one another:

Nam cum feras bestias videamus alacres et erectas vadere ut alteri bestiae noceant, non est incredibile putandum istius quoque animum ferum, crudelem atque inhumanum cupide ad inimici perniciem profectum. . . . (2.19.29)

For when we see wild beasts rush eagerly and resolutely to attack one another, we must not think it incredible that this creature, too [Ulysses]—a wild, cruel, inhuman spirit—set out passionately to destroy his enemy. . . .

There is not, it must be admitted, a complete correlation between the various illustrations of embellishment in this paragraph and the divisions of embellishment listed at 2.29.46 (*simile, exemplum, amplificatio, res iudicata*). Specifically, there is no illustration of *exemplum* (historical example).[16] Nevertheless, it is likely that this general comparison at 2.19.29 should be identified with the division of embellishment called *simile* at 2.29.46. The collocation of *simile* and *exemplum* (fictional comparison and historical example), which recalls Aristotle's equivalent collocation of παραβολή and παράδειγμα,[17] is also interesting. Here, as in Aristotle, fictional comparison and historical example form part of a juridical argument, primarily to provide proof. In Book IV the author will use the same collocation more than once but always within the context of style rather than argument.

Book IV of *ad Herennium* is the oldest systematic treatment of style in Latin[18] and, in view of the undocumented Hellenistic period, one of the basic analyses of style in ancient rhetoric.[19] The central discussion of comparison occurs in chapters 45–49, but terms of comparison also appear with some frequency elsewhere. A general, and marked, departure from Aristotle in stylistic doctrine is that metaphor and comparison are discussed separately, neither being subordinate to the other. Metaphor (*translatio*) comprises one of ten special embellishments of diction (*exornationes verborum*),[20] while comparison is discussed under the general heading of embellishments of thought (*exornationes sententiarum*).[21] Although the author treats comparison entirely apart from metaphor, terms of comparison occur in connection with two of metaphor's companion embellishments of diction, hyperbole (*superlatio*) and allegory (*permutatio*). Hyperbole is the sixth special

[16] In addition, *simile* is the first embellishment listed at 2.29.46, *amplificatio* the third. At 2.19.29 the possible illustration of *simile* comes at the end of the paragraph, and the first illustration in the paragraph is of *amplificatio*.

[17] *Rhet.* 2.20.1393a28–31.

[18] *De Inventione* does not include an analysis of style.

[19] Kroll 1074.

[20] 4.31.42–34.46. Caplan 332 note b points out that what the author means by these ten special embellishments, although he does not use the term, is *tropi* (tropes), which at first (and even in Quintilian) were not separated clearly from figures of diction and thought.

[21] 4.35.47–55.69.

embellishment (metaphor is the ninth) and is expressed either separately or through comparison (*cum conparatione*).[22] When expressed through comparison, the method used is equivalance or superiority, and examples are given:

> Cum conparatione aut a similitudine aut a praestantia superlatio sumitur. A similitudine, sic: "Corpore niveum candorem, aspectu igneum ardorem adsequebatur."[23] A praestantia, hoc modo: "Cuius ore sermo melle dulcior profluebat."[24]   (4.33.44)

> Hyperbole with comparison is formed from either equivalence or superiority. From equivalence as follows: "His body attained a snowy whiteness, his face a fiery zeal."[25] From superiority, as follows: "From his mouth flowed speech sweeter than honey."

As the examples (in the form of ablatives of respect and comparison) show, *comparatio* here denotes broadly a figure of comparison, while *similitudo* is used nonfiguratively in a sense of "likeness," "resemblance," "equivalence."[26]

The tenth special embellishment of diction, allegory (*permutatio*), can be expressed in three ways. One of these is through *similitudo*, and the example given is a general comparison with a strong admixture of metaphor:

---

[22] 4.33.44.

[23] Compare *Iliad* 1.104 and 10.437 for similar expressions.

[24] This phrase is applied to Nestor at *Iliad* 1.249.

[25] I use a more literal translation here in preference to Caplan's free "his body was as white as snow, his face burned like fire."

[26] R. M. Gummere, "De variis similitudinum generibus apud poetas Latinos ante aetatem Augusteam" (unpub. diss., Harvard University 1907) 37A, constructs a chart designed to show that simile moves toward metaphor through twelve phases and that therefore the two are really one. The ablative of comparison and the cases of respect form two of these phases and thus are both simile and metaphor. Gummere's dissertation, useful in many other ways, is surely in error on this point. It should be noted that a very similar subdivision of hyperbole occurs in [Demetrius] *On Style* 124 and is labeled καθ' ὁμοιότητα (in the form of likeness).

Ea dividitur in tres partes: similitudinem, argumentum, contrarium. Per similitudinem sumitur cum translationes plures frequenter ponuntur a simili oratione ductae, sic: "Nam cum canes funguntur officiis luporum, cuinam praesidio pecuaria credemus?"

(4.34.46)

It [allegory] assumes three aspects: comparison, argument, and contrast. It operates through a comparison when a number of metaphors originating in a similarity in the mode of expression are set together, as follows: "For when dogs act the part of wolves, to what guardian, pray, are we going to entrust our herds of cattle?"

Allegory in the form of argument also makes use of *similitudo*, and the example is one of metaphorical likeness:

Per argumentum tractatur cum a persona aut loco aut re aliqua similitudo augendi aut minuendi causa ducitur, ut si quis Drusum Graccum nitorem obsoletum dicat.[27]   (4.34.46)

An Allegory is presented in the form of argument when a similitude is drawn from a person or place or object in order to magnify or minify, as if one should call Drusus a "faded reflection of the Gracchi."

A second example of allegory through *similitudo* is then given to show how an argument can be put forward by means of the metaphor contained in the *similitudo*:

. . . in illo primo quod a similitudine ducitur, per translationem argumento poterimus uti. Per similitudinem, sic: "Quid ait hic rex atque Agamemnon noster, sive, ut crudelitas est, potius Atreus?"   (4.34.46)

. . . in the first [type] above, drawn from a comparison, we can through the metaphor make use of argument. In an Allegory operating through a comparison, as follows: "What says this king —our Agamemnon, or rather, such is his cruelty, our Atreus?"

[27] The last part of the sentence, as Caplan remarks, clearly contains some corruption.

Although all these examples are built *on similitudo*, it must be kept in mind that they are not examples *of similitudo* but of allegory.[28] Hence, the meaning "likeness, resemblance" is as dominant here as "comparison."

A final preliminary instance of a term of comparison comes in the treatment of *expolitio* (refining),[29] one of the embellishments of thought (*exornationes sententiarum*), the stylistic category under which comparison also is discussed. *Expolitio* is defined as the ability to continue on the same topic and yet appear to be saying something new. This is accomplished either by repeating the original idea with differing vocabulary, delivery, and treatment, or by expanding the original idea. After outlining the means of repetition, the author of *ad Herennium* proceeds to seven ways of expanding the idea:

> Sed de eadem re cum dicemus, plurimis utemur commutationibus. Nam cum rem simpliciter pronuntiarimus, rationem poterimus subicere; deinde dupliciter vel sine rationibus vel cum rationibus pronuntiare; deinde adferre contrarium . . . deinde simile et exemplum—de quo suo loco plura dicemus; deinde conclusionem. . . . (4.43.56–44.56)

> But when we descant upon the same theme, we shall use a great many variations. Indeed, after having expressed the theme simply, we can subjoin the Reason, and then express the theme in another form, with or without the Reasons; next we can present the Contrary . . . then a Comparison and an Example (about these I shall say more in their place); and finally the Conclusion. . . .

A *tractatio* (treatment) follows,[30] illustrating expansion of the basic

[28] Similarly, both metaphor and comparison are present in the examples of allegory, but this is not to say that the two are being treated together. They simply can be found together within a third kind of embellishment.

[29] 4.42.54–44.58. As Caplan 365 note c points out, *expolitio* is the Latin term for the Greek χρεία, which was a common kind of προγύμνασμα (model exercise).

[30] Caplan 370 note d mentions that this is the first extant illustration of a Greek χρεία or of a Latin *expolitio*.

theme of a wise man's duty to undergo all perils for the safety of his country. The example given for *simile* is a long illustrative comparison.

> Ita uti contemnendus est qui in navigio non navem quam se mavult incolumem, item vituperandus qui in rei publicae discrimine suae plus quam communi saluti consulit. Navi enim fracta multi incolumes evaserunt; ex naufragio patriae salvus nemo potest enatare. (4.44.57)

He who in a voyage prefers his own to his vessel's security deserves contempt. No less blameworthy is he who in a crisis of the republic consults his own in preference to the common safety. For from the wreck of a ship many of those on board escape unharmed, but from the wreck of the fatherland no one can swim to safety.

This model of *simile* is followed by the story of Decius Mus as a model of *exemplum*, and so within the context of *expolitio* fictional comparison and historical example are again juxtaposed.

The promise of further discussion of *simile* and *exemplum* (*de quo suo loco plura dicemus*) is fulfilled at 4.45.59 with the beginning of the central analysis of comparison. As the minutiae of this analysis will be treated in some detail, it is well to begin by outlining the whole:[31]

Similitudo/simile, 4.45.59–48.61:
(a) Method: by contrast. Purpose: to embellish.
(b) Method: by negation. Purpose: to prove.
(c) Method: by conciseness. Purpose: to clarify.
(d) Method: by detailed comparison. Purpose: to make vivid.

Exemplum, 4.49.62.

Imago, 4.49.62.
(a) Purpose: praise.

[31] In general form this is the chart drawn up by Caplan lviii.

(b) Purpose: censure, in order to arouse:
   (i) hatred
   (ii) envy
   (iii) contempt.

A definition of *similitudo* announces the general character of analysis of the term:

> Similitudo est oratio traducens ad rem quampiam aliquid ex re dispari simile.[32] Ea sumitur aut ornandi causa aut probandi aut apertius dicendi aut ante oculos ponendi. Et quomodo quattuor de causis sumitur, item quattuor modis dicitur: per contrarium, per negationem, per conlationem, per brevitatem.[33]   (4.45.59)

Comparison is a manner of speech that carries over an element of likeness from one thing to a different thing. This is used to embellish or prove or clarify or vivify. Furthermore, corresponding to these four aims, it has four forms of presentation: Contrast, Negation, Detailed Parallel, Abridged Comparison.

The opening sentence states that *similitudo* affirms a resemblance between two objects.[34] There are four kinds of *similitudo*, each with a different purpose and each with a characteristic method of presentation.

The first, with the purpose of decorating or embellishing (*ornandi causa*), presents itself through contrast. An example is given:

[32] *Simile*, which was the actual term of comparison in the discussion of *expolitio* and at 2.29.46, is merely a neuter adjective here meaning "like." Later on, however, it will be found once again as a term of comparison synonymous with *similitudo*. Its dual function is simply an ambiguous terminological feature.

[33] There is perhaps a slight corruption here, since the *similitudo per brevitatem* is eventually discussed before the *similitudo per conlationem*. The text therefore may better read in the order: *per contrarium, per negationem, per brevitatem, per conlationem*. The third purpose, *apertius dicendi* (greater clarity) is now correctly answered by what turns out to be the third method, *per brevitatem*; and the fourth purpose is answered by the correct fourth method. It seems unlikely that the author would have committed this slip.

[34] The implications of the precise wording of this definition are discussed below, p. 80.

Ornandi causa sumitur per contrarium sic: "Non enim, quemadmodum in palaestra qui taedas candentes accipit celerior est in
cursu continuo quam ille qui tradit, item melior imperator novus
qui accipit exercitum quam ille qui decedit; propterea quod de-
fatigatus cursor integro facem, hic peritus imperator imperito
exercitum tradit."   (4.46.59)

In the form of a contrast, in order to embellish, Comparison is
used as follows: "Unlike what happens in the palaestra, where he
who receives the flaming torch is swifter in the relay race than he
who hands it on, the new general who receives command of an
army is not superior to the general who retires from its command.
For in the one case it is an exhausted runner who hands the torch
to a fresh athlete, whereas in this it is an experienced commander
who hands over the army to an inexperienced."

A surprising feature is immediately apparent. The purpose of this
type of *similitudo* is to embellish (*ornare*); is it to be inferred thereby
that none of the other types is truly an embellishment (*exornatio*)?
This would be exceedingly strange, since the discussion of *similitudo* is as one of the embellishments of thought (*exornationes
sententiarum*). The answer involves, at least in part, a weakness
in the author's approach. So bound is he to an organization of four
purposes and four methods for *similitudo* that his categories at
times become artificial and form early instances of the kind of
overclassification that appears increasingly in ancient rhetoric.
Quite obviously all four types of *similitudo*, as embellishments of
thought, seek to embellish. To this extent the special purpose of
ornare given to the first type is meaningless. On the other hand,
ornare does have meaning in suggesting that, while the purposes
of the remaining three types can be pinpointed even further—to
prove, to clarify, to make vivid—the *similitudo per contrarium* does
little but simply and blatantly embellish something that could be
expressed equally well in a straightforward statement were there
no desire to set off the thought stylistically. The author explains

his meaning in just this way,[35] and his words seem a trifle apologetic:

> Hoc sine simili satis plane et perspicue et probabiliter dici potuit, hoc modo: "Dicitur minus bonos imperatores a melioribus exercitus accipere solere;" sed ornandi causa simile[36] sumptum est, ut orationi quaedam dignitas conparetur.   (4.46.59)

This [the example just given] could have been expressed quite simply, clearly, and plausibly without the Comparison, as follows: "They say that usually it is inferior generals who take over the command of armies from superior." But the Comparison is used for embellishment, so as to secure a certain distinction for the style.

Although the *similitudo per contrarium* must be comparative in form, no additional formal restrictions seem implied. In the example, the words *quemadmodum* (in the way that) and *item* (likewise) bring the comparison close to the form of a simile, but there is no further indication of a specific way (beyond that of contrast) in which the *similitudo* is to be expressed. It is reasonable to suppose that such a comparative contrast as "he who receives the torch is fresher than he who gives it, but the new general who receives command is not superior to him who relinquishes it" would also be classified as a *similitudo ornandi causa per contrarium*.

If the first type of *similitudo* seeks only to embellish, the second has, of all four, the least to do with embellishment. Its purpose and method are stated together with an example:

> Per negationem dicetur probandi causa hoc modo: "Neque equus indomitus, quamvis bene natura conpositus sit, idoneus potest esse ad eas utilitates quae desiderantur ab equo; neque homo

---

[35] He says of no other type of *similitudo* that it is equally well expressed by a simple statement.

[36] *Simile* reappears twice here as a noun and term of comparison synonymous with *similitudo*.

indoctus, quamvis sit ingeniosus, ad virtutem potest pervenire."[37]

(4.46.59)

In the form of a negation and for the purpose of proof, Comparison will be used as follows: "Neither can an untrained horse, however well-built by nature, be fit for the services desired of a horse, nor can an uncultivated man, however well-endowed by nature, attain to virtue."

Further explanation of how this kind of *similitudo* achieves its purpose of proof follows:

Hoc probabilius factum est quod magis est veri simile non posse virtutem sine doctrina conparari, quoniam ne equus quidem indomitus idoneus possit esse. Ergo sumptum est probandi causa. . . .

(4.46.59)

This idea has been rendered more plausible, for it becomes easier to believe that virtue cannot be secured without culture, when we see that not even a horse can be serviceable if untrained. Thus the Comparison is used for the purpose of proof. . . .

The author concludes by restating the negative character of the *similitudo*:

dictum autem per negationem; id enim perspicuum est de primo similitudinis verbo. (4.46.59)

and moreover [the comparison] is presented in the form of a negation, as is clear from the first word of the Comparison.

The *similitudo per negationem* presents another kind of difficulty from the *similitudo per contrarium*. Its purpose, proof (*probatio*), would seem quite alien to embellishment. Should this type of *similitudo* then be considered essentially different from *similitudines* that are embellishments? Certainly Aristotle separated compari-

[37] A similar comparison is attributed to Socrates by Xenophon, *Memorabilia* 4.1.3.

sons of proof and style distinctly.[38] Not quite the same separation need be made, however, in *ad Herennium*. The whole work, unlike Aristotle's *Rhetoric*, is not a general, even a philosophical, treatment of rhetoric but a practical handbook designed specifically to instruct Gaius Herennius in the techniques of forensic rhetoric. Thus, even those parts of the work dealing with features of style are not meant to include anything that could not be of use in the courts. All the types of *similitudo*, just as much as they are embellishments, are elements of forensic rhetoric, the essential function of which is to prove or refute. The second type of *similitudo* simply acts very secondarily as an embellishment in addition to being an element of law court rhetoric. Thus once again the author of *ad Herennium* has made a classification that is in part unnatural but from which some meaning can be extracted. The first two types of *similitudo* are the extremes of the case: one is a studied embellishment with but a tenuous connection to practical court rhetoric, the other is a decided aid to proof and only distantly an embellishment. The author's concluding remark on the *similitudo per negationem* calls attention to the negative form of the example he has used. His phrase, "as is clear from the first word of the Comparison," may mean that this type of *similitudo* will consistently begin with a negative, but in fact the language does not seem to generalize beyond the immediate example. The *similitudo per negationem*, it would appear, will always be restricted in form to the extent that it will be constructed on a negative base; but within these limits there will be variety of form.[39]

The third kind of *similitudo* (in fact, the synonymous term *simile* is used in this section) stands more on a middle ground than

[38] And the *similitudo per negationem* recalls Aristotle's παραβολή by using an example reminiscent of Socrates, just as Socrates is said by Aristotle to have used παραβολή. See the previous note and above, Chap. II n. 5.

[39] And, indeed, the opening words of the first type of *similitudo* (*non enim*) show that a negative beginning does not automatically classify a *similitudo* as one *per negationem*.

either of the first two. Its purpose is to clarify and its method of
presentation is through conciseness. Purpose and method are com-
patible with both embellishment and practical oratory. The author
gives an example in the form of a simile:

> Sumetur et apertius dicendi causa simile—dicitur per brevi-
> tatem—hoc modo: "In amicitia gerenda, sicut in certamine cur-
> rendi, non ita convenit exerceri ut quoad necesse sit venire possis,
> sed ut productus studio et viribus ultra facile procurras." (4.47.60)

> A Comparison will be used also for greater clarity—the pre-
> sentation being in abridged form—as follows: "In maintaining a
> friendship, as in a footrace, you must train yourself not only so
> that you succeed in running as far as is required, but so that, ex-
> tending yourself by will and sinew, you easily run beyond that
> point."

The particular features of this type of *similitudo* are discussed in a
fairly straightforward manner, but in reverse logical order. The
author of *ad Herennium* first states, rather haphazardly, how this
type of *similitudo/simile* gives greater clarity to a situation and
secondly explains what he means by the phrase "the presentation
being in abridged form." It then becomes apparent, however,
that the method of presentation is what really defines the purpose
of the *similitudo*.

"The presentation being in abridged form" is explained as
follows:

> Dictum autem simile est per brevitatem, non enim ita ut in ceteris
> rebus res ab re separata est, sed utraeque res coniuncte et confuse
> pronuntiatae.   (4.47.60)

> The Comparison is moreover presented in abridged form, for one
> term is not detached from the other as in the other forms, but the
> two are conjoined and intermingled in the presentation.

The *simile* does not separate the terms of subject and comparison
but blends them together, the images of the comparison being

applied metaphorically to the subject. A "detached" version of the example might read: "In a race one must train not only to run as far as is required but also, by straining will and strength, to be able easily to run further; in maintaining a friendship one must be able to give greater evidence of friendship than expected." In the real example, images of running are applied to friendship, and the same words describe both the subject (maintaining a friendship) and the comparison (running a race). The result is that the actual comparison consists only of *sicut in certamine currendi* ("as in a footrace"), the description of the race belonging grammatically to the subject of maintaining a friendship. The term *brevitas* (abridged form) seems therefore to refer both to the condensing of the separate descriptions of subject and comparison into one and to the consequent brevity of the comparison itself. The author maintains that when a *similitudo/simile* is thus condensed its application is more easily seen and the subject under consideration gains greater clarity. For instance, he says, if someone were faced by the present example of *similitudo per brevitatem*, he would not be able to criticize those who are kind to a friend's children even after the friend's death without realizing the poor reasoning of his criticism.[40] In his analysis of the *similitudo per brevitatem* the author of *ad Herennium* recalls Aristotle. This is the most metaphorically oriented of all the types, and it is also the most instructive to a listener—precisely Aristotle's outlook on comparison. Almost certainly, however, the author should be thought of as following a Hellenistic source and not Aristotle directly. Quintilian will be seen to argue the opposite, that comparison with an admixture of metaphor distracts the listener.[41]

[40] As mentioned, this explanation of how the example gives clarity to a situation comes, illogically, before the author's explanation of "abridged form." I have presented the two aspects of the *similitudo* in what seems to be their logical order.

[41] *Inst. Orat.* 5.11.23 (see below, pp. 198ff). Perhaps Quintilian consciously opposes Aristotle's view, but this does not mean that he is opposing *ad Herennium* as well. He seems not to have been aware of the work; see Caplan viii.

The fourth and last kind of *similitudo* has as its purpose vividness; its method of presentation is by detailed comparison.

> Ante oculos ponendi negotii causa sumetur similitudo—dicetur per conlationem—sic. . . .　　　　　　　　　　(4.47.60)

> A Comparison will be used for vividness, and be set forth in the form of a detailed parallel, as follows. . . .

The example is an extremely long simile (more than half a page in Caplan's Loeb text). The comparative part describes a lyre player who is magnificently dressed and of imposing appearance but who sings and moves his body distastefully and is consequently derided all the more by his audience because of the high expectations he had engendered. The subject part answers by describing a man born nobly, of great wealth and many natural gifts but lacking virtue and all the arts that teach virtue, and consequently scorned all the more by good men because of his many advantages. Each feature of the lyre player parallels a feature of the man: his robes correspond to the man's background, his personal attractiveness to the man's natural gifts, his rousing of great expectations in the audience to the man's rousing of great hopes among good men, his disgraceful performance to the man's surprising lack of virtue, his derision by the audience to the man's rebuff by good men. The author of *ad Herennium* then states that this kind of *similitudo* achieves its purpose of vividness through the extensive embellishment of both its parts and that the method of presentation is *per conlationem* (by detailed parallel) because, as is clear from the example, all the corresponding items of the subject and comparative parts are expressed and correlated:

> Hoc simile exornatione utriusque rei, alterius inertiae alterius stultitiae simili ratione conlata, sub aspectus omnium rem subiecit. Dictum autem est per conlationem, propterea quod proposita similitudine paria sunt omnia relata.　　　　　　(4.47.60)

This Comparison, by embellishing both terms, bringing into relation by a method of parallel description the one man's ineptitude and the other's lack of cultivation, has set the subject vividly before the eyes of all. Moreover the Comparison is presented in the form of a detailed parallel because, once the similitude has been set up, all like elements are related.

The particular mention of *exornatio* (embellishment) suggests that this type of *similitudo*, like the first, is also more of a decoration than a practical embellishment. But there is no trace of the slightly apologetic tone displayed in the earlier type by the author's admission that the point could have been made equally well through a simple statement as through a *similitudo per contrarium*. In fact, there are two indications that the author of *ad Herennium* considers the *similitudo per conlationem* to be exemplary. First, at 2.29.46,[42] one of the possible defects of *simile* is said to occur when it does not possess *parem rationem conparationis* ("a proper ground for the comparison"). Conversely, the *similitudo* under consideration is presented through "detailed parallel because, once the similitude has been set up, all like elements are related" (*paria sunt omnia relata*). Although *parem* at 2.29.46 carries the sense of "proper" while *paria* in the present phrase means "like," a "proper" base for comparison would seem to refer to a comparison of "like" things. Thus the general defect mentioned in 2.29.46 is avoided, and its opposite virtue incorporated, in the *similitudo per conlationem*. Second, at 4.44.57, in the discussion of *similitudo* as an element of *expolitio*,[43] the example given of *similitudo*, though shorter than the one just analyzed, would also be classified as a *similitudo per conlationem* in that every detail of one of its parts corresponds to a detail of the other part. Both a general remark about and a general example of *similitudo*, therefore, anticipate characteristics of the *similitudo per conlationem*.

After the lengthy exposition of the purpose and method of the

four types of *similitudo/simile*, *ad Herennium* completes its remarks
with some general observations that are not wholly congruent
with what has preceded. The first is a firm statement advising that
care be taken to phrase the subject part of a comparison in a way
that is suited to the imagery of the comparative part:

> In similibus observare oportet diligenter ut, cum rem adferamus
> similem cuius rei causa similitudinem adtulerimus, verba ad simi-
> litudinem habeamus adcommodata.   (4.48.61)

> In Comparisons we must carefully see to it that when we present
> the corresponding idea for the sake of which we have introduced
> the figure we use words suited to the likeness.

The author explains with an example which is a simile. If we say,
"just as *swallows stay* with us in *summertime* but are driven to leave
us by the *cold*,"[44] we should continue with the same imagery in
the subject part by using metaphor (*ex eadem similitudine nunc per
translationem verba sumimus*) and say "so false friends *stay* with us
in the peaceful *time* of life, but as soon as they see the *winter* of our
fortune they all *fly away*."[45] The author of *ad Herennium* does not
add an example of a faulty continuation of the *similitudo*, but he
appears to have in mind something like this: "Just as swallows
stay with us in the summer but are driven away by the cold, so
false friends embark on our ship of state when the breeze is fair
but clamor to be free of us when there is a storm." The change of
imagery from swallows and the seasons to the ship of state and
weather involves an unpleasant departure from the continuity of
the original comparison.

The author's second point concerns the ease of invention of
similitudines if one will only look at the world about him. A further step is necessary, however: to determine out of all that is
observed just what is suitable for each type of *similitudo*:

---

[44] My emphases.
[45] 4.48.61; my emphases.

Sed inventio similium facilis erit si quis sibi omnes res, animantes et inanimas, mutas et eloquentes, feras et mansuetas, terrestres, caelestes, maritimas, artificio, casu, natura conparatas, usitatas atque inusitatas, frequenter ponere ante oculos poterit, et ex his aliquam venari similitudinem quae aut ornare aut docere aut apertiorem rem facere aut ponere ante oculos possit.   (4.48.61)

But the invention of Comparisons will be easy if one can frequently set before one's eyes everything animate and inanimate, mute and articulate, wild and tame, of the earth, sky, and sea, wrought by art, chance, or nature, ordinary or unusual, and can amongst these hunt out some likeness which is capable of embellishing or proving or clarifying or vivifying.

This is the first such list of sources of comparison to occur, and the range of possibilities is sweeping. The list almost certainly is not a product of the author's own imagination but has been taken from a Hellenistic model. It would be worth knowing if the original compiler of the list had one particular person, Homer for instance, in mind, but only conjecture is possible on this point. In any case, the author's repetition of all four purposes of *similitudo* shows that he intends the list of sources to be comprehensive.

The final general comment about *similitudo* qualifies somewhat the first:

Non enim res tota totae rei necesse est similis sit, sed id ipsum quod conferetur similitudinem habeat oportet.   (4.48.61)

The resemblance between the two things need not apply throughout, but must hold on the precise point of comparison.

The earlier observation emphasized that the imagery in the subject part of the *similitudo* must logically continue the idea used in the comparative part. Now the emphasis shifts from imagistic consistency to the extent of exact resemblance necessary: the two parts of a *similitudo* must correspond only on the particular points for which the comparison was created. No example is offered, but the author's intention seems clear. If the point to be illustrated is once again the inconstancy of false friends and if the image used is of swallows, then when one says "false friends are inconstant in times of trouble" one must not go on to phrase the comparative part "swallows stay in summertime," but rather "swallows fly away in wintertime." Additional subordinate details may occur in either part that do not find correspondence in the other part. One might say, "swallows, who rear their young and teach them to fly in the summertime, fly away in wintertime," without being compelled to add corresponding descriptive detail in the subject part. There is a deviation here from the previous treatment of the four kinds of *similitudo*, none of which illustrated the freedom implied in this passage for discursiveness in one part of a comparison without equivalent discursiveness in the other part. The author has, it seems, been a bit careless in making a general observation about *similitudo* that is not corroborated in his presentation of the actual types.

The discussion of *similitudo* as one of the *exornationes sententiarum* (embellishments of thought) can now be summarized. Two terms, *similitudo* and *simile*, are used interchangeably. There seems to be no difference whatsoever between them except that *simile* occurs also as an adjective. To a much greater extent than in Aristotle, the aim in *ad Herennium* is to subdivide comparison into all possible compartments. At times the divisions are not very meaningful, as in the purpose of embellishment (*ornare*) for the *similitudo per contrarium* and proof (*probare*) for the *similitudo per negationem*: in these two cases the author has merely obscured the basic components of *similitudo* by repeating them as attributes of particular types. The feeling that minute subdivision is necessary in analysis of a figure of style is a characteristic of ancient rhetoric that developed between Aristotle and the first century B.C. and became prevalent thereafter.[46] It is apparent that, like Aristotle,

---

[46] Kennedy 266 notes of this passion for classification and subdivision: "No doubt the primary reason for this elaboration is the fact that any discipline, once it begins self-analysis, carries on the process relentlessly."

the author of *ad Herennium* does not lay down dicta on the form of *similitudines*. The *modi* of his four types are best understood not as "forms" but as "methods of presentation"—that is, by contrast, by negation, by conciseness, by detailed comparison. A fair number of the examples of *similitudo* are couched in the form of simile; even more are not.[47] Thus, taken as a group, the examples present *similitudo* in a considerably wider context than is covered by "simile." Finally, *ad Herennium* suggests no relationship between *similitudo*, an embellishment of thought, and metaphor, a special embellishment of diction, beyond their joint classification as features of style. The figure to which *similitudo is* closely bound by the author is historical example (*exemplum*).

Historical example is the embellishment of thought treated directly after *similitudo*. It is discussed only briefly. The author does little more than emphasize its closeness to *similitudo*; indeed he feels the two figures so firmly joined that he assigns exactly the same four purposes to *exemplum* as he has to *similitudo*.

> Rem ornatiorem facit . . . apertiorem . . . probabiliorem . . . ante
> oculos ponit. . . .   (4.49.62)

> It [*exemplum*] renders a thought more brilliant . . . clearer . . .
> more plausible . . . more vivid. . . .

The purposes of these two embellishments of thought are equivalent; but their subject matter is different, since an *exemplum* will be taken from something actually said or done in the past and the person who said or did it will be specified.[48] No illustration of *exemplum* is given, but *ad Herennium* refers the reader to the earlier

---

[47] Including a final instance of *similitudo* near the end of Book IV, where it is used as one of the means of producing emphasis (*significatio*). The example, at 4.54.67, clearly presents the term as referring to a comparison of general resemblance, *Noli, Saturnine, nimium populi frequentia fretus esse; inulti iacent Gracci* ("Do not, Saturninus, rely too much on the popular mob—unavenged lie the Gracchi").

[48] 4.49.62.

instance of *exemplum* in the treatment of refinement (*expolitio*) as typical, the illustration there being the tale of Decius Mus.[49]

The discussion of *imago* that follows comprises the second half of the central analysis of comparison in *ad Herennium*. There is no indication by the author that *imago* stands in any special bond to *similitudo* and *exemplum* beyond the fact that it, too, is one of the embellishments of thought. It is treated immediately after the other two, but proximity does not necessarily ally *imago* to them any more than it does the embellishment immediately preceding them, antithesis (*contentio*). In addition, there are no cross-references between the discussions of *imago* and *similitudo* as there are between *exemplum* and *similitudo*. Passages on comparison in other treatises[50] confirm a note by Caplan at the beginning of *ad Herennium*'s analysis of *similitudo*, "this figure and the next two [*exemplum* and *imago*] form a common triad in post-Aristotelian rhetoric,"[51] and also his note at the beginning of the discussion of *imago*, "in post-Aristotelian rhetoric this appears as a special figure, separate from *similitudo* . . . to which it is yet closely akin."[52] But the text of *ad Herennium* states only that *similitudo* and *exemplum* are a related pair and that *imago* is another *exornatio sententiarum*.

There are no figurative uses of *imago* in *ad Herennium* apart from the present passage. The word occurs several times in the section on memory in Book III,[53] but always in the sense of "pictorial image," one of the basic aids to memory. It seems, therefore, to be a more restricted figure for the author[54] than *similitudo*, which

---

[49] 4.44.57.

[50] See, e.g., *de Inventione* 1.30.49; below, p. 95.

[51] Caplan 376 note b.

[52] *Ibid.*, 385 note c.

[53] 3.16.28–24.40. This is the oldest extant Latin discussion of memory in a rhetorical work. *Similitudo* also occurs in it, as at 3.20.33, in a general sense of "likeness," "resemblance."

[54] The author's approach is thus comparable to Aristotle's restricted use of εἰκών, for which *imago* is the normal Latin equivalent.

occurs in figurative contexts throughout the treatise. The discussion of *imago* opens with a definition:

> Imago est formae cum forma cum quadam similitudine[55] conlatio. Haec sumitur aut laudis aut vituperationis causa. (4.49.62)

> Simile is the comparison of one figure with another, implying a certain resemblance between them. This is used either for praise or censure.[56]

Interpretation of the definition becomes somewhat puzzling when it is compared with the opening definition of *similitudo*. The two are quite similar:

> Similitudo est oratio traducens ad rem quampiam aliquid ex re dispari simile. (4.45.59)

> Comparison is a manner of speech that carries over an element of likeness from one thing to a different thing.

Both *similitudo* and *imago* are said to place side by side two *res*, or *formae*, in such a way that a likeness between the two is effected; once again the author of *ad Herennium* appears in some degree to have succumbed to overclassification. But certain distinctions are made between the two *exornationes*: it is indicated that a *similitudo* starts with two unlike components,[57] while *imago* starts with two components that basically resemble one another. An additional, and more obvious, difference lies in their purposes. *Similitudo* is

---

[55] It is interesting that the author feels free to use *similitudo* in this general sense of "resemblance" so soon after the discussion of *similitudo* as stylistic comparison. *Conlatio* seems here to refer to the *act* of comparison, not to any *figure* of comparison.

[56] The two purposes of *imago*, praise and censure, raise a suspicion that the author has adapted for forensic speaking a bit of stylistic analysis intended originally to apply to epideictic oratory.

[57] The key phrase is *ad rem quampiam aliquid ex re dispari*, which Caplan undertranslates by "from one thing to a different thing." Something like "to one thing from a dissimilar thing" would be better.

used to embellish, to prove, to clarify, to make vivid. The purpose of *imago* is defined as neither stylistic nor didactic but as emotional and personal: it is employed either for praise or blame.

Only one example is given of an *imago* of praise:

> Laudis causa, sic: "Inibat in proelium corpore tauri validissimi, impetu leonis acerrimi simili." (4.49.62)

> For praise, as follows: "He entered the combat in body like the strongest bull, in impetuosity like the fiercest lion."[58]

The *imago* of censure, on the other hand, is said to arouse three different emotions: hatred, envy, contempt. An example of each is given:

> Vituperationis, ut in odium adducat, hoc modo: "Iste qui cotidie per forum medium tamquam iubatus draco serpit dentibus aduncis, aspectu venenato, spiritu rabido, circum inspectans huc et illuc si quem reperiat cui aliquid mali faucibus adflare, ore adtingere, dentibus insecare, lingua aspergere possit." Ut in invidiam adducat, hoc modo: "Iste qui divitias suas iactat sicut Gallus e Phrygia aut hariolus quispiam, depressus et oneratus auro, clamat et delirat." In contemptionem, sic: "Iste qui tamquam coclea abscondens retentat sese tacitus, cum domo totus ut comedatur aufertur."
> (4.49.62)

> For censure, so as to excite hatred, as follows: "That wretch who daily glides through the middle of the Forum like a crested serpent, with curved fangs, poisonous glance, and fierce panting, looking about him on this side and that for someone to blast with venom from his throat—to smear it with his lips, to drive it in with his teeth, to spatter it with his tongue."[59] To excite envy, as

---

[58] The source of this *imago* is unknown, but Caplan 385 note d notes the resemblance of the second clause to Aristotle's opening example of εἰκών, "leapt on the foe as a lion" (*Rhet.* 3.4.1406b21). It is improbable that the author of *ad Herennium* had access to a text of the *Rhetoric*. If the example stems in any way from Aristotle the line would be indirect: through Hellenistic treatises that drew upon Aristotle.

[59] This example seems to derive from Demosthenes, *Against Aristogeiton* 1.52. The sources of the other two are unknown.

follows: "That creature who flaunts his riches, loaded and weighed down with gold, shouts and raves like a Phrygian eunuch-priest of Cybele or like a soothsayer." To excite contempt, as follows: "That creature, who like a snail silently hides and keeps himself in his shell, is carried off, he and his house, to be swallowed whole."

With these examples in mind it may be asked whether, aside from their different purposes, the principal distinction between *similitudo* and *imago* does indeed lie, as their definitions initially suggest, in the fact that one creates an artificial resemblance between two things while the other compares two essentially similar things. The subject matter of the opening example of each momentarily bears out the distinction. That the first type of *similitudo* compares "by contrast" is itself evidence that the comparison artificially likens dissimilar objects. The comparison in the *imago* of praise, on the other hand, between a warrior and a bull or lion is a traditional one for the very reason that it is founded on an essential likeness in doughtiness of the objects compared. From this point on, however, it is increasingly less arguable that the examples of *similitudo* and *imago* illustrate the distinction suggested by their definitions. Comparison between an untrained horse and an uncultivated man, between maintaining a friendship and running a race, and between a falsely magnificent lyre player and a man endowed with false virtues would seem to be based on at least as much natural resemblance as comparison between a loathsome creature in the forum and a crested serpent, a fellow flaunting wealth and a Phrygian priest of Cybele, 'and a recluse and a snail. From this standpoint, it almost looks as if the definitions of *similitudo* and *imago* have been derived from the subject matter of the first example of each.

Perhaps, however, the distinction between artificial and natural resemblance is meant to be illustrated by the structure, rather than the subject matter, of the examples of *similitudo* and *imago*. In fact this approach proves somewhat more fruitful. The four examples of *imago* are constructed, with minor variations, as follows: subject and main verb; specific comparison; description of varying length applicable directly to the comparison and metaphorically to the subject.[60] What all four examples of *imago* have in common, as a result of this basic structure, is that none has an extended, separate description of both subject and comparison, and all introduce the subject before the comparison. In contrast, three of the four kinds of *similitudo* do have extensive, separate descriptions of both their parts, and the same three kinds begin with the comparative part and end with the subject part. The first of these two generally consistent structural differences between *similitudo* and *imago* is enlightening. In the examples of *imago*, where the description can apply equally, either metaphorically or directly, to the subject and comparative parts,[61] the implication is that the two parts bear a certain essential resemblance to one another (*formae cum forma cum quadam similitudine*). In all but the third type of *similitudo* (the one *per brevitatem*), on the other hand, the comparative part is presented with descriptive detail, then the subject is presented with different descriptive detail; the "equal but separate" situation suggests that two essentially unlike things are being juxtaposed so as to display a resemblance to each other (*traducens ad rem quampiam aliquid ex re dispari simile*). The only significance that can be attached to the second structural difference between *similitudo* and *imago* (that is, the former is all but once in the order comparison/subject, whereas the latter is always in the order subject/comparison) would seem to be that the "subject first" order of *imago* indicates a *visual* kind of com-

[60] Once, in the second type of *imago* of censure, this descriptive portion comes before the specific comparison. And in the *imago* of praise there is no descriptive section at all but simply the subject, a verb, and the comparison.

[61] For instance, in the last type of *imago* of censure, the whole second half of the example "who . . . silently hides and keeps himself in his shell, is carried off, he and his house, to be swallowed whole" describes at the same time the recluse (metaphorically) and the snail (directly).

parison[62] that accords with the nonrhetorical meaning of the term.

The one *similitudo* that does not fit the normal pattern is the *similitudo* of conciseness, the purpose of which is greater clarity (*per brevitatem apertius dicendi causa*). Its order is subject/comparison, and it does not have separate description of subject and comparative parts.[63] The latter feature, indeed, brings about the very conciseness that is the special characteristic of the type,[64] but this does not obviate the result: the structure of this *similitudo* is contrary to all the others and completely equivalent to the examples of *imago*. In partial extenuation it may be said that the author appears more concerned with the purpose and method of the various kinds of *similitudo* and *imago* than with their structure. Nevertheless, the only discernible difference between the two embellishments that is suggested by their actual definitions seems to be a structural one, and in this respect the *similitudo per brevitatem* remains an anomaly.

Two other possible distinctions between *similitudo* and *imago* remain to be considered. If *imago* is direct and visual, while *similitudo* is extended (through separate descriptions), one might conclude that a consistent difference in length could be observed, with *imago* a short and *similitudo* a long comparison. The examples of *similitudo* are, on the whole, longer than those of *imago*, but the first type of *imago* of censure is as long as any type of *similitudo* except that expressed by detailed comparison (*per conlationem*). *Ad Herennium*, therefore, presents a situation analogous to that in Aristotle: the relative length or brevity of a comparison is not decisive for its classification as a certain kind of comparison.

[62] That is to say, the subject is already in the mind's eye as the comparison unfolds.

[63] The example, it will be recalled, runs: "In maintaining a friendship, as in a footrace, you must train yourself not only so that you succeed in running as far as is required, but so that, extending yourself by will and sinew, you easily run beyond that point."

[64] See above, p. 72.

Second, is Caplan's particular distinction between *similitudo* as "comparison" and *imago* as "simile" necessary? Every example of *imago* is in form a simile. Furthermore, as has been mentioned, apart from this single discussion there are no rhetorical instances of *imago* in *ad Herennium* that might present the term in a broader contextual background. It is easy to see the basis of Caplan's translation; nevertheless, there are opposing indications. The author makes no recommendations for the precise verbal form of either *similitudo* or *imago*. His sole stated concerns are with purpose, method, and general structure. More significantly, there is duplication of verbal form—all the examples of *imago* are similes, as are some of the examples of *similitudo*. If the passage on *imago* were a discussion of "simile" there should not be other similes within a different *exornatio*; all should be grouped under the same heading. In fact, the particular verbal form of a comparison is, like the length, not the key to its classification.[65]

The foregoing negative aspects of *ad Herennium*'s approach to comparison can be balanced by a summation of its positive features. First, the author conceives of two different kinds of figurative comparison, *similitudo* and *imago*,[66] with *similitudo* much the more general term. His division is similar to Aristotle's, but both his terms of comparison come within the category of stylistic embellishment, while one of Aristotle's terms (εἰκών) belonged to style and the other (παραβολή) to proof.[67] Second, neither type of comparison is connected with metaphor, a significant change from Aristotle. *Similitudo* is closely related to historical

[65] M. L. Clarke, *Rhetoric at Rome* (London 1965) 35, also somewhat restricts the real nature of *ad Herennium*'s discussion of comparison when, using "simile" to represent both *similitudo* and *imago*, he says: "The lengthy treatment of the simile in *ad Herennium* shows that its use was carefully taught in the rhetorical schools." "Comparison" and "illustration" would be the soundest translations of *similitudo* and *imago*.

[66] *Comparatio* and *collatio* have occurred, but only in broad contexts and never to denote a specific rhetorical figure. *Simile* often serves as a synonym of *similitudo*.

[67] As mentioned, however (above, p. 70), all of *ad Herennium*'s embellishments are designed for use in forensic speeches, where proof is basic.

example (*exemplum*), paralleling Aristotle's treatment of παραβολή and παράδειγμα. *Imago* is presented as an entirely independent embellishment, with no stated connection either to
similitudo or *exemplum*, although it seems certain that the three
already constituted a standard rhetorical group. Third, while
similitudo and *imago* are alike in being embellishments of thought,
they differ in purpose, method, and structure (*similitudo* effecting
an artificial, *imago* a natural, resemblance). Finally, *ad Herennium*'s
analytic, categorizing discussion of terms of comparison is
strikingly divergent from Aristotle's intellectual, didactic, teleo-
logical approach and serves to illuminate the rhetorical trends that
had evolved during the undocumented Hellenistic period.

CHAPTER IV

CICERO

One might reasonably anticipate that Cicero's several rhetorical works would furnish something like a full discussion of terms of comparison. Sadly, this is not the case. Cicero makes frequent use of terms of comparison but never really undertakes any detailed treatment of them. In fact, only the youthful and incomplete *de Inventione* does more than give random attention to comparison.

To be sure, the general absence of highly *technical* discussions of comparison in Cicero is *not* altogether unpredictable. It has often been pointed out that in rhetorical theory Cicero reaches back beyond the technical Hellenistic age to the broader Aristotelian approach to rhetoric and, even further back, to the pre-Platonic view that philosophy and the art of persuasion are not incompatible.[1] In the midst of the overall development of ancient rhetoric along lines of increasingly lifeless and automatic classifications, Cicero injects a temporary antidote of refreshing *humanitas* in his continuing search for the ideal orator. The early and derivative *de Inventione* alone falls outside the period in which the mature Cicero made this search the underlying goal of his rhetorical works. Thus, for *de Inventione* to contain a fuller technical discussion of comparison than any other Ciceronian work is natural, since it is closest in character to the Hellenistic treatises that thrived on such discussions. On the other hand, it must not be thought that all of Cicero's mature rhetorical works are non-technical. The *Partitiones Oratoriae* and *Topica* are highly technical,

---

[1] Kroll 1087; Solmsen, *AJP* 62 (1941) 49-50; Kennedy 278.

and his other works, the *de Oratore*, *Brutus*, *Orator*, and *de Optimo Genere Oratorum*, if not technical in basic purpose, nevertheless contain technical sections, including several discussions of embellishment, figures of thought, and metaphor. What is disappointing, then, is that Cicero's most complete treatment of comparison, in the *de Inventione*, represents only what he had been taught. His mature and more perceptive works, by contrast, though dealing in some detail with rhetorical figures closely akin to comparison, never concede to comparison itself more than the scantiest outline of a discussion.

It is not only in the rhetorical works that terms of comparison occur; they are scattered throughout the philosophical works as well. The testimony is spread widely, and it seems sensible to treat the rhetorical works first and then to check whatever conclusions are forthcoming by the use of the terms in the philosophical works. As in *ad Herennium*, all of the several Latin terms of comparison (*comparatio*, *collatio*, *similitudo*, *simile*, *imago*) appear, but they are not of equal significance.

The *de Inventione* is the earliest extant rhetorical treatise in Latin. It would seem to precede *ad Herennium* (the earliest *complete* treatise) by a few years[2] without serving in any way as a source for the slightly later work. The case is rather, as has been noted,[3] that both treatises are mutually dependent upon earlier Latin and Hellenistic works and very possibly upon a common teacher. As it survives, *de Inventione* constitutes the first section of a projected five-part treatise, of which another section would have dealt exclusively with style (*elocutio*)—wherein comparison would most naturally have been considered. Thus, although the single part of the work that remains (on subject matter) is not commonly used

---

[2] The *terminus post quem* is 91 B.C., since there are references to events of that year, and the work must have been written within a very few years of this date since Cicero labels it in *de Oratore* I.2.5, *pueris aut adulescentulis . . . commentariolis* ("the notebooks of my boyhood, or rather of my youth").

[3] See above, p. 57.

for a treatment of comparison, it is here that Cicero's fullest discussion appears.[4]

In addition to one central section on terms of comparison in *de Inventione* there are a good many isolated instances of various terms, which will be noted first.[5] *Comparatio* occurs several times but always means "comparison" in a general way and, as in *ad Herennium*, does not refer to the stylistic figure of comparison. An instance from Book I illustrates: quite early, after the four possible issues of a case have been defined and discussed, the question of whether the case (*causa*) is simple or complex is considered. If the case is complex, it will consist either of several questions or of *comparatio*, which then is defined and illustrated:

> ex conparatione, in qua per contentionem, utrum potius aut quid potissimum, quaeritur, ad hunc modum: "utrum exercitus in Macedoniam contra Philippum mittatur, qui sociis sit auxilio, an teneatur in Italia, ut quam maximae contra Hannibalem copiae sint".[6] (1.12.17)

The case involves comparison when various actions are contrasted and the question is which one is more desirable or which is most desirable to perform, in this fashion: "Should an army be sent to Macedonia against Philip to support our allies, or should it be kept in Italy so that the greatest possible force may oppose Hannibal?"[7]

Comparatio is clearly being used very broadly, and no narrower application is to be found in *de Inventione*.[8]

[4] It may be recalled, however, that παραβολή was discussed during the treatment of subject matter in Aristotle's *Rhetoric*.

[5] Although the research for this chapter and for chap. III was finished before Abbott/Oldfather/Canter, *Index Verborum in Ciceronis Rhetorica* (Urbana 1964) became available, the work has been a valuable check against overlooking significant passages on comparison.

[6] Ströbel's Teubner text is used for *de Inv*.

[7] The Loeb translation by H. M. Hubbell, *Cicero, de Inventione, de Optimo Genere Oratorum, Topica* (Cambridge, Mass., 1949), is used.

[8] Further illustrations of its use occur at 1.11.15 and, in greater length, at 2.24.72–26.78.

After a brief analysis of simple and complex cases and some further discussion of the issues, Cicero devotes the remainder, and the major part, of Book I to the seven parts of an oration: exordium, narration, partition, proof, refutation, digression, and peroration. An isolated instance of *similitudo* occurs in the section on narrative. One of the three kinds of narrative is that in which a digression is made[9] for any one of four purposes:

> ... aut criminationis aut similitudinis aut delectationis non alienae ab eo negotio, quo de agitur, aut amplificationis causa. ...
>
> (1.19.27)
>
> ... for the purpose of attacking somebody, or of making a comparison, or of amusing the audience in a way not incongruous with the business in hand, or for amplification. ...

There is no further indication of the precise meaning of *similitudo*. Another slightly less isolated instance of the term occurs in Book II. Near the beginning of a long analysis of forensic speeches, the first kind of case discussed is that in which the issue is one of fact (*constitutio coniecturalis*). If, for example, the prosecutor alleges the act to have been committed on impulse, he will be more believable if he explains how a certain passion can lead to crime. This may be done

> ... et exemplorum commemoratione, qui simili inpulsu aliquid commiserint, et similitudinum conlatione. ... (2.5.19)
>
> ... by citing examples of those who have done something under a similar impulse and by collecting parallels. ...

Collatio appears here in a nonrhetorical sense of "bringing together, collecting."[10] There are no illustrations of *similitudo*, but there is the by now familiar collocation of historical example and a term of comparison. The same juxtaposition occurs slightly later

---

[9] There is a certain amount of confusion and overlapping here, since Cicero also lists digression (*digressio*) as an independent part of a speech.

[10] At 2.50.150, however, it is used to mean, broadly, "comparison."

on in the analysis of the issue of fact when Cicero describes how the defense counsel must deny the presence of any strong impulse and attribute the crime to some mild emotion. In doing this

> . . . et exempla et similitudines erunt proferundae. . . .   (2.8.25)

> . . . he will have to offer examples and parallels. . . .

Once again no illustrations are offered.

A final preliminary instance of a term of comparison occurs in Book I in the long section on proof (*confirmatio*). Cicero states that there are four attributes of actions. The third of these is the adjunct of an action, which refers to something which is greater than, less than, or equal to the action. It may also be: similar to the action (*quod simile erit ei negotio, quo de agitur*), contrary to it, its negative, or in the relation to it of genus, part, or result. The adjunct that is *simile* is defined a few lines later:

> simile autem ex specie conparabili aut ex conferunda atque as-
> simulanda natura iudicatur.   (1.28.42)

> Similarity is decided on the basis of comparable appearance and
> natural characteristics which can be set side by side and likened
> one to another.

No examples are given, and all that can be said is that *simile* is used nonfiguratively as an adjunct of an action with two subdivisions whose particular characteristics are not given.[11]

The central mention of comparison in *de Inventione* (1.29.46–30.49) is only moderately more informative than the isolated

---

[11] Hubbell, *Cicero, de Inventione* 81, in a somewhat misdirected footnote refers to a section of C. Marius Victorinus' commentary on *de Inventione* (C. Halm, *Rhetores Latini Minores* [Leipzig 1863] 227). The passage referred to is actually Victorinus' comment on the kind of adjunct that is greater, less, or equal. Victorinus does have a comment on the adjunct *simile* (Halm 228), but it is not based on Cicero's own words but on the standard approach to comparison in the late technical treatises (e.g., it automatically divides *simile* into three parts, whereas Cicero specifies only two). The comment is therefore of little use in supplying information about what *Cicero* means in the present passage.

passages. After discussing the attributes of action, Cicero begins a fresh section (1.29.44) with the statement that every argument in proof must be either probable or certain (*aut probabilis aut necessaria*). The probable argument is defined:

> Probabile autem est id, quod fere solet fieri aut quod in opinione positum est aut quod habet in se ad haec quandam similitudinem, sive id falsum est sive verum. (1.29.46)

That is probable which for the most part usually comes to pass, or which is a part of the ordinary beliefs of mankind, or which contains in itself some resemblance to these qualities, whether such resemblance be true or false.

The first two areas of *probabile* are illustrated; then the third is subdivided further and illustrated:

> similitudo autem in contrariis et ex paribus et in iis rebus, quae sub eandem rationem cadunt, maxime spectatur. in contrariis, hoc modo: "nam si iis, qui inprudentes laeserunt, ignosci convenit, iis, qui necessario profuerunt, haberi gratiam non oportet." [12] ex pari, sic: "nam ut locus sine portu navibus esse non potest tutus, sic animus sine fide stabilis amicis non potest esse." [13] in iis rebus, quae sub eandem rationem cadunt, hoc modo probabile consideratur: "nam si Rhodiis turpe non est portorium locare, ne Hermocreonti quidem turpe est conducere." [14] (1.30.46–47)

Resemblance is seen mostly in contraries, in analogies, and in those things which fall under the same principle. In contraries, as follows: "For if it is right for me to pardon those who have wronged me unintentionally, I ought not to be grateful to those who have assisted me because they could not help it." In analogies, thus:

---

[12] The three examples in the passage all derive ultimately, if not directly, from Aristotle, the first one from *Rhet.* 2.23.1397a13–16.

[13] *Eud. Eth.* 7.2.1237b12 supplies the latter part of this example.

[14] This third example derives from *Rhet.* 2.23.1397a25ff, where it is attributed to a certain tax gatherer, Diomedon. Aristotle makes no mention of Rhodians or Hermocreon.

"For as a place without a harbor cannot be safe for ships, so a mind without integrity cannot be relied on by friends." In the case of those things which fall under the same principle, probability is considered after this fashion: "For if it is not disgraceful for the Rhodians to farm out their customs-duties, neither is it disgraceful for Hermocreon to take the contract."

Cicero is using *similitudo* as an element of probable proof; it thus constitutes the quality of resemblance, rather than a stylistic figure of comparison, in certain kinds of argument. Nevertheless, there are points of contact between it and the embellishing *similitudo* in *ad Herennium*. Both *de Inventione* and *ad Herennium* have a kind of *similitudo* that is presented through contrast. Second, the examples in *de Inventione*, like all but one in *ad Herennium*, contain equal development of both their parts and are in the order comparison/subject. Third, there is freedom in the form of the examples here, as there was in *ad Herennium*. Two of the examples of argument by *similitudo* are conditional comparisons, the other is a simile.

Cicero proceeds to a second brief passage on comparison, inserted somewhat enigmatically, that is both instructive and tantalizing. His remarks on *similitudo* would seem to have concluded the analysis of probable proof (*probabile*), but he now redefines *probabile* quite differently from his definition at 1.29.46:

> Omne autem—ut certas quasdam in partes tribuamus—probabile, quod sumitur ad argumentationem, aut signum est aut credibile aut iudicatum aut comparabile. (1.30.47)

> For the sake of making definite subdivision we may say that all probability that is used in argument is either a sign, or something credible, or a point on which judgement has been given, or something which affords an opportunity for comparison.

The opening phrase appears to indicate that Cicero is here dividing *probabile* into precise types rather than into the more general areas of the previous definition, but difficulties attend this interpretation. It would be hard to demonstrate that "a sign, or something credible, or a point on which judgement has been given, or something which affords an opportunity for comparison" are really more precise divisions than "what for the most part usually comes to pass, or is a part of the ordinary beliefs of mankind, or contains in itself some resemblance to these qualities." Indeed, the examples show that "something credible" (*credibile*) and "what is a part of the ordinary beliefs of mankind" (*quod in opinione positum est*) are almost synonymous.[15] In addition, "something which affords an opportunity for comparison" (*comparabile*) and "what contains in itself some resemblance to these qualities" (*quod habet in se ad haec quandam similitudinem*) both involve comparison. It is doubtful, therefore, that this second discussion of *probabile* is a mere refinement of the first discussion. It is more likely that Cicero is giving two independent accounts of *probabile*, drawing either on two sources or on one source that itself contained two accounts. Certain elements in the two accounts are parallel, certain are divergent; neither is subordinate to the other.

In this second discussion of *probabile*, Cicero follows his four-fold division of the term with definitions and examples of the first three divisions (*signum, credibile, iudicatum*). The fourth type, *comparabile*, is defined but with no examples:

conparabile[16] autem est, quod in rebus diversis similem aliquam rationem continet. eius partes sunt tres: imago, conlatio, exemplum. imago est oratio demonstrans corporum aut naturarum

---

[15] *Credibile* is said to be that "which is supported by the opinion (*opinione firmatur*) of the auditor without corroborating evidence," and the example given is: "There is no one who does not wish his children to be safe and happy" (1.30.48). The two examples given earlier (1.29.46) for *quod in opinione positum est* are "punishment awaits the wicked in the next world" and "philosophers are atheists."

[16] *Comparabile*, though a general heading for comparison here, did not develop into a recurring term of comparison in Latin. It appears not to have been used again until Victorinus' commentary on *de Inventione*.

similitudinem. conlatio est oratio rem cum re ex similitudine con-
ferens. exemplum est, quod rem auctoritate aut casu alicuius
hominis aut negotii confirmat aut infirmat. (1.30.49)

Lastly, probability which depends on comparison involves a certain principle of similarity running through diverse material. It
has three subdivisions, similitude, parallel, example. A similitude
is a passage setting forth a likeness of individuals or characters. A
parallel is a passage putting one thing beside another on the basis
of their resemblances. An example supports or weakens a case by
appeal to precedent or experience, citing some person or historical event.

The triad of terms, *imago, collatio, exemplum* ("similitude, parallel,
example"), must be equivalent to the triad *similitudo, exemplum,
imago* in *ad Herennium*, despite the fact that only two terms are
common to both triads and that the terms in *ad Herennium* are
among the embellishments of thought while in *de Inventione* they
are elements of probable proof. The first difference indeed may be
explicable as an effort to avoid confusion in terminology. Cicero
has already designated *similitudo* as the main heading in the first
account of comparison, and he may be seeking to avoid its use as
a subordinate heading in the second account by employing *collatio* in its stead. He does use the term, of course, in the definitions
of both *imago* and *collatio* in a broad sense of "similarity," but
this could be a further cause for bringing forward a different term
as the actual partner of *imago* and *exemplum*.

In the absence of examples, it is impossible to be doctrinaire on
the question of whether Cicero would have illustrated his triad of
terms in much the same way as did the author of *ad Herennium*.
The definitions given by Cicero and by the author, however, are
sufficiently different to suggest that Cicero's illustrations would
have been at least somewhat divergent. The two definitions of
exemplum are essentially the same:

Exemplum supports or weakens a case by appeal to precedent or experience, citing some person or historical event.

(de Inv. 1.30.49)

Exemplum is the citing of something done or said in the past, along with the definite naming of the doer or author.

(ad Her. 4.49.62)

But the element of comparing two dissimilar things that was present in *ad Herennium*'s definition of *similitudo* is absent from Cicero's definition of *collatio*:

Collatio is a passage putting one thing beside another on the basis of their resemblances.

(de Inv. 1.30.49)

Similitudo is a manner of speech that carries over an element of likeness to one thing from a dissimilar thing.[17]

(ad Her. 4.45.59)

And the definition of *imago* in *de Inventione* differs considerably from that given for *imago* in *ad Herennium*:

Imago is a passage setting forth a likeness of individuals or characters.

(de Inv. 1.30.49)

Imago is the comparison of one figure with another, implying a certain resemblance between them.

(ad Her. 4.49.62)

On the one hand it seems clear that the triad in *de Inventione* of *imago, collatio, exemplum* corresponds as a group to *similitudo, exemplum, imago* in *ad Herennium* and that both triads stem from a standard rhetorical classification. It seems equally clear that this classification was not immovably rigid and that varying analyses could be given within the broad agreement that the triad consisted of historical example and two kinds of comparison.

A last statement by Cicero has the effect of increasing the reader's disappointment over the absence of examples for his

[17] I depart here from Caplan's translation. For the reason, see above, chap. III n. 57.

triad of terms. He concludes his account of *comparabile* with a tantalizing promise:

> horum exempla et descriptiones in praeceptis elocutionis cognoscentur. (1.30.49)

> Instances and descriptions of these principles [*imago, collatio, exemplum*] will be given with the rules for style.

The only part of the work that has survived is that on subject matter (*inventio*), so this promise remains unfulfilled[18] and we are left guessing even more about Cicero's second account of comparison than about the first.

It might finally be asked what correspondence exists between *similitudo*, the main heading of Cicero's first account of comparison, and *comparabile*, the main heading of the second. There is in fact little beyond their parallel position as headings of the separate accounts. They are subdivided quite differently, and to some degree *similitudo* enjoys more correspondence with the *collatio* division of *comparabile*: like *collatio* it, too (elsewhere in *de Inventione*, at 2.5.19 and 2.8.25), appears in collocation with *exemplum*.[19]

---

[18] Hubbell, *Cicero, de Inventione* 90 note a, is quite mistaken in referring the reader to 1.42.78ff for the execution of this promise to illustrate the divisions of *comparabile*. At 1.42.78 Cicero takes up the refutation of all the parts of argumentation he has outlined earlier in the book. 1.44.82 deals with the refutation of *comparabile*, but all Cicero does is list the ways in which something said to be *comparabile* can be shown not to be so, by differences in time, place, and so on. This passage in no way gives "instances and descriptions" of *imago, collatio,* and *exemplum*.

[19] Victorinus, quite on his own, finds complete correspondence between Cicero's *comparabile* and *simile*, which was treated as one of the adjuncts of an action at 1.28.42. Although Cicero himself gives no details of his own understanding of *simile*, Victorinus (Halm 228) subdivides it into the same triad as Cicero subdivides *comparabile*, and Victorinus gives almost the same examples for these subdivisions of *simile* as he does for the subdivisions of *comparabile*. It cannot

A fragmented picture of comparison emerges from *de Inventione*. No term of comparison is associated at any point with metaphor; three (*similitudo, imago, collatio*) are variously associated with historical example. The latter two, together with *exemplum*, correspond to the rhetorical group of *similitudo, exemplum, imago* in *ad Herennium*. *Imago*, as is the case in *ad Herennium*, is used as a term of comparison in only one passage in *de Inventione*. Predictably, considering the nature of the treatise, comparison is advanced much more as an element of proof than of style. Finally, *de Inventione* contains no discussion of simile.

Almost forty years passed before Cicero wrote again on the subjects of rhetoric and oratory. The great work marking his new involvement with these subjects, *de Oratore*, contains a good many instances of terms of comparison, a few of which are important. As in *de Inventione*, terms of comparison appear both in isolation and in groups, both in broad and in figurative contexts.

Comparatio occurs in *de Oratore* in the same very general sense of "comparison" in which it was used in *de Inventione* and in *ad Herennium*. At *de Oratore* 1.60.257, the term refers to the act of comparing the work of one student with that of another. At 2.85.348, in the section on panegyric, Antonius remarks that a worthwhile policy in panegyric is to make a *comparatio* of the person being praised with other outstanding men. In neither instance does *comparatio* denote an actual figure of comparison.

Simile appears in alternation with *similitudo*, but the term is also used by itself in the section of Book II in which Antonius discusses arrangement.[20] He remarks that an orator's opening words should be carefully formed but that some speakers, in particular Philippus,[21] start out completely unprepared. Philippus, he says, has a rejoinder:

---

be said that the correspondence Victorinus finds between *comparabile* and *simile* is indicated at all in Cicero's text.

[20] 2.78.316.

[21] L. Marcius Philippus, consul in 91 B.C.—the dramatic date of *de Oratore*.

... et ait idem, cum bracchium concalfecerit, tum se solere
pugnare.[22]   (2.78.316)

... what he says about it is that his way is to warm up his biceps
first and then start fighting.[23]

But, Antonius continues, Philippus misses the point,

neque attendit eos ipsos, unde hoc simile ducat, primas illas hastas
ita iactare leniter. ...   (2.78.316)

not observing that even the professionals from whom he derives
this metaphor[24] when throwing the spear deliver their first
throws gently. ...

Simile refers here to a stylistic figure, but the element of comparison plays a minor role, the figure consisting essentially of a
metaphorical likeness.

Imago, like *simile*, appears in connection with *similitudo*, but it
too occurs once independently in a rhetorical context—as well as
frequently in a pictorial sense of "image" in the discussion of
memory (2.86.351ff).[25] At 3.54.207 it is listed by Crassus without
definition or illustration among the figures of diction, as opposed
to the figures of thought just outlined by Crassus. There is no
indication of a precise meaning,[26] but it is noteworthy that there

[22] Wilkins' OCT is used for *de Oratore* and all subsequent rhetorical works of
Cicero.
[23] The Loeb translation by E. W. Sutton and H. Rackham, *Cicero, de Oratore,*
Books I and II (London 1942), is used.
[24] Although a metaphor is certainly presented, the Loeb translation of *simile* by
"metaphor" is not quite accurate. *Translatio* is the regular term for metaphor. A
better rendering would be "likeness" or "illustration."
[25] This pictorial use of *imago* is entirely analogous to the use of the term in *ad
Herennium*'s discussion of memory (3.16.28–24.40) and to the use of εἰκών in
Aristotle's *de Memoria* 450b21–451a15.
[26] H. Rackham's Loeb volume, *Cicero, De Oratore Book III, De Fato, Paradoxa
Stoicorum, De Partitione Oratoria* (Cambridge, Mass., 1942) 167, is reasonably
vague in translating "indication of similarity."

has been a change in classification from *ad Herennium*, where *imago* was one of the figures of thought in collocation with *similitudo* and *exemplum*. *Imago* has been disengaged in this passage and placed among the figures of diction;[27] *similitudo* and *exemplum*, on the other hand, are retained by Crassus among the figures of thought:

> . . . tum duo illa, quae maxime movent, similitudo et exemplum.
>
> (3.53.205)
>
> . . . then two extremely effective figures, comparison and example.

Similitudo as in *ad Herennium* and *de Inventione*, so in *de Oratore*, is the most widely used term of comparison, whether referring to an actual figure of comparison or in a broader sense of "resemblance," "likeness." To illustrate the latter, at 1.56.240 Antonius claims that eloquence will win an argument when the law is uncertain, and he recounts an incident in which Servius Galba swayed the opinion of Publius Crassus over an unclear point of law by a sportive eloquence that included adducing *multas similitudines* ("a number of analogies") to the issue at hand. Again, at 2.36.152 Catullus remarks on the similarity of the rhetorical principles of Antonius and Aristotle, and he graciously suggests that one reason for this may be a general resemblance between Antonius' native talent and that of Aristotle:

> . . . sive tu similitudine illius divini ingeni in eadem incurris vestigia. . . .[28]   (2.36.152)
>
> . . . whether it be that through likeness to that godlike genius you fall into the same track. . . .

[27] A. S. Wilkins, *M. Tulli Ciceronis de Oratore Libri III* (Oxford 1879–1892) III 123, is not helpful in his note on *imago* when he refers for analogous usage to the *ad Herennium* passage and also to *de Inventione* 1.30.49. In the latter, *imago is* used analogously in that it is not a figure of thought, but it still is a member of a rhetorical triad; *imago* in the present *de Oratore* passage is independent of the surrounding figures of diction.

[28] See also 2.17.71, 2.23.96, and 2.23.98 for passages closely analogous to this one.

Finally, at 2.88.359, in the discussion of memory, a somewhat curious phrase occurs. Antonius states that memory of words is given clarity by a large variety of images. But there are many words (*multa verba*) that connect parts of a sentence/speech (*membra orationis*), and

> quae formari similitudine nulla possunt.　　　　　(2.88.359)

these cannot be formed by any use of simile.

The *multa verba* are prepositions and conjunctions, as Sutton and Rackham point out,[29] but their translation is mistaken: Cicero's meaning is that in the case of connectives it is not possible to picture resemblances or likenesses (*similitudine*) as is possible with nouns and verbs.[30]

Of the passages in which *similitudo* is used to refer more explicitly to a figure of comparison, the first comes at 1.28.130, where Crassus is expounding the perfection that must accompany the orator. He illustrates by pointing to the excellence that Roscius demands in a player but never finds, and he transfers this comparison from acting to speaking:

> Itaque ut ad hanc similitudinem huius histrionis oratoriam laudem dirigamus, videtisne. . . .　　　　　(1.28.130)

And so, to take this comparison with this player as our standard of an orator's merit, do you not see. . . .

At 2.40.168 Antonius is sketching the doctrine of topics, consisting both of intrinsic and extrinsic arguments, and he illustrates each topic. One of them is *similitudo*:

> Ex similitudine autem: "si ferae partus suos diligunt, qua nos in liberos nostros indulgentia esse debemus?"　　　　　(2.40.168)

---

[29] Sutton/Rackham 470 note c.

[30] J. S. Watson, *Cicero On Oratory and Orators* (New York 1860), sees this well: ". . . for there are many words which . . . connect the members of our speech, that can not possibly be represented by any thing similar to them."

Then, as a deduction from resemblance, we have: "If the wild beasts cherish their young, what tenderness ought we to bear to our children!"

The illustration is a conditional comparison;[31] but there is also, as Sutton and Rackham make clear, a strong admixture of "resemblance" in the meaning of *similitudo* here, as can be seen from the next topic, which is *ex dissimilitudine* ("from difference").[32] The whole list of topics outlined in 2.39.162–40.173 is practically identical to a list used in the *Topica*, where a slightly fuller passage on *similitudo* occurs.[33]

At 2.66.265–266 there is a considerably more complex passage. C. Julius Caesar Strabo Vopiscus is discussing wit. Sections 248–263 define and illustrate seven kinds of verbal wit, sections 264–290 eight[34] kinds of wit of matter. The first of these is *similitudo*, which is subdivided:

> Est etiam ex similitudine, quae aut conlationem habet aut tam-
> quam imaginem.   (2.66.265)

> Another source of such pleasantry is resemblance, involving either comparison or something like portraiture.

Several points are noteworthy. Two terms of comparison have been classified under a third main term, a procedure exactly like the subclassification in *de Inventione* of *comparabile* into *collatio* and *imago*. From the recurring triad of two terms of comparison and historical example only the last is missing in the present passage, and in a sense it can be found nearby. Caesar has begun his dis-

---

[31] It is very like the third type of *similitudo* ("the case of those things which fall under the same principle") at *de Inv.* 1.30.47; see above, p. 93.

[32] It should be noted that this illustration of *similitudo* resembles the usual character of the term in *ad Herennium* in the equal development of its two parts.

[33] See below, p. 115.

[34] The precise number is disputed. Wilkins II 328 says there are six main headings. Sutton/Rackham xxi say nine, and their count is the more accurate except that they list *imago* as a separate heading, whereas Cicero specifically subordinates it to *similitudo*.

cussion of wit of matter by saying that it is more effective, but also more difficult, than verbal wit. It involves narrative, which is always demanding, and it also involves drawing upon history:

> Trahitur etiam aliquid ex historia, ut, cum Sex. Titius se Cassandram esse diceret, "multos" inquit Antonius "possum tuos Aiaces Oileos nominare." (2.66.265)

> Material is derived too from history, as when Sextus Titius was describing himself as a Cassandra, and Antonius commented, "I can name many who played Ajax, the son of Oileus, to your Cassandra."

The term *exemplum* does not occur; furthermore, historical material is a general category that can be used in any kind of wit of matter. But it is clear that *exemplum* is being discussed, and the two subdivisions of *similitudo* appear immediately afterwards. Cicero in effect is again presenting the common rhetorical triad, though more loosely than in *de Inventione*.

The inclusion of *imago* under the category of wit of matter (*facetiae rerum*) is interesting. In its one independent appearance in *de Oratore*, in Book III,[35] *imago* is one of Crassus' figures of diction (*verborum*), as opposed to figures of thought (*sententiarum*). Much the same contrast of categories is present here in the distinction between verbal wit, *facetiae verborum*,[36] and wit of matter, *facetiae rerum* (Wilkins describes *rerum* as "substance of thought,"[37] that is, *sententiarum*). In this case, however, *imago* is not regarded as belonging to the category of diction (*verborum*) but of matter/thought (*rerum/sententiarum*). The discussion of wit is spoken by Caesar, while Crassus is the speaker in Book III when *imago* is considered a figure of diction; but it seems less likely that Cicero assigns two different views of *imago* to two different speakers than that he is simply inconsistent on this point. *Imago*, therefore, in

[35] 3.54.207; see above, p. 99.
[36] Within which is listed metaphor.
[37] Wilkins II 328.

this passage in Book II, is treated as an embellishment of thought; in Book III it changes to one of diction.

Illustrations are provided for both subdivisions of *similitudo*. The first example of *collatio* is a retort by Gallus to Marcus Scaurus, who is defending Piso[38] on a charge of paying large bribes to a lieutenant, Magius. Scaurus' defense is to point out that Magius is poor and needy. Gallus counters that Magius has squandered the sum of money:

> "erras," inquit "Scaure; ego enim Magium non conservasse dico, sed tamquam nudus nuces legeret, in ventre abstulisse."
>
> (2.66.265)

> "You are missing the point, Scaurus, for I do not assert that Magius still has this fund, but that he has tucked it away in his paunch, like a naked man who goes nutting."

Cicero's second example of *collatio* is a disparaging remark attributed to his own grandfather, Marcus Cicero, about the effect of Greek influence on Rome:

> "nostros homines similis esse Syrorum venalium: ut quisque optime Graece sciret, ita esse nequissimum." (2.66.265)

> [Marcus Cicero said] that our contemporaries were like the Syrian slave-market: "the better knowledge they had of Greeks, the more worthless were their respective characters."

Two examples of *imago* are given also; but, unlike *collatio*, a definition of *imago* precedes the examples.

> Valde autem ridentur etiam imagines, quae fere in deformitatem aut in aliquod vitium corporis ducuntur cum similitudine turpioris. (2.66.266)

> Caricatures also provoke loud laughter: as a rule they are levelled against ugliness or some physical defect, and involve comparison with something a little unseemly.

[38] Gallus' identity is unknown, according to Wilkins II 329. Piso is probably the consul of 112 B.C.

Once the exaggerated nature of a figure aiming at jest is allowed for,[39] it can be seen that this definition resembles the more sober one given for *imago* in *de Inventione*:

> imago est oratio demonstrans corporum aut naturarum simili-
> tudinem.   (*de Inv.* 1.30.49)

A similitude is a passage setting forth a likeness of individuals or characters.

In both cases personal characteristics are the subject matter for *imago*, and both passages mention the presence in *imago* of comparison by resemblance (*similitudo*).[40] The first example of *imago* actually consists not of any spoken jest but merely of a silent humorous comparison that Caesar reports having once made himself about Helvius Mancia[41] by pointing to a Cimbrian shield captured by Marius in the Gallic War of 101 B.C. that depicted a Gaul with contorted body, protruding tongue, and hanging jowls. The second example is a remark made by Caesar to a Titus Pinarius who kept twisting his chin as he spoke:

> "tum ut diceret, si quid vellet, si nucem fregisset. . . ."[42]
>   (2.66.266)
> [I said] that the time for observations, if he wished to say anything, would come when he had finished cracking his nut. . . .

---

[39] The very presence of the exaggerated nature of raillery has led to the reasonable suggestion that this passage is a rare instance in Latin rhetorical prose of the Greek game of εἰκασμός, several examples of which were seen in pre-Aristotelian rhetorical literature (see above, chap. I n. 43). G. Monaco, "Un particolare tipo di facezia nel *de Oratore*," *Atti del 9 Congresso Internazionale di Studi Ciceroniani* (Rome 1961) I 61–64, sets forth the evidence and argues that one further reminiscence of εἰκασμός is in Quintilian *Inst. Orat.* 5.11.24 (see below, p. 201f).

[40] Because of the limits in terminology, *similitudo* in the *de Oratore* passage is both the general heading for *collatio* and *imago* and also part of the definition of *imago*.

[41] Of unknown identity according to Wilkins II 330.

[42] Wilkins II 330 suggests that the *oratio recta* would have been "*tum dic, si quid vis, si nucem fregeris.*"

The point is that Pinarius's idiosyncrasy made him look as though he were trying to break a nut in his mouth.

The personal and descriptive character of the *imago* type of comparison is apparent from the opening remarks and the two examples. There is no corresponding opening definition of *collatio*, and its particular nature as a comparison of jest remains less clear. Both examples are in form similes, but nothing more can be made of this as Cicero expresses no view on a desired form for *similitudo* or either of its subdivisions.[43] The two examples describe both their subject and comparative parts; in this they differ from the examples of *imago* that describe only the object brought forward in comparison while they resemble the usual character of examples of *similitudo* in *ad Herennium*, *de Inventione*, and elsewhere in *de Oratore*. Aside from these observable features, it can only be said of *collatio* that it serves as a subordinate part of *similitudo*, which is an element of wit of matter.

Finally, Cicero does not completely restrict *similitudo* and its divisions to the realm of jest. In the slightly earlier section 263, he remarks that all methods of jesting can also be used for serious purposes. One can suppose, therefore, that Cicero would feel that *similitudo* and its divisions of *collatio* and *imago* have a function in serious oratory as well as in jest, although the terms do not actually appear as a group elsewhere in *de Oratore*.

One of the two significant passages on comparison in *de Oratore* occurs at 2.66.265–266. The second, at 3.39.157, is all the more interesting because its authenticity has been seriously challenged. In this part of Book III Crassus discusses the means by which an orator may embellish his style. The first is through vocabulary—use of single words—and Crassus specifies three possibilities: use of a rare word, use of a new word, or use of a transferred word (that is, a metaphor).[44] Then, shortly after the beginning of what

[43] It is noteworthy nonetheless that this is the only use, and these the only examples, of *collatio* in *de Oratore*.

[44] 3.38.152. My comments that follow on this vexed passage have been made separately in *AJP* 90 (1969) 215–219.

will be a lengthy exposition of metaphor, a sentence concluding
a brief initial development of two kinds of metaphor is followed
by a new thought: definition of metaphor in terms of its relation
to *similitudo*.

Ergo haec translationes quasi mutuationes sunt, cum quod non
habeas aliunde sumas, illae paulo audaciores, quae non inopiam
indicant, sed orationi splendoris aliquid arcessunt; quarum ego
quid vobis aut inveniendi rationem aut genera ponam?
[Similitudinis[45] est ad verbum unum contracta brevitas, quod
verbum in alieno loco tamquam in suo positum si agnoscitur,
delectat, si simile nihil habet, repudiatur]; sed ea transferri oportet,
quae. . . .   (3.38.156–39.157)

Consequently the metaphors in which you take what you have
not got from somewhere else are a sort of borrowing; but there is
another somewhat bolder kind that do not indicate poverty but
convey some degree of brilliance to the style. However there is no
need for me to put before you[46] the method of inventing these or
their classification.
[A metaphor is a short form of *similitudo*, contracted into one
word; this word is put in a position not belonging to it as if it were
its own place, and if it is recognizable it gives pleasure, but if it
contains no similarity it is rejected.] But only such metaphors
should be used as. . . .

Bake first questioned the genuineness of the bracketed sentence,[47] on grounds of lack of appropriateness and intelligibility,
and deleted the opening clause, *similitudinis . . . brevitas.* Sorof ex-

[45] The paragraph indication is mine; Wilkins' OCT has none. Brackets here
and below are Wilkins'.

[46] Rackham's Loeb edition proposes *exponam* for *ponam* at this point and
translates "to give you a lecture on."

[47] The rhetorician Julius Victor (fourth century A.D.), while reproducing the
argument and much of the phrasing of *de Orat.* 3.155–158, omits section 156 and
this sentence (Halm 431f). His omission would be of weight if he did not elsewhere make similar doctrinal omissions of matter that is surely genuine; e.g., he
skips all the way from section 150 to 155 in his analysis.

punged the whole sentence.[48] Harnecker deleted the second word of the sentence, *est*, and the phrase *quod . . . positum*.[49] Sorof was supported by Wilkins,[50] and editors since have generally fallen in line.[51] But the case for expunging, the whole or the part, does not seem secure. The passage is also, if genuine, more important than has been acknowledged.

The connection with the previous sentence is admittedly harsh. A singular *translatio* (metaphor) must be understood, and this is difficult in face of the preceding plurals.[52] Lambinus suggested that *translatio omnis similitudinis . . .* be read;[53] Schütz, *est autem translatio similitudinis. . . .*[54] Either one forms an adequate transition, though *translatio* is left at some distance from *contracta brevitas*. If the sentence is indeed inappropriate and generally unintelligible, however, restoration of a suitable transition is likely to be wasted effort.

The arguments of the sentence's critics are several, but their variety alone is confusing and contradictory. Each of three editors, as noted, questions the latinity of a different part of the passage; for these critics, a differing amount of the passage has seemed appropriate within the context. Such disparate judgments of the sentence do not inspire particular faith in any single one. In fact, the latinity seems passable except for the transition. *Brevitas* in the nominative appears with a genitive at *de Oratore* 1.5.17. *Agnoscere* is found in a similar passive phrase at *Brutus* 10.41;

[48] J. Bake, *M. Tulli Ciceronis De Oratore Libri Tres* (Amsterdam: F. Muller, 1863); G. Sorof, *M. Tullii Ciceronis De Oratore Libri Tres* (Berlin: Weidmann, 1875).

[49] In his 6th ed. (1886) of Piderit's 1859 ed. of *de Oratore*.

[50] Wilkins III 86–87.

[51] For example, Firmani (1899), Cima (1900), Bornecque (1930), Rackham (1942). Klotz (1900) and Richard (1932) are exceptions.

[52] But it is made easier by considering the new thought as starting a fresh paragraph.

[53] In his 1566 ed.

[54] In the 1814 ed., part of his complete Cicero; his 1805 ed. of *de Oratore* does not question the passage.

repudiare in similar passive phrases at *de Oratore* 3.48.185 and 49.192. Harnecker himself supplies parallels for the phrase *quod . . . positum* from *de Oratore* 3.38.153, 38.155, and 41.165.[55] On the other hand, Bake's deletion makes the rest of the sentence, *quod verbum . . . repudiatur*, grammatically impossible, a difficulty he overcomes only with the severe proposal that *quod verbum . . . repudiatur* be placed between sections 155 and 156.[56]

If the latinity, except for the transition, is acceptable, is the sentence appropriate? To most critics the crux is the sudden definition of metaphor in terms of *similitudo* and, conversely, the technical use of *similitudo* to denote a rhetorical figure of comparison. Bake and Sorof object that metaphor has already been defined in sections 155 and 156; Wilkins joins them in arguing that this technical use of *similitudo* is unique in the present discussion of metaphor. One can answer that metaphor has indeed been defined, and in some detail, as a means of embellishing style, but that this does not make superfluous a brief definition of it in terms of a related rhetorical figure. Next, it is true that *similitudo* appears several times elsewhere in the discussion of metaphor, even a second time in section 157, and always in the more general sense of "resemblance," "similarity."[57] Nevertheless, as we have seen, Cicero does use *similitudo* to describe a figure of comparison in a good many passages of *de Oratore*; and for one whose lack of concern over consistency in technical vocabulary is apparent the

[55] His view that these verbal parallels indicate interpolation in our passage can work the other way, of course. Cicero may simply be repeating the same or similar phrases in different sections of this connected part of Book III.

[56] Bake also emends *ponam* to *exponam* at the end of 156. Rackham is therefore quite wrong to assign this conjecture to himself; see n. 46 above.

[57] Compare 3.38.155; 39.158; 40.161; 40.162; 41.163. For instance, the second use of *similitudo* in section 157 comes after Cicero, having said that metaphor should make clearer what one means, has given an example of several verses from Pacuvius in which most of the verbs are metaphorical. He adds: *omnia fere, quo essent clariora, translatis per similitudinem verbis dicta sunt* (almost everything is said in words transferred [used metaphorically] through resemblance, so as to make them clearer). *Simile* also occurs several times in these sections in a synonymous sense of "resemblance"; cf. 3.40.161; 41.163; 41.164.

sudden figurative use here of *similitudo* does not seem noticeably out of character. The sequence of meaning, then, in sections 156–157 is as follows: I do not need to describe the kind of metaphor that is stylistically brilliant. Metaphor (in general) is a figure of comparison shortened to one word; if the word is recognized the metaphor is sound and gives pleasure, if not the metaphor must be rejected. Here are some examples of successful metaphors. Section 157, in other words, concentrates attention on the brevity of metaphor and on the consequent importance of recognizing the similarity between the subject matter and the metaphorical word. None of this seems inappropriate or unduly obscure.

Two external facts give limited support to the internal arguments for authenticity. The *de Oratore* is not an interpolated work. To follow Sorof and Wilkins is to assume an interpolation possibly longer than any other in the whole work.[58] This is a negative indication, but it makes the burden of proof slightly heavier for those who would expunge. Secondly, the critics willingly point to Quintilian 8.6.8–9 as a similar definition of metaphor with comparison as a referent, but to them the Quintilian passage, in contrast to the Ciceronian, fits its context easily. Cousin has demonstrated, however, that Quintilian's whole discussion of metaphor in that part of Book VIII follows, broadly and in several details, Cicero's discussion of metaphor both before and after section 157.[59] Clearly Cicero's discussion is a model for Quintilian;[60] it may well be asked why Quintilian, adhering to

[58] Wilkins' text recognizes no interpolation of more than half a line in Book I, more than two of two lines each in Book II (22.90; 66.268), or more than two of one line each (7.28; 9.35) in Book III except for the present passage, which occupies three lines in his text.

[59] J. Cousin, *Etudes sur Quintilien* (Paris 1936) I 439ff. Having made this point, and writing after the Ciceronian sentence had been generally condemned, Cousin does not quite take the logical further steps. He quotes the *de Oratore* passage as genuine but does not support his view with the specific arguments he himself has brought to light.

[60] Kennedy 274 points out a similarity on an even larger scale between Quintilian 8.1–9.1 and the whole discussion of style in Book III of *de Oratore*.

his model in most respects, would insert a technical definition absent from the model.[61]

Despite infelicities of style in the passage, more problems are created than solved by its deletion—hardly an inducement to tamper with the manuscript tradition. If one accepts the sentence, while allowing for some such transitional conjecture as that of Lambinus or Schütz, Cicero will have made two innovations in rhetorical theory. First, he has coupled metaphor and comparison. Although this is very much the norm in earlier Greek theory, specifically in Aristotle, in the earliest Latin treatises (*ad Herennium* and *de Inventione*) metaphor and comparison have been consistently separated. The *de Oratore* passage is the first in Latin rhetoric to recall the Aristotelian coupling of metaphor and comparison as closely connected features of style. Quintilian 8.6.8–9 is a second instance, but in general Latin rhetorical writers remain non-Aristotelian in this matter, and even Cicero and Quintilian follow Aristotle only in these single passages. Second, Cicero has defined metaphor by its relation to comparison, making comparison the principal, metaphor the subordinate, figure. In Aristotle the case was very much the opposite, and the *de Oratore* sentence marks the first instance in which a reversal of the Aristotelian position is expressed. It seems, then, both that *de Oratore* 3.39.157 should be retained as genuine and that in it Cicero has made a modest contribution to ancient critical theory.

The interesting and significant character of these last two comments on comparison in *de Oratore* is not maintained in the remainder of Cicero's rhetorical works, and the pertinent passages in them may be treated with dispatch. The *Partitiones Oratoriae*, of uncertain and disputed date,[62] is the most purely technical of all Cicero's rhetorical writings.[63] It utilizes two terms of comparison,

[61] For the Quintilian passage, see below, pp. 229ff.

[62] A date of 54 or 53 is probable, but the work could be as late as 46 or 45.

[63] Kennedy 329 points out, though, that even in his most technical work Cicero avoids endless lists of rhetorical terms and continues to express the belief that oratory is not possible without philosophy.

similitudo and *simile*, in three brief passages, each one pairing the term with historical example. At 11.40, when dealing with the structure of a speech under the general heading of *confirmatio* (proof), Cicero tells his son, for whose instruction the treatise was designed, that the greatest corroboration of a probable truth is

primum exemplum, deinde introducta rei similitudo.

first an example, next the introduction of a parallel case.[64]

At 16.55, under the heading of *peroratio* (peroration), amplification is listed as a major element; two especially (*maxime*) effective ingredients of amplification are *similitudines et exempla* ("analogies and instances"). Finally, at 36.126, Cicero states in his remarks on forensic speaking that both the prosecution and the defense will support their definition and interpretation of a particular word *similibus exemplisque* ("by means of parallels and instances").

Cicero's history of oratory, the *Brutus*, probably written during the early months of 46 B.C., contains two instances of *similitudo* and three of *comparatio*. At 38.143, in his encomium of Crassus, Cicero says that in handling questions Crassus was ready and fertile *argumentorum et similitudinum* ("in argument and in analogies"[65]). In a sense *similitudo* is again allied with *exemplum*: a few sentences later (39.145) Cicero speaks of the famous case of Manius Curius in which Crassus and Scaevola opposed one another, and he stresses the *argumentorum exemplorumque copia* ("the wealth of arguments and precedents") that Crassus brought to bear. The pairing of both *similitudo* and *exemplum* with *argumentum* within the space of a few sentences suggests a kinship between the two of them as well. At 74.259 there is a more general use of *similitudo*. In a short description of L. Aurelius Cotta,[66] Cicero states that Cotta's preference for an archaic manner of speaking kept him as

---

[64] Rackham's Loeb translation.

[65] The Loeb translation by G. L. Hendrickson and H. M. Hubbell, *Cicero, Brutus and Orator* (Cambridge, Mass., 1939), is used.

[66] The tribune of 103 B.C.

far as possible *a similitudine* ("from resemblance") to Greek pronunciation. The three instances of *comparatio* all occur in precisely the same phrase, *sine comparatione*,[67] and present the word in its usual broad sense of "comparison" or "act of comparison." No rhetorical figure is involved in any of the passages.

The brief *de Optimo Genere Oratorum* was written as a preface to Cicero's lost (if ever completed) translations of Aeschines' *Against Ctesiphon* and Demosthenes' *On the Crown* and composed probably in 46 B.C., perhaps between *Brutus* and *Orator*.[68] It contains but a single instance of one term, *similitudo*. The word occurs in a nonfigurative context that recalls the view toward metaphor in *de Oratore*, specifically the need for a word used metaphorically to contain a real and easily apparent resemblance (*similitudo*) to the thing with which it is equated. At 2.4 Cicero, in discussing eloquence, stresses the desirability of a good choice both of words used in their proper sense (*verba propria*) and words used metaphorically (*verba translata*). He then remarks:

in propriis ut lautissima eligamus, in translatis ut similitudinem secuti verecunde utamur alienis.

We should choose the most elegant "proper" words; in the case of metaphorical words we should seek after resemblance and shy away from ones which are far-fetched.[69]

In *Orator*, Cicero's defense of his own oratorical practices, written toward the end of 46 B.C., there is again only one term of comparison, *similitudo*. It occurs several times, all but once in its general sense of "similarity," "resemblance." In two of these instances the context is once more the "resemblance" necessary

---

[67] 35.134; 47.173; 52.193.

[68] A date as early as 52 B.C. has been suggested; the relation of the treatise to *Brutus* and *Orator* is uncertain.

[69] My translation. Hubbell's Loeb translation is off the mark: "Of 'proper' words we should choose the most elegant, and in the case of figurative language we should be modest in our use of metaphors and careful to avoid far-fetched comparisons."

in good metaphor.[70] Only at 40.138 does *similitudo* appear in a more figurative context. A long list of thirty-nine figures of thought is given; *similitudo* and *exemplum* appear in consecutive phrases:

> ut comparet similitudines; ut utatur exemplis.

> he [the orator] will use comparisons[71] and examples.

The collocation is familiar and recalls in particular *de Oratore* 3.53.205, where *similitudo* and *exemplum* were also listed among the figures of thought. There *imago* was to be found among the verbal figures. In *Orator* a short list of verbal figures precedes the figures of thought, but *imago* is not mentioned.

The last of Cicero's rhetorical works, the *Topica*, written in 44 B.C., contains two somewhat fuller discussions of comparison. Each discussion is in turn foreshadowed by an earlier brief mention of comparison. Despite Cicero's own belief that he was summarizing Aristotle's *Topica* from memory for his friend, the lawyer Trebatius, his immediate source was undoubtedly some Hellenistic treatise that he took to be Aristotle's own work. The doctrines reflected are Hellenistic rather than Aristotelian, and many parts of the work simply do not occur in Aristotle.[72]

The less complex of the two sequences in the *Topica* of a brief, then a fuller discussion of comparison involves the term *comparatio*. At 4.23 the argument *ex comparatione* forms the last of an introductory list of intrinsic (inherent, as opposed to extrinsic or external) topics. *Comparatio* refers, as it has elsewhere, to the act of comparing one thing with another—here the greater with the

---

[70] 27.92; 39.134. "Resemblance to something" is the context three times: 55.184, *propter similitudinem sermonis* ("because of the resemblance to ordinary conversation"); 57.191, *propter similitudinem veritatis* ("because of the similarity to actual speech"); 59.201, *poematis similitudinem* ("the semblance of poetry").

[71] Hubbell's "similes" in the Loeb edition seems restrictive.

[72] Kroll 1065, 1088 stresses Antiochus of Ascalon as an important influence on Cicero's *Topica* and also as a probable transmitter of Aristotle's doctrines.

less, the less with the greater, and equal with equal. Examples of these processes are given, and each is in form a causal condition.[73] Then, at 18.68–71, the topic of argument *ex comparatione* is entered into in considerably greater detail, with Cicero emphasizing that, whether the comparison be drawn between things that are greater, less, or equal, consideration must be made of

> numerus species vis, quaedam etiam ad res aliquas adfectio.
>
> (18.68)
>
> quantity, quality, value, and also a particular relation to certain things.[74]

The ensuing treatment of all these headings reinforces the impression conveyed by 4.23 that *comparatio* is used by Cicero in the *Topica* strictly as a term of legal argumentation. It does not extend at all into use as a stylistic feature of oratory.

The second sequence of discussion of comparison involves *similitudo*. Its relatively brief mention comes at 3.15, slightly earlier than *comparatio* in the list of intrinsic topics for argument. Arguments *a genere* (from genus) and *a forma* (from species) are illustrated, and Cicero continues:

> A similitudine hoc modo: Si aedes eae corruerunt vitiumve faciunt quarum usus fructus legatus est, heres restituere non debet nec reficere, non magis quam servum restituere, si is cuius usus fructus legatus esset deperisset.

> An argument is based on similarity or analogy in the following manner: If one has received by will the usufruct of a house, and the house has collapsed or is in disrepair, the heir is not bound to restore or repair it, any more than he would have been bound to replace a slave of which the usufruct had been bequeathed, if the slave had died.

[73] For instance, the comparison of the greater with the less: *si in urbe fines non reguntur, nec aqua in urbe arceatur* ("since there is no action for regulating boundaries in the city, there should be no action for excluding water in the city").

[74] Hubbell's Loeb translation.

The next intrinsic topic is the argument *a differentia*, and there is clearly a contrast between this argument "from difference" and the argument *a similitudine*. The example is in form a conditional comparison, paralleling the conditional form of the example of *similitudo* in the list of intrinsic topics at *de Oratore* 2.40.168.[75]

In this first mention of *similitudo*, Cicero's use of the term is along purely legal grounds. The later, more detailed treatment of the argument *a similitudine* at 10.41–45 suggests that he understands a stylistic element as well in the term and he indicates this in his opening remark on the broadness of the topic:

> Similitudo sequitur, quae late patet, sed oratoribus et philosophis magis quam vobis. (10.41)

> Similarity comes next. This is an extensive topic, but of more interest to orators and philosophers than to you jurists.

The application of *similitudo*, Cicero implies, extends beyond the single sphere of law—with which the jurisconsult Trebatius is solely concerned—to the grander fields of oratory and philosophy where the stylistic embellishment of an argument is more fitting. There are five types of argument from *similitudo*. The first is *inductio* (induction), the Greek ἐπαγωγή, which, Cicero points out, Socrates often used.[76] It is defined and illustrated:

> Sunt enim similitudines quae ex pluribus conlationibus perveniunt quo volunt hoc modo: Si tutor fidem praestare debet, si socius, si cui mandaris, si qui fiduciam acceperit, debet etiam procurator. (10.42)

> For example, there are certain arguments from similarity which attain the desired proof by several comparisons, as follows: If

[75] See above, p. 101.

[76] This kind of argument is thus set in a long rhetorical tradition, going back to Aristotle's statement (*Rhet.* 2.20.1393b4) that Socrates frequently made use of arguments involving παραβολή (a part of παράδειγμα, the rhetorical equivalent of ἐπαγωγή).

honesty is required of a guardian, a partner, a bailee, and a trustee, it is required of an agent.

The example sets up a resemblance in the form of a conditional comparison and is parallel in form to the general example of *similitudo* at 3.15. The phrase *ex pluribus conlationibus* ("by several comparisons") refers to the series of conditional subjects (guardian, partner, etc.), and so *collatio* in itself denotes "parallel (case)" more than any figure of comparison.

The second type of *similitudo* is again defined in terms of *collatio*, which here does seem to mean a definite kind of figure:

> Alterum similitudinis genus conlatione sumitur, cum una res uni, par pari comparatur hoc modo: Quem ad modum, si in urbe de finibus controversia est, quia fines magis agrorum videntur esse quam urbis, finibus regendis adigere arbitrum non possis, sic, si aqua pluvia in urbe nocet, quoniam res tota magis agrorum est, aquae pluviae arcendae adigere arbitrum non possis. (10.43)

> Another kind of argument from similarity rests on comparison, when one thing is compared to one, equal to equal, as follows: If there is a dispute about boundary lines in the city you could not require arbitration for the regulation of boundaries, because the whole matter of boundary regulation applies to country property rather than to city; on the same principle, if rain-water does damage in the city you could not require arbitration for excluding rain-water, since the whole matter applies rather to country property.[77]

There is considerable similarity between the structure of this *similitudinis genus conlatione* and the *similitudo per conlationem* in *ad Herennium*. In both, every detail in one part of the comparison finds a parallel in the other part, and the present passage carries the parallelism even further than *ad Herennium* does by repeating words and phrases (*magis; adigere arbitrum non possis*) in both parts

[77] The subject matter of this example is, of course, the same as that of the *comparatio* that argued from the greater to the less. Only the form of presentation differs. See n. 73 above.

of the comparison. The resemblance to the embellishing *similitudo per conlationem* of *ad Herennium* furthers the likelihood that the sphere of the argument *a similitudine* is conceived of as going beyond the purely legal to the stylistic. In actual form, the *quem ad modum* . . . *sic* sequence of the example creates a simile, but the more basic form is one of parallel conditions contained within the *quem ad modum* . . . *sic* frame; and this conditional form is natural to legal argumentation and has already been seen in the first type (*inductio*) of *similitudo*, as well as in the earlier example of *similitudo* at 3.15.

Each of the remaining three types of argument *a similitudine* provides additional evidence of the stylistic function assigned in the *Topica* to the term. The third type, *exemplum*,[78] does this by inference, in that Cicero elsewhere associates historical example with comparison as an element of stylistic embellishment (for example, at *de Oratore* 3.53.205 and at *Orator* 40.138). The last two types, *ficta exempla* (nonhistorical, fictitious examples) and ὑπερβολή (hyperbole) are more explicit in that Cicero speaks of each as belonging less to jurisprudence than to oratory in general.

The conclusions to be drawn from the various discussions of comparison in Cicero's rhetorical works are, in part, as diffuse as might be expected in a body of writing that spans almost half a century and that in addition has the contrasting character of being at one time, as in *de Oratore*, highly original and at another, as in *de Inventione* and the *Topica*, wholly derivative. Certain usages and ideas, however, recur quite consistently. *Similitudo* (with *simile* on occasion used synonymously) clearly embraces the widest scope of the various terms of comparison. Its use is split between a general sense of "similarity," "resemblance," and a figurative sense of "comparison," and the two are at times juxtaposed. *Collatio*, a less frequent term, is usually a subdivision of *similitudo* and often means a figure of comparison in which both

---

[78] 10.44. Aristotle's *Topica* also associates historical example (παράδειγμα) and a term of comparison (παραβολή); see above, p. 26.

parts are developed equally and with corresponding detail. *Comparatio* regularly refers to the process of comparison but on occasion denotes an actual figure of comparison. *Comparabile* occurs once, in *de Inventione*, as a major heading of rhetorical figures of comparison and historical example. *Imago* is hard to classify. It slips in and out of the triad of historical example and two terms of comparison. It is rarely illustrated, but when it refers to a type of comparison the focus is on personal characteristics and description. The different terms of comparison are couched on occasion in the form of simile, but verbal form is never the essential ingredient of any of them.

Cicero's overall views of comparison conform in the main to those expressed in *ad Herennium*, which is to say that both reflect Hellenistic doctrines equally. The close partner of comparison continues to be historical example. Only once in Cicero, in the vexed passage at *de Oratore* 3.39.157, are metaphor and comparison associated, and here their relation is the reverse of that found in Aristotle. As in Aristotle and *ad Herennium*, there is no distinction drawn between comparisons of different length. Comparison belongs to every section of oratory, and to philosophy as well; it serves as an embellishment of style, as an element of proof, as a type of argument, and it can be used to advantage in all the various parts (for example, exordium, peroration) of a speech.

It remains to survey briefly Cicero's use of terms of comparison in the philosophical works,[79] noting any variations from his approach to comparison in the rhetorical works. Instances of *imago* are swiftly covered, since there are none in a rhetorical context in the philosophical treatises. *Comparatio* is employed rarely and in a very analogous fashion to the rhetorical writings, namely to

[79] H. Merguet, *Lexikon zu den philosophischen Schriften Cicero's* (Hildesheim 1961), is indispensable for such a survey. An examination of Merguet's *Lexikon zu den Reden des Cicero* (Hildesheim: G. Olms, 1962) revealed no rhetorical instances of terms of comparison in the speeches. Oldfather/Canter/Abbott, *Index Verborum Ciceronis Epistularum* (Urbana 1938), list a single rhetorical use of *similitudo*, at *ad Familiares* 9.16.6, referring to a simile of the tragedian Accius.

denote the process or act of comparison;[80] once it comes somewhat closer to signifying a figure of comparison.[81] *Collatio* occurs several times but always in connection with *similitudo* or *simile* and is best treated with them. *Similitudo* is again the term most frequently used and of the widest range of meaning, with *simile* serving as an occasional synonym. The great number of appearances of *similitudo* in the general sense of "similarity," "resemblance," need not be listed or illustrated.[82] The much smaller number of instances in which it and *simile* refer to a figure can be dealt with chronologically.[83]

In the *Academica*, written in the spring of 45 B.C., there is a passage in which *similitudo* does not quite denote a rhetorical figure but still is used more technically than in its general sense of "similarity." In Book II, toward the end of his defense of skepticism against Lucullus' attacks, Cicero refers to Zeno's demonstrations with his fingers and hands—intended to indicate the philosophical stages of visual appearance (*visum*), assent (*adsensus*), and comprehension (*comprehensio*)—and adds the phrase:

> qua ex similitudine etiam nomen ei rei, quod ante non fuerat, κατάληψιν imposuit.[84] (2.47.145)

and from this illustration he gave to that process the actual name of *catalēpsis*, which it had not had before.[85]

---

[80] See, e.g., *de Officiis* 1.17.58.

[81] At *de Finibus* 3.10.34, which will be quoted shortly in connection with *similitudo* and *collatio*.

[82] For the complete list see Merguet, *Lexikon zu den philosophischen Schriften* III 540–541. Typical instances are *Tusculan Disputations* 1.33.80, 4.13.30; *de Amicitia* 14.50; *de Divinatione* 2.26.55; *Academica* 2.14.43.

[83] The philosophical treatises involved were all written within the space of a year, and one would not expect to see any noticeable changes in terminology or rhetorical doctrine from the first to the last. Chronological treatment, while logical, is not so important here as in the rhetorical works that were separated by a large time span.

[84] Mueller's Teubner text is used for all the philosophical works.

[85] The Loeb translation by H. Rackham, *Cicero, de Natura Deorum, Academica* (London 1933), is used.

The meaning *similitudo* bears in this context of philosophical "analogy" or "illustration" is one that recurs elsewhere in the philosophical works.[86]

In the *de Finibus*, written in the summer of 45 B.C., there are four separate comments on comparison. The first, at 3.10.33–34, is obscure. Cato, expounding Stoic ethics, comes here to the definition and nature of the Good. He first explains how in general concepts of things are created in the mind, then specifies which of these general methods results in a conception of the Good. *Similitudo* and *collatio* are two of the methods, and it is *collatio* that will lead toward the Good:

> Cumque rerum notiones in animis fiant, si aut usu aliquid cognitum sit aut coniunctione aut similitudine aut collatione rationis, hoc quarto, quod extremum posui, boni notitia facta est.
>
> (3.10.33)
>
> Now notions of things are produced in the mind when something has become known either by experience or by combination of ideas or by likeness or by analogy. The fourth and last method in this list is the one that has given us the conception of the Good.[87]

Then the process of *collatio* is explained in slightly more detail but with no great clarity:

> Cum enim ab iis rebus, quae sunt secundum naturam, ascendit animus collatione rationis, tum ad notionem boni pervenit.
>
> (3.10.33)
>
> The mind ascends by analogy from the things in accordance with nature till finally it arrives at the notion of Good.

No examples of the process of *similitudo* or *collatio* are given, and it is hard to know their exact nature and meaning and what is conceived to be the difference between them. In the rhetorical writings *collatio* is usually a subdivision of *similitudo*, but here it is

---

[86] Compare *de Fin.* 3.6.22.

[87] The Loeb translation by H. Rackham, *Cicero, de Finibus Bonorum et Malorum* (London 1914).

quite separate and independent. In addition, the term does not occur by itself but in the less than clear phrase *collatione rationis*. Rackham's "likeness" and "analogy" for *similitudine* and *collatione rationis* are reasonable enough guesses, but some confusion results because elsewhere he renders *similitudo* and *simile* by "analogy" or "illustration."[88] Use of the terms in the rhetorical works might suggest something slightly more precise, such as "comparison through resemblance" and "comparison by detailed parallel," but doubt must remain over Cicero's true meaning. In a final sentence in the next section, Cato states that the Good is absolute and is therefore also recognized by its own properties, that is, not only from *collatio*. He illustrates his point by a simile comparing honey and the Good, saying of honey that, like the Good, it is perceived to be sweet by its own flavor and *non comparatione cum aliis* ("not by comparison with other things").[89] *Comparatio* does not refer as much to the simile as to the process of comparison. Nevertheless, it is associated with the actual figure of comparison more closely than usual.

Slightly further on in Book III, Cato puts forward the Stoic doctrine that lasting happiness is no more desirable than brief happiness. He then says of the Stoics, *utunturque simile* ("and they use this illustration"),[90] and a simile follows comparing the satisfactory functioning of shoes, whether many or few, and the satisfactory functioning of something chosen for its propriety, whether there is much or little of it. *Simili* clearly refers to the philosophical method of illustrative analogy.

At *de Finibus* 4.23.64 Cicero is rebutting Cato's exposition of Stoicism, in particular the doctrine put forward at 3.14.48 (just after the section discussed above) that wisdom and happiness are incapable of degree. Cicero says, referring to Cato's specific words at 3.14.48:

[88] In the next two passages discussed from the *de Finibus*, for example.
[89] 3.10.34.
[90] 3.14.46.

Atque hoc loco similitudines eas, quibus illi uti solent, dissimillimas
proferebas. (4.23.64)

It was at this point that you brought forward those extremely
false analogies which the Stoics are so fond of employing.

The *similitudines* used by Cato in 3.14.48 that Cicero thinks false
and lacking in resemblance (*dissimillimas*) are two similes comparing (1) a man who is only just below the surface of the water
but is still drowning and (2) puppies who have almost opened
their eyes but are still blind, with someone who has made great
but not complete progress toward happiness and is therefore
utterly miserable. Cicero repeats both of Cato's *similitudines*, not
at all in the form of similes but as conditional or causal comparisons. He subverts with irony the *similitudo* of the puppies, for
instance, as follows:

et, quoniam catuli, qui iam dispecturi sunt, caeci aeque et ii, qui
modo nati, Platonem quoque necesse est, quoniam nondum vide-
bat sapientiam, aeque caecum animo ac Phalarim fuisse. (4.23.64)

Again, since puppies on the point of opening their eyes are as
blind as those only just born, it follows that Plato, not having yet
attained to the vision of wisdom, was just as blind mentally as
Phalaris.

It is apparent that Cato's comparisons have been termed *similitudines* by reason of their character as (perhaps false) analogies, not
by reason of their simile form.

Somewhat further on in Book IV, Cicero has shifted to a refutation of the Stoic doctrine that all sins are equal. He debates
with an imagined opponent whom he calls upon to support the
Stoic doctrine. The opponent retorts:

Ut, inquit, in fidibus pluribus, si nulla earum ita contenta nervis sit,
ut concentum servare possit, omnes aeque incontentae sint, sic
peccata, quia discrepant, aeque discrepant; paria sunt igitur.
(4.27.75)

Suppose, says my opponent, of a number of lyres not one is so
strung as to be in tune; then all are equally out of tune; similarly
with transgressions, since all are departures from rule, all are
equally departures from rule; therefore all are equal.

Cicero rebukes his opponent for delivering a false argument: all
the lyres are out of tune, but not necessarily equally out of tune.
And he concludes:

Collatio igitur ista te nihil iuvat.   (4.27.75)

So your comparison does not help you.

A few sentences later he puts another argument into his opponent's mouth and labels it, with a bit of verbal display, a *simile
dissimile*:

Ecce aliud simile dissimile. Ut enim, inquit, gubernator aeque
peccat, si palearum navem evertit et si auri, item aeque peccat, qui
parentem et qui servum iniuria verberat.   (4.27.76)

Here is another of these false analogies: A skipper, says my ad-
versary, commits an equal transgression if he loses his ship with a
cargo of straw and if he does so when laden with gold; similarly a
man is an equal transgressor if he beats his parent or his slave without due cause.

Although both these comparisons possess the form of similes, they
are more basically examples of Stoic illustrative analogies through
comparison, just as were the *similitudines* in the previous passage.
In fact, all three terms, *similitudo, collatio, simile*, appear to be used
synonymously in this part of *de Finibus*, a predictable relation for
similitudo and *simile* but a somewhat surprising one for these two
and *collatio*, especially after *collatio* has been distinguished from
similitudo at 3.10.33. There is a degree of contradiction in Cicero's
use of terms of comparison in *de Finibus*; but all of them can denote comparisons that seek to prove a point by demonstrating a
detailed resemblance between two things.

In the *Tusculan Disputations*, written just after *de Finibus* in July of 45 B.C., there is a single mention of comparison that presents *similitudo* and *collatio* in the most common relation in which they have already been observed. In the fourth *Disputation* Cicero discusses from various points of view the proposition that the wise man is not free from all disorders of the soul. He approaches the problem first from the Stoic position and proposes to relate a favorite Stoic comparison:

> Atque ut ad valetudinis similitudinem veniamus eaque conlatione utamur aliquando, sed parcius, quam solent Stoici. . . .
>
> (4.12.27)
>
> Now to come to the analogy of health and to make use at last of this comparison (but more sparingly than is the way of the Stoics). . . .[91]

There follows a lengthy simile that compares several disorders of the body with several of the soul. As often, *similitudo* is the main heading and signifies "illustrative comparison," "analogy," while *collatio* signifies, within this heading, a type of comparison by detailed parallel.

De Natura Deorum, written still later in the prolific summer of 45, contains an interesting passage on comparison in each of its three books. In Book I, *similitudo* appears in close succession in sections 96 and 97. In section 96 it carries a broad meaning of "resemblance," "likeness,"[92] but in section 97 more of a figure is present. The Academic criticism of Epicureanism is being expounded by Cotta, who at this point is hammering particularly at Epicurean anthropomorphism. One of his arguments consists of noting resemblances between different animals and between animals and man in order to show that man does not have sole

[91] The Loeb translation by J. E. King, *Cicero, Tusculan Disputations* (Cambridge, Mass.: Harvard University Press, 1945) is used.

[92] The actual phrase is *ad similitudinem deorum* (toward a resemblance to the gods).

claim to reason. His argument takes the form of reversing a
similitudo used by the Epicureans:

> Ipsa vero quam nihil ad rem pertinet, quae vos delectat maxime,
> similitudo! Quid? canis nonne similis lupo? atque, ut Ennius,
> > Simia quam similis, turpissuma bestia, nobis!
>
> (1.35.97)

Then take your favourite argument from resemblance: how
utterly pointless it really is! Why, does not a dog resemble a
wolf?—and, to quote Ennius,
> How like us is that ugly brute, the ape!

The original Epicurean *similitudo* would be "a dog is *not* like a
wolf." Cotta scorns this as ridiculous and claims that a more sensible *similitudo* would be "a dog *is* like a wolf," or "an ape *is* like
us." His *similitudines* are similes, but his concern (as the Loeb
translation indicates) is whether a true or false resemblance is
being expressed.

In the second book of *de Natura Deorum*, Balbus, in his exposition of Stoicism, reports the arguments used by Zeno to show
that the world is animate and rational. He enlivens the report by
a *similitudo* that Zeno was accustomed to use:

> Idemque similitudine, ut saepe solet, rationem conclusit hoc modo:
> "Si ex oliva modulate canentes tibiae nascerentur, num dubitares,
> quin inesset in oliva tibicinii quaedam scientia? Quid, si platani
> fidiculas ferrent numerose sonantes? idem scilicet censeres in
> platanis inesse musicam. Cur igitur mundus non animans
> sapiensque iudicetur, cum ex se procreet animantis atque sapien-
> tis?"
>
> (2.8.22)

Furthermore he proved his argument by means of one of his
favourite comparisons, as follows: "If flutes playing musical
tunes grew on an olive-tree, surely you would not question that
the olive-tree possessed some knowledge of the art of flute-play-
ing; or if plane-trees bore well-tuned lutes, doubtless you would
likewise infer that the plane-trees possessed the art of music; why

then should we not judge the world to be animate and endowed with wisdom, when it produces animate and wise offspring?"

This extended conditional comparison is again an argument by detailed analogy, and *similitudo* seems to stand here both for a type of illustrative comparison and for its particular structure by close parallel—a dual function more usually filled, as in the *Tusculan Disputations* passage, by *similitudo* in conjunction with *collatio*.

The two terms appear jointly in a passage in the third book. At section 70 Cotta, who has been refuting the Stoic doctrines propounded by Balbus in the second book, argues against the specific double doctrine that human reason is a divine gift and that the gods look after the best interests of men. After Cotta ridicules these beliefs by pointing to the harm reason has wrought among men, Cicero employs the same rhetorical subtlety as in *de Finibus* and has Cotta manufacture for an imagined opponent a reply to his argument.

> Huic loco sic soletis occurrere: non idcirco non optume nobis a dis esse provisum, quod multi eorum beneficio perverse uterentur; etiam patrimoniis multos male uti, nec ob eam causam eos beneficium a patribus nullum habere.   (3.28.70)

> This line of argument is usually met by your school thus: it does not follow, you say, that the gods have not made the best provision for us because many men employ their bounty wrongly; many men make bad use of their inheritances, but this does not prove that they have received no benefit from their fathers.

To which Cotta rejoins gleefully:

> Quisquamne istuc negat? aut quae est in collatione ista similitudo?
>   (3.28.70)
> Does anybody deny this? and where is the analogy in your comparison?

Similitudo and *collatio* are connected here in the way that by now seems the norm: *similitudo* is the major figure denoting "illustrative analogy," while *collatio* indicates the type of comparison drawn.[93]

One final comparison in the philosophical works disregards this "normal" pattern. In Book II of *de Divinatione*, written during the fall of 45 and the winter of 44 B.C., at section 38, Cicero discusses with his brother Quintus the haphazard character of sacrifices in which the nature of the entrails seems to vary not by divine guidance but by the random choice of one victim over another. Once again he has an imaginary opponent reply:

> At enim id ipsum habet aliquid divini, quae cuique hostia obtingat, tamquam in sortibus, quae cui ducatur. (2.17.38)

> Oh! but someone will say, "The choice itself is a matter of divine guidance, just as in the case of lots the drawing is directed by the gods!"[94]

Cicero retorts confidently to his invisible opponent:

> Mox de sortibus; quamquam tu quidem non hostiarum causam confirmas sortium similitudine, sed infirmas sortis conlatione hostiarum. (2.17.38)

> I shall speak of lots presently; although you really do not strengthen the cause of sacrifices by comparing them to lots; but you do weaken the cause of lots by comparing them with sacrifices.

Similitudo and *collatio* appear here to be completely synonymous in referring to a simile with equal, though sparse, development of

---

[93] A. S. Pease, *M. Tulli Ciceronis De Natura Deorum* (Cambridge, Mass., 1958) II 1153, argues that this whole section of *N.D.* is confusing in its organization and seems to contain at least one revision or amplification of Cicero's original draft. This difficulty need not apply, it would seem, to the brief passage on comparison, where the text and meaning seem clear enough. .

[94] The Loeb translation by W. A. Falconer, *Cicero, de Senectute, de Amicitia, de Divinatione* (Cambridge, Mass.: Harvard University Press, 1923).

both its parts. Just why Cicero should use them so when they are as a rule distinct elsewhere is not clear, but the reason may be a stylistic desire to further the antithesis in his statement by employing different terms in each part.

Consideration of the philosophical treatises does not force any change in the conclusions already drawn concerning Cicero's theories of comparison. Indeed, as the closely contemporary character of the philosophical writings might lead one to expect, there is even somewhat more regularity in them than exists in the disparate rhetorical works. *Similitudo* remains the most frequent and basic term, very often denoting philosophical argument by analogy. *Collatio* is a more restricted term and usually, in subordinate juxtaposition with *similitudo*, refers to a comparison constructed by close parallel. Although the two most commonly bear this relation to each other, they also appear as equal and separate terms at *de Finibus* 3.10.33 and as wholly synonymous terms at *de Finibus* 4.27.75–76 and *de Divinatione* 2.17.38. Cicero's usage, therefore, is by no means absolutely uniform. More often than in the rhetorical works the comparisons are similes in form. But there are clear instances (*de Finibus* 4.23.64, for example) showing that no single form is requisite for the comparisons. Here, as in the rhetorical treatises, it can be said without reservation that Cicero displays no thought of simile as an independent rhetorical figure.

CHAPTER V

GREEKS OF THE FIRST CENTURIES
B.C. AND A.D.

Dionysius Thrax, Philodemus, [Demetrius] *On Style,*
Dionysius of Halicarnassus, [Longinus] *On the Sublime.*

Diffuseness marked Cicero's views of comparison. The same
quality belongs to the writers, spanning more than a century,
treated in this chapter. No common thread unites them: the first
was a grammarian, the second an Epicurean, and, while the last
three may have belonged to the same Augustan intellectual circle,
the precise dates of [Demetrius] and [Longinus] are not known,
making the connection far from sure. Very roughly, the writers
fall contemporary with Cicero or between him and the next
Latin writers of interest, the Senecas; their treatment within a
single chapter is largely a convenience.

It must not be thought that these Greek authors are typical of
the kind of Hellenistic rhetoric mentioned often as the main
source of *ad Herennium* and so much of Cicero. Each of the five is
a special case in this respect. Dionysius Thrax simply was not a
rhetorician; Philodemus belonged to a sect that scarcely deigned
to recognize rhetoric as a legitimate pursuit; Dionysius of
Halicarnassus and [Longinus] were literary critics rather than
rhetoricians; *On Style* is a rhetorical work but with considerably
broader aims than the technical treatises of the Hellenistic age. In
each instance the doctrines expressed simply do not fit rhetorical

tradition as easily as those in *ad Herennium,* Cicero, and subsequent writers. Nor were these authors particularly influential on later generations. In short, here is something of a real interlude in a survey of ancient theories of comparison.

Dionysius Thrax is the earliest figure of the group, and his small handbook of grammar, containing a bare mention of terms of comparison, almost certainly precedes in date both *ad Herennium* and *de Inventione.* An Alexandrian who taught at Rome, his dates are unknown, but he is said to have studied with Aristarchus and to have taught Tyrannion. On this basis Cohn places his life from 170–90 B.C.,[1] and a date of around 100 B.C. has been suggested for the handbook.[2] The section on the adverb (τὸ ἐπίρρημα)[3] gives a list of the different things that adverbs express; twelfth is:

Τὰ δὲ παραβολῆς ἢ ὁμοιώσεως, οἷον ὡς ὥσπερ ἠύτε καθάπερ.[4]

(19.12)

Some are characteristic of παραβολή or ὁμοίωσις, such as "as," "just as," "as when," "even as."

Of the two terms of comparison used, one (παραβολή) has appeared in a technical sense as early as Aristotle, while the other (ὁμοίωσις) has up to this point occurred only rarely, and then in a general sense of "likeness." One has no way of telling whether Dionysius uses the terms synonymously or distinctly. Again, any of the four ἐπιρρήματα listed would, if set in front of a comparison, create a simile. But Dionysius does not say that παραβολή and ὁμοίωσις cannot exist without the adverbs, only that among all adverbs these are the particular ones that signal παραβολή and ὁμοίωσις. In other words, the adverbs are natural, but not essential, features of the terms of comparison.

---

[1] L. Cohn, "Dionysius" no. 134, *RE* 5 (1903) 977.

[2] Kennedy 269.

[3] This covers somewhat more ground than the English "adverb."

[4] The text of G. Uhlig, *Dionysii Thracis Ars Grammatica* (Leipzig 1883) 79. The scholia, ed. by A. Hilgard in *Grammatici Graeci* I (Leipzig: B. G. Teubner, 1901), do not shed light on Dionysius' brief entry.

The exact dates of the Epicurean Philodemus, whose prose works have been partially recovered from Herculaneum, are unknown.[5] He was a native of Gadara and studied at Athens with the Epicurean Zeno. At some later date he became a member of the household of L. Calpurnius Piso Caesoninus, consul in 58 B.C. Hubbell places the date of the *Rhetorica* at around 75 B.C.;[6] others prefer a slightly later floruit from 70–40 B.C.[7] Philodemus certainly did not live much beyond the latter date.[8] Under the influence of Zeno he took the position, against most Epicureans, that a certain kind of rhetoric, namely epideictic, was an art.[9] He was also interested in style, again emulating Zeno, even though Epicureans in general condemned such interests. The *Rhetorica* consists of a Ὑπομνηματικόν (*Dissertation*) in one book and a Περὶ ῥητορικῆς (*On Rhetoric*) in seven books.[10] The *Dissertation*, circulated privately, was criticized by other Epicureans; *On Rhetoric* was written as a reply and restatement of Philodemus' views. Some repetition in the two parts results. The passages containing mention of comparison come from the fragments of Books IV and V of *On Rhetoric* and from the *Fragmenta Incerta*.[11]

The first passage, from Book IV, is perhaps of greatest interest. Book IV in general criticizes various claims of the different rhetorical schools.[12] A particular complaint that Philodemus makes

[5] R. Philippson, "Philodemos" no. 5, *RE* 19 (1938) 2445, suggests a birthdate of around 110 B.C.

[6] H. M. Hubbell, *The Rhetorica of Philodemus* (New Haven 1920) 259.

[7] See, for example, G. P. Goold, "A Greek Professorial Circle at Rome," *TAPA* 92 (1961) 180.

[8] Philippson 2446.

[9] Kroll 1131 comments on the trend toward epideictic oratory in Greece at this time.

[10] See the introduction to S. Sudhaus, *Philodemi Volumina Rhetorica* (Leipzig 1892–1896), a work of primary importance.

[11] C. J. Vooijs and D. A. Van Krevelen, *Lexicon Philodemeum* (Purmerend and Amsterdam 1934–1941).

[12] Hubbell, *Rhetorica of Philodemus* 253, suggests that Philodemus' special foes were Nausiphanes and the Peripatetics.

is against the faulty understanding of metaphor in the schools, and near the end of the complaint he states:

> "Ἔνιοι δέ φασιν καὶ
> τῆς ὁμοιώσεως ἕνεκεν αὐ-
> τ[ῆς] λαμβάνεσθαι τὰς με-
> ταφοράς· οὐ [μὲν] τῆς ὁμοι-
> ώσ]εως αὐτῆς καθ' αὑτὴν
> ὁρ]μωμένης ἀλλὰ διὰ τὴ[ν
> χρείαν [ἕ]ν[εκα] τῆς μεταφο-
> ρᾶς. . . .] [13]

Some say that they use metaphors for the sake of the comparison or resemblance; not however resemblance *per se*, but [through the need . . . of metaphor . . .].[14]

Both a similarity to and a difference from certain comments on metaphor in Cicero can be seen here. The passage ascribes to some (ἔνιοι) the view that metaphors are used because of the resemblance (ὁμοίωσις) contained in them. This is a quite parallel emphasis to that placed by Cicero on the necessary presence of resemblance in metaphor.[15] The second part of the Philodemus fragment, however, seems to go further than Cicero by suggesting that even the element of resemblance is less important than the plain need for metaphor. The fragment does not make clear whether this additional point is Philodemus' own or a further view of the ἔνιοι.

Book V of *On Rhetoric* contains a "detailed discussion of the disadvantages of rhetoric, with a comparison of the wretched life of the rhetor with the happy life of the philosopher."[16] One of

---

[13] Sudhaus I 177 (col. XVIII 2–9); here, and elsewhere, I follow Sudhaus' text uncritically.

[14] Hubbell's translation, *Rhetorica of Philodemus* 298. Sometimes Hubbell paraphrases more than translates. Where, as here, he does not cover the whole fragment given by Sudhaus, I translate in brackets what remains.

[15] *De Oratore* 3.39.157; *de Optimo Genere Oratorum* 2.4.

[16] Hubbell, *Rhetorica of Philodemus* 253.

Philodemus' points is that the philosopher, contrary to the charges of his opponents, is indeed knowledgeable in those practical aspects of life that can lead to better management of a city. He continues:

Οἱ
δὲ σοφισταὶ καὶ λελήθα-
σιν εἰκόνας ἑαυτῶν πα-
ρατ[ιθέν]τες. Αἱ γὰρ τού-
τ[ων δι]ατριβα[ὶ .]νο .
εἰς πόλιν δ[ὲ κ]αὶ εἰς ἀ[γο-
ρὰν οὐκ εἰσίασιν οὐδὲ τὸν
βίον ὅλως ὠφελοῦσιν.[17]

The sophists have unawares made a simile which applies to themselves; for it is their profession which does not enter into civil life and the assembly, and is of no help to human life.[18]

Hubbell's "simile" seems too narrow, since there is none in the surrounding text. What εἰκόνας does designate is the "image" or "illustration" of useless pleasure-seeking, which the sophists try to apply to philosophers but which really fits themselves. εἰκών thus carries much the same sense as was often the case in Plato and other pre-Aristotelian writers.

Among the *Fragmenta Incerta* there appear to be three instances of παραβολή,[19] though some doubt attends two of these: one is a complete restoration of the word and the other a restoration of all but the initial π. In both passages the restorations present παραβολή as denoting a general comparison between philosophy and rhetoric. The first reads:

Διὸ] καὶ προ[ώμεθα ταῦτα,
εἰ μὴ εὐλο[γώτεραί τι-

[17] Sudhaus I 245 (cols. XIII 31–35, XIV 1–3).
[18] Hubbell, *Rhetorica of Philodemus* 314.
[19] The term also appears in the fragments of Book I of *On Rhetoric* (Sudhaus I 5), but with the nonrhetorical meaning of "objection."

νέ[ς] εἰσιν [παραβολαὶ γνη-
σίας φι[λοσοφίας καὶ ῥη-
τορικῆ[ς.²⁰

Therefore let us pass over this unless there are more sensible comparisons to be made between philosophy and rhetoric.²¹

The second is:

$$\overset{\text{ἔτι}}{}$$

μᾶλλ[ον δ᾽ ἦν καταγ]έλαστος, ὅτι π[αραβολὰς] προστέ-
θεικεν [ῥητορικῆς] τε καὶ φιλοσοφίας.²²

He was still more ridiculous in adding comparisons between rhetoric and philosophy.²³

The third instance of παραβολή would seem to refer to an actual figure of comparison:

μόνον γὰρ ἃ [σημ]αίνεται διὰ παρα[βολ]ῶν εἰκάζουσιν.²⁴

[Only those things which are clear do they compare through παραβολαί.]

Since εἰκάζουσιν already contains the general sense of "compare," "make comparisons," διὰ παρα[βολ]ῶν must denote something more specific, namely "through figures of comparison," but no further features of the παραβολαί are indicated.

In the fragments of Book V of *On Rhetoric* a term of comparison, σύγκρισις, occurs that neither here nor elsewhere in the ancient testimony refers to a figure of comparison and thus is not of great significance for this study. It is used by Philodemus, however, in a manner synonymous with the two restored instances of

---

²⁰ Sudhaus II 180–181 (frag. d I 1–6).
²¹ Hubbell, *Rhetorica of Philodemus* 343.
²² Sudhaus II 181 (frag. d III).
²³ Hubbell, *Rhetorica of Philodemus* 343.
²⁴ Sudhaus II 186 (frag. e XI).

παραβολή[25] (that is, in a broad sense of "comparison") and may be mentioned briefly at this point. The term appears as early as Aristotle, in three passages of the *Topica*,[26] denoting broadly in each case "comparison" or "process of comparison." It is also found, like παραβολή and ὁμοίωσις, in the handbook of Dionysius Thrax among the things that adverbs (ἐπιρρήματα) express. The particular adverbs are μᾶλλον (more) and ἧττον (less),[27] and σύγκρισις here refers to comparison of degree. In Philodemus the term expresses still another general comparison between philosophy and rhetoric:

> Νῦν [τοίν]υν
> ἐπέλθωμεν αὐτῶν καὶ
> τὰς κατ' ἄλλον τρ[όπον τ]ῆς
> ῥητορικῆς τῆι φ[ιλοσο]φί-
> αι συγκρίσεις.[28]

Let us now take up the comparison of rhetoric and philosophy in another fashion.[29]

The use here and in Aristotle of σύγκρισις is extremely analogous to the normal application of *comparatio* in *ad Herennium* and in Cicero.[30] Since the term does not extend to figures of comparison, its usage will not be examined further.

The meager compass of Philodemus' use of terms of comparison does not allow many conclusions. Four terms have appeared, εἰκών, ὁμοίωσις, παραβολή, and σύγκρισις, but no passage has

---

[25] In fact, where παραβολαί has been restored completely the reading could just as easily be συγκρίσεις.

[26] *Top.* 1.5.102b15; 3.4.119a1–11; 8.5.159b25.

[27] Uhlig 83; Dionysius' words are, Τὰ δὲ συγκρίσεως, οἷον μᾶλλον ἧττον (some adverbs are characteristic of σύγκρισις, such as "more" and "less").

[28] Sudhaus II 146 (frag. III 26–30).

[29] Hubbell, *Rhetorica of Philodemus* 308.

[30] Indeed, *ThLL* gives σύγκρισις as an equivalent in rhetoric to both *comparatio* and *collatio. Collatio*, however, has already been seen to refer often to a figure of comparison, whereas this is outside the regular sphere of *comparatio* and σύγκρισις.

really shed new light on views of comparison. Nevertheless, it is historically interesting simply to note the presence of these terms in such a figure as Philodemus: any problem in ancient rhetoric must deal in good measure with bits and pieces of evidence, and Philodemus provides further testimony, albeit fragmentary, on continuity of interest in comparison.

In the preface, mention was made of the problem of the technical treatise Περὶ τρόπων (*On Tropes*), ascribed by the Suda to Trypho Grammaticus, a grammarian of the late first century B.C. A rather lengthy analysis of terms of comparison appears under the heading περὶ ὁμοιώσεως, and if the work were genuinely Trypho's it should have been the next subject here. As stated earlier, however, Wendel[31] is correct in arguing that the Suda wrongly assigns the work to the first-century grammarian. All the manuscripts are late; only some bear Trypho's name, while others regard the author as anonymous. Περὶ τρόπων has all the marks of the late technical works and must lie close to the treatises of Herodian and Polybius Sardianus, probably in the third century A.D. Discussion of it is therefore deferred.[32]

The date of [Demetrius] *On Style* is, if anything, even more vexing than that of Περὶ τρόπων. Since the beginning of the nineteenth century, when the early Hellenistic figure Demetrius of Phalerum was rejected as a possible author, there has been general agreement that the work should be attributed to an *auctor incertus*. No such consensus has developed over the date of composition, though, and there seems little possibility of one in the immediate future, as controversy has sprung up anew in recent years. A date somewhere in the first century A.D. commanded wide support in the latter part of the nineteenth century

[31] Wendel 739.
[32] But an outline of the section on comparison will be given below, pp. 252–256, as an example of the approach to comparison in the late technical treatises.

and the early twentieth. Rhys Roberts spoke for it in great and lucid detail, and Radermacher argued similarly. Kroll initiated a return to a much earlier, Hellenistic date,[33] and Grube, in giving this view its fullest statement, has specified a date in the early third century B.C.[34] The early date has been accepted by some but rejected by more,[35] and the balance of opinion must be said to rest presently with the more traditional first-century A.D. date— a view that will be maintained in this study. Indeed, certain points of terminology arise in analyzing *On Style*'s understanding of comparison that strengthen the case for an A.D. date.[36]

[33] W. Rhys Roberts, *Demetrius on Style* (Cambridge, Eng., 1902); L. Radermacher, *Demetrii Phalerei qui dicitur De Elocutione libellus* (Leipzig. 1901); Kroll 1078–1080.

[34] Grube, *A Greek Critic* 22–56. His candidate for author is an unknown Alexandrian scholar, perhaps named Demetrius. In briefer compass his arguments are repeated in *The Greek and Roman Critics* (Toronto 1965) chap. v.

[35] Acceptance: Kennedy 286. Rejection: Goold 178–189; J. M. Rist, "Demetrius the Stylist and Artemon the Compiler," *Phoenix* 18 (1964) 2–8 (Grube answers both Goold and Rist in "The Date of Demetrius *On Style*," *Phoenix* 18 [1964] 294–302); and most recently Schenkeveld, *Studies in Demetrius On Style* 135–148. See also my review of Grube's *The Greek and Roman Critics* (*AJP* 88 [1967] 251–254). Two particularly strong points made by Goold are: (1) it bears little fruit for Grube to show that in the early third century certain words in use are closely related to other words that were felt by Roberts to indicate a late date; (2) Grube's feeling, shared by Kroll, that *On Style* displays a broad enough critical interest to be close in spirit and therefore in date to Theophrastus also does not prove very much, since the same broad approach to criticism existed among critics of the first century A.D. such as Dionysius and [Longinus]. Goold also refutes the possibility that the author of *On Style* is mentioned in Philodemus and shows that the Demetrius named is Demetrius of Phalerum. Less conclusive is his suggestion that the author *is* referred to in Dionysius of Halicarnassus' *Epistula ad Ammaeum* 1.1 and *is* mentioned by name in the *Epistula ad Pompeium* 3. Still, the basic thesis that the author may well have belonged to the same Augustan professorial circle as Dionysius, Caecilius, Theodorus, and Manilius, and would have been the only Peripatetic member of the circle, is highly attractive.

[36] The title itself, Περὶ ἑρμηνείας, as opposed to Aristotle's and Theophrastus' word for "style," λέξις, may be of significance. Roberts, *Demetrius on Style* 32, suggests that the use of ἑρμηνεία rather than λέξις for "style" may reflect the Isocratean school of rhetoric, but this does not seem conclusive in view of the generally Peripatetic character of *On Style* as stressed by Solmsen, *AJP* 62 (1941) 184.

The first reference to comparison in the work does not actually contain a noun term of comparison, but another technical term that recurs interestingly in Quintilian. The opening sections of *On Style* discuss the periodic style and the period; the historical, rhetorical, and conversational periods are analyzed in succession. Sections 22–24 turn to periods consisting of antithetical members (ἐξ ἀντικειμένων κώλων περίοδοι) wherein the antithesis may be one of thought or it may be verbal. The author says of the latter:

> Κατὰ δὲ τὰ ὀνόματα μόνον ἀντικείμενα κῶλα τοιάδε ἐστίν, οἷον ὡς ὁ τὴν Ἑλένην παραβαλὼν τῷ Ἡρακλεῖ φησιν, ὅτι "τῷ μὲν ἐπίπονον καὶ πολυκίνδυνον τὸν βίον ἐποίησεν, τῆς δὲ περίβλεπτον καὶ περιμάχητον τὴν φύσιν κατέστησεν."[37] ἀντίκειται γὰρ καὶ ἄρθρον ἄρθρῳ, καὶ σύνδεσμος συνδέσμῳ, ὅμοια ὁμοίοις, καὶ τἆλλα δὲ κατὰ τὸν αὐτὸν τρόπον . . . καὶ ὅλως ἓν πρὸς ἕν, ὅμοιον παρ' ὅμοιον, ἡ ἀνταπόδοσις.[38]   (23)

Members which are only verbally contrasted may be illustrated by the comparison drawn between Helen and Hercules: "to the man he gave a laborious and perilous life, while he caused the woman's beauty to be admired and coveted." Here article is opposed to article, connective to connective, like to like, from the beginning to the end. . . . The correspondence of one thing with another, of like with like, runs throughout.

The salient feature of this comparison of contrast is the antithetical verbal correspondence of its two parts, every detail in one matching a detail in the other. *On Style* describes this characteristic with the term ἀνταπόδοσις. Similar features have been noticed in the *similitudo per collationem* in *ad Herennium* and in the general use of *collatio* in Cicero. ἀνταπόδοσις appears half a dozen times in Aristotle, but always in the nonrhetorical sense of

---

[37] The example comes, with minor differences, from Isocrates' *Encomium on Helen* 17.

[38] The text and translation used throughout are Roberts', *Demetrius On Style*.

"payment," "obligation," "return."[39] This is its first use as a technical term of rhetoric.[40] It reappears in Quintilian,[41] and the first-century A.D. parallel helps to suggest, in this one small matter, a late date for *On Style*. The term seems to have developed as part of rhetorical vocabulary sometime during the Hellenistic period, and *On Style*'s easy use of it indicates a position at the end, rather than the beginning, of the development. The only word of comparison in the passage is the participle παραβαλών, but from this it cannot be assumed that *On Style* would designate the comparison a παραβολή. The two principal verbs expressing comparison, παραβάλλω and εἰκάζω, are used freely throughout Greek rhetoric with all the several noun terms of comparison,[42] not just with those nouns linguistically related. It remains uncertain what term *On Style* might have employed to describe the present comparison.

Following his introductory remarks on the period and certain other elements of style, the author divides the main body of *On Style* into four parts, analyzing in each a basic style: the grand (μεγαλοπρεπής), the elegant (γλαφυρός), the plain (ἰσχνός), and the forceful (δεινός). There is at least one mention of comparison in each part, usually within discussion of the diction appropriate to the particular style. By far the most important and detailed treatment comes in the first, the grand style. But the decreasing attention given comparison in the remaining styles stems at least in part not from any diminished appropriateness of comparison in the styles, but from the fact that succeeding treatments can be shortened by using the first as a base.[43]

[39] Compare *Nicomachean Ethics* 1133a3; 1163a11.

[40] But the verb ἀνταποδιδόναι occurs in a similar rhetorical sense in Aristotle, *Rhet.* 3.4.1407a16.

[41] *Inst. Orat.* 8.3.77; see below, p. 222.

[42] For example, the phrase in Philodemus, διὰ παρα[βολ]ῶν εἰκάζουσιν.

[43] At section 274, for instance, there is a reference back to section 89; see below, p. 154. This feature is true of the work as a whole. The opening analysis of the grand style contains several digressions, of which Schenkeveld 17 says: "In the

On Style depends substantially upon Aristotle's *Rhetoric* for many of its tenets, natural enough in view of the Peripatetic leanings of the author.[44] A typical example is that, within discussion of the diction of the grand style, *On Style* approaches comparison as a subordinate branch of metaphor. Sections 78–90 analyze metaphor; passages on comparison arise at various places but always from the context of metaphor. This debt to Aristotle could be used to argue for an early date. *Ad Herennium* and most of Cicero have shown that the general movement in Hellenistic rhetoric was to separate metaphor and comparison and to associate comparison with historical example. The close and subordinate relation of comparison to metaphor in *On Style* might suggest that the treatise was written before this Hellenistic separation occurred. But because one exception to the separation has already been found in *de Oratore* 3.39.157 and another will occur in Quintilian, the situation in *On Style* is far from decisive for the date.

The subject of metaphor, then, is raised in connection with diction of the grand style. The diction must be impressive and unusual, and metaphor is the essential element:

> Τὴν δὲ λέξιν ἐν τῷ χαρακτῆρι τούτῳ περιττὴν εἶναι δεῖ καὶ ἐξηλλαγμένην καὶ ἀσυνήθη μᾶλλον· οὕτω γὰρ ἕξει τὸν ὄγκον, ἡ δὲ κυρία καὶ συνήθης σαφὴς μέν, λειτὴ δὲ καὶ εὐκαταφρόνητος.
>
> Πρῶτα μὲν οὖν μεταφοραῖς χρηστέον· αὗται γὰρ μάλιστα καὶ ἡδονὴν συμβάλλονται τοῖς λόγοις καὶ μέγεθος.   (77–78)

The diction used in this style should be grandiose, elaborate, and distinctly out of the ordinary. It will thus possess the needed

---

treatment of the grand style, objections [to digressions] will be only slight if we bear in mind that this is the first style under discussion and that therefore Demetrius will often feel himself forced to more general remarks. . . ."

[44] This Peripatetic character may help explain the absence from the work of that ecstatic enthusiasm for Demosthenes so prevalent in late antiquity and already visible, for instance, in *On the Sublime*.

gravity, whereas usual and current words, though clear, are un-
impressive and liable to be held cheap.

In the first place, then, metaphors must be used; for they impart
a special charm and grandeur to style.

One is reminded of *Rhetoric* 3.2,[45] where Aristotle makes the
same point of the importance of metaphor to impressive diction,
and undoubtedly the author is following Aristotelian tradition
here. He also appears to draw on the *Rhetoric* in the phrase
μάλιστα καὶ ἡδονὴν συμβάλλονται ("they impart a special
charm"). Yet, whereas Aristotle's ascription of extreme pleasant-
ness to metaphor was another way of ascribing to it immediate
instructiveness,[46] neither here nor elsewhere does *On Style*
attempt to identify pleasure with instruction.

After some comments on the composition of metaphors, including the point that they should be based on a real resemblance
(ἐκ τοῦ ὁμοίου),[47] *On Style* makes the statement:

Ἐπὰν μέντοι κινδυνώδης ἡ μεταφορὰ δοκῇ, μεταλαμ-
βανέσθω εἰς εἰκασίαν· οὕτω γὰρ ἀσφαλεστέρα γίγνοιτ' ἄν. (80)

When the metaphor seems daring, let it for greater security be
converted into a simile.

We have seen the idea of modifying bold metaphors ascribed to
both Aristotle and Theophrastus in *On the Sublime*.[48] No such
idea actually occurs anywhere in Aristotle, and *On Style* in not
mentioning any names seems simply to be following a general
Peripatetic tradition.[49] The author goes on to describe in some
detail the term of comparison (εἰκασία) he has just used:

---

[45] See also *Poetics* 22.

[46] *Rhet.* 3.10; see above, pp. 39–42.

[47] Recalling passages in both Cicero and Philodemus.

[48] Above, p. 54; see also below, p. 157.

[49] Schenkeveld 93 argues for Theophrastus as the originator of the idea, and
this seems probable.

εἰκασία δ' ἐστὶ μεταφορὰ πλεονάζουσα, οἷον εἴ τις τῷ "τότε
τῷ Πύθωνι τῷ ῥήτορι ῥέοντι καθ' ὑμῶν"⁵⁰ προσθεὶς⁵¹ εἴποι,
"ὥσπερ ῥέοντι καθ' ὑμῶν." οὕτω μὲν γὰρ εἰκασία γέγονεν καὶ
ἀσφαλέστερος ὁ λόγος, ἐκείνως δὲ μεταφορὰ καὶ κινδυνωδέ-
στερος.   (80)

A simile is an expanded metaphor, as when, instead of saying "the
orator Python was then rushing upon you in full flood," we add a
word of comparison and say "was like a flood rushing upon you."
In this way we obtain a simile and a less risky expression, in the
other way metaphor and greater danger.

εἰκασία occurs for the first time as a term of comparison in *On
Style*. Its next appearance is in Plutarch. In addition, εἰκών, by
far the most common term of comparison before and in Aristotle,
is not used at all in *On Style* except at section 227 in the sense of
"mirror," "image." Each of these terminological features reinforces the arguments for a late date.

In the present passage, the author defines εἰκασία along very
similar lines to Aristotle's several definitions of εἰκών in the
Rhetoric, and he seems to think of εἰκασία as a simile. The only
difference between the examples of metaphor and εἰκασία is the
addition in the latter of an introductory word of comparison, the
formal mark of simile. The Demosthenic example does not occur
in connection with εἰκών in Aristotle, but much of the rest of
On Style's opening definition of εἰκασία clearly imitates Aristotle.
It will be recalled that Aristotle proceeds, in his opening discussion of εἰκών, to give a good many examples that show his
apparent definition of simile to be illusory. No such modifying
section follows *On Style's* first statement on εἰκασία. The author

⁵⁰ The example is adapted, not quite word for word, from Demosthenes, *On
the Crown* 136.
⁵¹ προσθεὶς, in this passage that strongly follows Aristotle, may be an argument for reading at *Rhet.* 3.10.1410b18 (with the Θ and Π groups of manuscripts)
μεταφορὰ διαφέρουσα προσθέσει, rather than, with Ross, προθέσει. See above,
chap. II n. 43.

merely adds that Plato's style employed metaphors more than εἰκασίαι and is therefore considered more risky than Xenophon's style with its preference for εἰκασίαι. The subject of εἰκασία is then put aside temporarily, and *On Style* returns to metaphor for the next several sections.

Within these sections there are two passages, illustrating the dependence on Aristotle of *On Style*'s views on metaphor, that are related indirectly to comparison. In section 81 the author reports Aristotle's opinions on the best kind of metaphor, that which achieves vividness (ἐνέργεια). His report is quite accurate, and in using a Homeric verse also cited by Aristotle he correctly interprets a misleading Aristotelian phrase:

Ἀρίστη δὲ δοκεῖ μεταφορὰ τῷ Ἀριστοτέλει ἡ κατὰ ἐνέργειαν καλουμένη, ὅταν τὰ ἄψυχα ἐνεργοῦντα εἰσάγηται καθάπερ ἔμψυχα, ὡς τὸ ἐπὶ τοῦ βέλους·

      ὀξυβελὴς καθ' ὅμιλον ἐπιπτέσθαι μενεαίνων,[52]
καὶ τὸ

      κυρτὰ φαληριόωντα.[53]
πάντα γὰρ ταῦτα, τὸ "φαληριόωντα" καὶ τὸ "μενεαίνων," ζωτικαῖς ἐνεργείαις ἔοικεν.

In Aristotle's judgment the so-called "active" metaphor is the best,[54] wherein inanimate things are introduced in a state of activity as though they were animate, as in the passage describing the shaft:

Leapt on the foemen the arrow keen-whetted with eager wing,

and in the words:

      High-arched foam-crested.

All such expressions as "foam-crested" and "eager wing" suggest the activities of living creatures.

[52] *Iliad* 4.126.
[53] *Iliad* 13.799.
[54] Aristotle actually takes this a little further by specifying proportional metaphors as those most likely to contain ἐνέργεια and, therefore, as the best metaphors.

Aristotle prefaced his use of the second example with the phrase ἐν ταῖς εὐδοκιμούσαις εἰκόσιν (in popular comparisons),[55] apparently identifying κυρτὰ φαληριόωντα (high-arched foam-crested) as a comparison. As argued earlier,[56] Aristotle is really speaking of vivid metaphor *within* comparisons; On Style, by classifying κυρτὰ φαληριόωντα as metaphor possessing ἐνέργεια, has interpreted Aristotle's meaning with precision.

In section 85, *On Style* says a little more on the subject of making metaphors less bold. The views expressed are ascribed to ἔνιοι (some writers), and the tone of the passage suggests *On Style*'s accordance with these views:

> Ἔνιοι δὲ καὶ ἀσφαλίζονται τὰς μεταφορὰς ἐπιθέτοις ἐπιφερομένοις, ὅταν αὐτοῖς κινδυνώδεις δοκῶσιν, ὡς ὁ Θέογνις παρατίθεται τῷ τόξῳ "φόρμιγγα ἄχορδον" ἐπὶ τοῦ τῷ τόξῳ βάλλοντος· ἡ μὲν γὰρ φόρμιγξ κινδυνῶδες ἐπὶ τοῦ τόξου, τῷ δὲ ἀχόρδῳ ἠσφάλισται.

Some writers endeavour by the addition of epithets to safeguard metaphors which they consider risky. In this way Theognis applies to the bow the expression "lyre without chords" when describing an archer in the act of shooting. It is a bold thing to apply the term "lyre" to a bow, but the metaphor is guarded by the qualification "without chords."

The example cited in *On Style* is the same used by Aristotle to illustrate a proportional metaphor as opposed to a simple one (ἁπλοῦν).[57] *On Style* also supplies—which Aristotle did not—the author of the metaphor; but the identification is only partial, since "Theognis" could equally well be the elegiac poet Theognis of Megara or the tragedian of the same name.[58] Aristotle's passage

---

[55] *Rhet.* 3.11.1412a7.
[56] Above, p. 44.
[57] *Rhet.* 3.11.1413a1ff.
[58] Grube, *A Greek Critic* 82. Roberts, *Demetrius On Style* 228, argues at length against identification with Theognis of Megara. He maintains that the author is either Theognis Tragicus or that a corruption of some other name has occurred.

is undoubtedly in the author's mind, but he is also following other sources, as is clear both from the addition of Theognis' name and from the point made—which is quite different from Aristotle's. For Aristotle, "a bow is a lyre" and "a bow is a lyre without chords" illustrated a simple metaphor and a not simple proportional metaphor closely allied to comparison. For *On Style*, "a bow is a lyre" is a bold and potentially risky metaphor that can be made safer by adding such an epithet as "without chords." In a certain sense *On Style* and Aristotle are not altogether at odds. *On Style* terms a metaphor less bold if it contains an epithet, recalling section 80 in which comparison is said to be desirable when a metaphor is too bold. Aristotle allies his proportional metaphor, which contains an epithet ("a bow is a lyre without chords"), with comparison. Both authors thus hold in common that there is a connection between metaphor with an epithet and comparison.

It is interesting to speculate on the identity of *On Style*'s "some writers" (ἔνιοι). The inviting possibility is to link the present passage with that in *On the Sublime* in which Aristotle and Theophrastus were said to advocate that bold metaphors be softened. But there is little security in so doing, since the means of softening metaphor ascribed by *On the Sublime* to Aristotle and Theophrastus are parenthetical (or perhaps comparative) words, whereas *On Style*'s "some writers" use adjectival epithets. In addition, as has been seen, Aristotle in fact nowhere talks of softening metaphor,[59] and Theophrastus' views do not survive. All that can be stated categorically is that *On Style* attributes to past critics[60] methods of making metaphor less bold, and that *On the Sublime* attributes the same goal but different methods to Aristotle and Theophrastus.

[59] Roberts, *Longinus On the Sublime* 219, however, thinks it possible that such a comment on metaphor may have occurred in a lost portion of the *Poetics*.

[60] Radermacher, *Demetrii Phalerei libellus* 88, points to resemblances between comments made by *On Style* about metaphor and certain fragments of Philodemus, but the present passage does not figure in any of these resemblances.

On Style returns to comparison in section 89, and in addition to εἰκασία a second term is used, παραβολή. In Aristotle, παραβολή formed an element of rhetorical proof. In *On Style* the term is conceived of only as an element of style.[61] Two kinds of literary comparison, therefore, are discussed:

Ἐπὰν μέντοι εἰκασίαν ποιῶμεν τὴν μεταφοράν, ὡς προλέλεκ-
ται, στοχαστέον τοῦ συντόμου, καὶ τοῦ μηδὲν πλέον τοῦ
"ὥσπερ" προτιθέναι, ἐπεί τοι ἀντ᾽ εἰκασίας παραβολὴ ἔσται
ποιητική, οἷον τὸ τοῦ Ξενοφῶντος, "ὥσπερ δὲ κύων γενναῖος
ἀπρονοήτως ἐπὶ κάπρον φέρεται,"[62] καὶ "ὥσπερ ἵππος λυθεὶς
διὰ πεδίου γαυριῶν καὶ ἀπολακτίζων·"[63] ταῦτα γὰρ οὐκ εἰκα-
σίαις ἔτι ἔοικεν, ἀλλὰ παραβολαῖς ποιητικαῖς.

Τὰς δὲ παραβολὰς ταύτας οὔτε ῥᾳδίως ἐν τοῖς πεζοῖς λόγοις
τιθέναι δεῖ, οὔτε ἄνευ πλείστης φυλακῆς.   (89–90)

When we turn a metaphor into a simile in the way above described, we must aim at conciseness. We must do no more than
prefix some such word as "like," or we shall have a poetical image
in place of a simile. Take, for example, the following passage of
Xenophon: "like as a gallant hound charges a boar recklessly," and
"like as a horse when untethered bounds proudly prancing over
the plain." Such descriptions have the appearance not of simile but
of poetical imagery.

These images should not be used in prose lightly nor without
the greatest caution.

The author points to two main differences between παραβολή
and εἰκασία. The first is length. Aristotle had no such distinction; εἰκών compassed every kind of stylistic comparison, whereas

[61] Schenkeveld 100 remarks that this is the first instance in which παραβολή has been explicitly so labeled. But he argues that Theophrastus was probably the first to use παραβολή in this way.

[62] Xenophon, *Cyropaedia* 1.4.21, with very slight changes.

[63] The source of this παραβολή is unknown; Grube, *A Greek Critic* 83, is in-accurate in attributing it, as well as the first παραβολή, to the same Xenophon passage. Roberts is similarly inaccurate in his 1902 edition but correctly makes the source unknown in his later Loeb translation (1932).

παραβολή was part of proof. Both *ad Herennium* and Cicero used more than one term for stylistic comparisons, but length was not a criterion by which they were distinguished. *On Style* has added a new concept of comparison to the ancient testimony. While length appears to be the principal difference, the two terms also have separate areas of application. παραβολή is a poetic figure and should be used in prose only with care; the intended, though unexpressed, corollary is that εἰκασία is not poetic and may be used freely in prose. The point has been made indirectly already in section 80, where the importance of metaphor to prose is underlined and εἰκασία is termed a safer alternative to metaphor. The author does not say that παραβολή is completely out of place in prose—in fact, both his examples are from prose—only that its employment should be limited.

On Style's approach to literary comparison shows more sophistication and greater critical acumen than Aristotle's. Both authors treat comparison as a subordinate part of metaphor, but Aristotle's inclusive statement that comparison is, in contrast to metaphor, poetic and therefore to be used sparingly in prose cannot really be maintained in the case of a brief comparison. To take Aristotle's opening example, ὡς λέων ἐπόρουσεν (he went forward like a lion) simply is not more poetic than λέων ἐπόρουσεν (he went forward a lion).[64] It could be thought so only by someone who, preferring metaphor to comparison on every count as a prose figure, wished to believe all comparison poetic, hence less suited to prose. Aristotle's double commitment to the equivalence of intellectual pleasure with instruction and to the doctrine that metaphor is the most instructive of all elements of prose style created such a bias. The author of *On Style* has no similar predilection and therefore, in addition to discerning two divisions of literary comparison differing in structure and application, is able to recognize that a brief comparison is no more poetic, indeed is less bold, than a metaphor.

[64] Grube, *A Greek Critic* 37, 83, rightly emphasizes this point.

The two examples given of παραβολή are similes. Further, the author states that εἰκασία should differ from metaphor by no more than the addition of ὥσπερ (like), an introductory word of comparison. In both instances support seems to be lent to the apparent identification of εἰκασία with simile in the opening definition at section 80. But it is difficult to believe that *On Style* does mean to discuss simile in these various passages—and for much the same reasons as in *ad Herennium*'s analysis of *similitudo* and *imago*.[65] Roberts translates εἰκασία by "simile" and παραβολή by "poetical image,"[66] suggesting both that a simile is unpoetical and that παραβολή does not appear as a simile. But if the author intends εἰκασία to denote "simile," then παραβολή must do so, too. That is to say, in these sections εἰκασία is brief and prosaic, παραβολή longer and more poetic, but both share the form of simile; neither is more a simile than the other. If the author wishes to talk of simile, he has created the large and self-induced problem of using two contrasting terms for one figure. Why not use one term and state that there are different types of it? Some other interpretation seems necessary that will neither make one of the terms a truer simile than the other nor indeed force both terms within the single rubric of simile. The solution would seem to be to take εἰκασία and παραβολή as quite independent kinds of literary comparison, not bound to any precise verbal form and each possessing its own particular structure and sphere of use. The recurring simile form is not difficult to interpret. For εἰκασία it will be seen that the form is not absolute, and in section 172 the term will refer to an imagistic description. Where, as in the present passages, the author associates εἰκασία with the form of simile the reason may be, as in Aristotle, that the most obvious way to illustrate a brief comparison (as opposed to a metaphor) is through the addition of a single comparative word. For παραβολή the reason is twofold. Most of the examples of

[65] Above, p. 85.
[66] Grube is very similar: "simile" and "poetic comparison."

παραβολή used in *On Style* come from poetry, where comparisons almost always take the form of similes; the only examples from prose are the two in section 89. Here, having just mentioned ὥσπερ (like) as a typical signpost of εἰκασία and wishing now to show that the figure changes with length to παραβολή, the author may intentionally choose two παραβολαί containing ὥσπερ and thus similar to εἰκασία in all but length. Such an explanation of *On Style*'s intent does not alter the fact that almost all the illustrations of εἰκασία and παραβολή throughout the work are similes. Quite clearly the author feels that simile is the most natural form of literary comparison, but the verbal form can often be identical for both εἰκασία and παραβολή—and yet the two are distinct. It is not, then, the single figure simile that the author sets out to identify and analyze with his two terms.

This first discussion of comparison in *On Style*, as has been noted, is easily the most significant. Remaining passages will serve to confirm the conclusions reached here. In section 146, the subject is no longer the grand style but the elegant (γλαφυρός), more particularly the graces of diction in that style, and the grace treated at this point is that which comes from use of παραβολή:

> Ἐκ δὲ παραβολῆς καὶ ἐπὶ τοῦ ἐξέχοντος ἀνδρὸς ἡ Σαπφώ φησι,
>
> πέρροχος ὡς ὅτ' ἀοιδὸς ὁ Λέσβιος ἀλλοδαποῖσιν.[67]
> ἐνταῦθα γὰρ χάριν ἐποίησεν ἡ παραβολὴ μᾶλλον ἢ μέγεθος. . . .
> Σώφρων δὲ καὶ αὐτὸς ἐπὶ τοῦ ὁμοίου εἴδους φησί, "θᾶσαι, ὅσα φύλλα καὶ κάρφεα τοὶ παῖδες τοὺς ἄνδρας βαλλίζοντι, οἷόν περ φαντί, φίλα, τοὺς Τρῶας τὸν Αἴαντα τῷ παλῷ."[68] καὶ γὰρ ἐνταῦθα ἐπίχαρις ἡ παραβολή ἐστι, καὶ τοὺς Τρῶας διαπαίζουσα ὥσπερ παῖδας.   (146–147)

Grace may also spring from the use of imagery. Thus Sappho says of the man that stands out among his fellows:

[67] Sappho, frag. 106 (ed. Lobel/Page).
[68] Sophron, frag. 32 (ed. Kaibel).

> Pre-eminent, as mid alien men is Lesbos' bard.

In this line charm rather than grandeur is the outcome of the comparison. . . .

The same point is illustrated by Sophron, who writes:

> See, dear, what rain of leaf and spray
> The boys upon the men are showering,
> Thick as flew Trojan darts, they say,
> At Aias huge in battle towering.

Here again there is charm in the comparison, which makes game of the Trojans as though they were boys.

The phrase χάριν . . . μᾶλλον ἢ μέγεθος ("charm rather than grandeur") looks back to παραβολή as an element of the grand style, and these elegant παραβολαί are contrasted with those suitable for decorating a grand style. In construction, however, the two παραβολαί instanced here are quite comparable to the earlier ones in section 89. They are relatively extended comparisons; they are of a poetical nature (in addition to coming from poetry); and they are similes in form, although the lines from Sophron are in this respect very free.

In section 160 the subject is still graces of the elegant style, and charm (χάρις) is being explored further. The author specifically credits εἰκασία with this grace:

> Καὶ εἰκασίαι δ' εἰσὶν εὐχάριτες, ἂν τὸν ἀλεκτρυόνα Μήδῳ
> εἰκάσῃς, ὅτι τὴν κυρβασίαν ὀρθὴν φέρει.

> Comparisons, also, are full of charm—if (for instance) you compare a cock to a Persian because of its stiff-upstanding crest.

The indirect illustration comes from a brief simile that Euelpides uses to describe the Great King in Aristophanes' *Birds* 486–487.

The topic of charm continues through the next several sections of *On Style*, and the author digresses on the difference between the humorous (τὸ γελοῖον) and the charming (τὸ εὔχαρι). In section 172 εἰκασία is said to play a role in the humor of abusive nicknames:

> Περὶ δὲ σκωμμάτων μέν, οἷον εἰκασία τις ἐστιν· ἡ γὰρ ἀντί-
> θεσις εὐτράπελος. χρήσονταί τε ταῖς τοιαύταις εἰκασίαις, ὡς
> "Αἰγυπτία κληματίς," μακρὸν καὶ μέλανα, καὶ τὸ "θαλάσσιον
> πρόβατον," τὸν μῶρον τὸν ἐν τῇ θαλάσσῃ.

In nicknames a sort of comparison is implied, there being wit in a play on words. Writers may use such comparisons as "Egyptian clematis" of a tall and swarthy man, or "sea-wether" of a fool on the water.

This passage of jesting personal description has been alluded to earlier as an instance in which εἰκασία does not assume the form of simile. In addition, although the author makes no reference to it, his application of εἰκασία to jesting comparisons recalls the game of εἰκασμός/ἀντεικασμός (comparison and answering comparison) that has been observed in fifth- and fourth-century Greek literature and in Cicero's *de Oratore*.[69]

The third kind of style discussed in *On Style* is the plain (ἰσχνός). The author raises the subject of vividness (ἐνάργεια)[70] at section 209, remarking that it is very suitable to the plain style. Vividness is produced by exact narration and completeness of detail (ἐξ ἀκριβολογίας καὶ τοῦ παραλείπειν μηδὲν μηδ' ἐκτέμνειν), and the first illustration given is a παραβολή:

> οἷον "ὡς δ' ὅτ' ἀνὴρ ὀχετηγὸς"[71] καὶ πᾶσα αὕτη ἡ παραβολή·
> τὸ γὰρ ἐναργὲς ἔχει ἐκ τοῦ πάντα εἰρῆσθαι τὰ συμβαίνοντα, καὶ
> μὴ παραλελεῖφθαι μηδέν.   (209)

---

[69] See above, chap. I n. 43 and chap. IV n. 39. Mr. D. A. Russell and Miss D. Innes have, in correspondence, called my attention to this and other appearances of the game.

[70] This term is used here in much the same meaning as was ἐνέργεια in section 81 and in Aristotle's *Rhetoric*. Both words denote vividness: ἐνάργεια stresses the clearness and ἐνέργεια the vigor and activity will lead to that vividness.

[71] *Iliad* 21.259.

An instance is the Homeric simile which begins "As when a man draws off water by a runnel." The comparison owes its vividness to the fact that all the accompanying circumstances are mentioned and nothing is omitted.

The example is the first verse of a lengthy Homeric simile that does indeed go on to present in full and accurate detail a picture of a farmer constructing an irrigation canal. Nothing more is said of the παραβολή than that it exemplifies the quality of vividness in the plain style.

The fourth and last kind of style, the forceful (δεινός), contains a final notice of both εἰκασία and παραβολή. Section 272 states that the same diction can be employed as in the grand style but not toward the same end. The first component of diction mentioned is metaphor; then sections 273–274 move on to the two terms of comparison, saying that εἰκασία suits the forceful style but that παραβολή does not:

> Καὶ εἰκασίας λέγοντα, ὡς τὸ Δημοσθένους, "τοῦτο τὸ ψήφισ-
> μα τὸν τότ' ἐπιόντα τῇ πόλει κίνδυνον παρελθεῖν ἐποίησεν,
> ὥσπερ νέφος."[72]
> Αἱ παραβολαὶ δὲ τῇ δεινότητι οὐκ ἐπιτήδειαι διὰ τὸ μῆκος,
> οἷον τὸ "ὥσπερ δὲ κύων γενναῖος, ἄπειρος, ἀπρονοήτως ἐπὶ
> κάπρον φέρεται·"[73] κάλλος γὰρ καὶ ἀκρίβειά τις ἐν τούτοις
> ἐμφαίνεται, ἡ δὲ δεινότης σφοδρόν τι βούλεται καὶ σύντομον.

So, too, by the use of similes [force can be gained], as in Demosthenes' expression: "this decree caused the danger which then threatened the city to pass by like a cloud."

But poetical images do not suit the forcible style owing to their length: e.g. "like as a gallant hound, ignorant of danger, charges a boar recklessly." There is an air of beauty and finish about this sentence. But the forcible style demands a certain vehemence and terseness.

[72] Demosthenes, *On the Crown* 188.
[73] Xenophon, *Cyropaedia* 1.4.21.

εἰκασία is mentioned and illustrated immediately after, and in direct connection with, metaphor, and once again this may help to explain the simile form of the example. The author has just given an example of metaphor from *On the Crown*. Now he gives one of εἰκασία from the same speech, and he shows the close relation of εἰκασία to metaphor by making the least possible change in form from one figure to the other. It is interesting to note that the two passages in *On Style* in which εἰκασία does not appear in connection with metaphor contain either an indirect example (section 160) or an example that is not a simile (section 172). The same essential difference of length between εἰκασία and παραβολή that was set forth in section 89 under the grand style is repeated briefly here,[74] and even the same example of παραβολή from Xenophon. The author also recalls another earlier comment: παραβολή possesses ἀκρίβεια ("finish"), which is unsuited to the forceful style, and this looks back to the quality of ἀκριβολογία ("exact narration") that was so appropriately a feature of παραβολή in the plain style.[75]

On Style's views of comparison are both perceptive and refreshingly novel.[76] In one sense, it is true, the treatise is somewhat anachronistic in returning to the Aristotelian bond between metaphor and comparison from which both *ad Herennium* and Cicero (and, it would seem, Hellenistic treatises in general) had moved away. On the other hand, the work presents for the first time a division of comparison in terms of length and poetic character, distinctions that apparently had not occurred to Aristotle, the author of *ad Herennium*, or Cicero. The author is quite precise in stating which styles will readily accommodate

[74] The author assumes familiarity with his more detailed earlier remarks on the length of παραβολή.

[75] Roberts' "finish" and "exact narration" do not sufficiently reflect the connection between the two Greek words. Grube's "precision" and "precise language" are much better.

[76] This is not to insist that the author originated the views he expresses, only that they have not been seen before in the testimony.

εἰκασία and παραβολή. παραβολή will be used only sparingly in any kind of prose style; but, granted that restriction, both figures will find a place in the grand and elegant styles, while παραβολή is also suited to the plain style and εἰκασία to the forceful. The last two classifications seem illogical. The poetical παραβολή would more naturally suggest forcefulness and the prosaic εἰκασία plainness, but the author makes no reference to εἰκασία within the plain style and explicitly excludes παραβολή from the forceful. We are left with this odd division.

Only one of Dionysius of Halicarnassus' many critical works, *de Compositione Verborum*, contains mention of terms of comparison. In the *Ars Rhetorica* there is quite a detailed analysis of comparison; in the best manuscript, however, *Parisinus* 1741, only a later hand ascribes the work to Dionysius, and without doubt it belongs to the age of the late technical treatises although it may contain remnants of Dionysius' doctrines.[77] Again, near the end of one of the literary letters, the *Epistula ad Cn. Pompeium*,[78] the phrase καὶ μάλιστα κατὰ τὰς παραβολάς (and especially in his comparisons) occurs in reference to Theopompus' errors in the treatment of subject matter. Kiessling emended the manuscript reading of παραβολάς to παρεμβολάς (and especially in his digressions),[79] however, bringing about a better, and surely correct, sense.

In *de Compositione Verborum* itself, a nonrhetorical instance of a term of comparison occurs in chapter 22. One of Dionysius' observations on the twelve opening periods of Thucydides 1.1 concerns hiatus, and of it he says: ". . . of hiatus between vowels in the twelve periods there are almost thirty instances, together with παραβολάς of semi-vowels and mutes which are dissonant,

---

[77] W. Rhys Roberts, *Dionysius of Halicarnassus, The Three Literary Letters* (Cambridge, Eng., 1901) 5.

[78] Goold 173 suggests this Pompeius as the author of *On the Sublime*.

[79] As reported by Roberts, *The Three Literary Letters* 126.

harsh, and hard to pronounce."[80] παραβολάς has no comparative sense but means "juxtaposition," "meeting."

Only in chapter 11 of *de Compositione Verborum* does a term of comparison appear in a figurative sense: the term is not παραβολή, but εἰκών. The chapter discusses the sources of stylistic charm and beauty. Dionysius emphasizes that not only are rhythm and melody important but also variety and appropriateness, which can be as effective and give as much pleasure as the first two qualities. As witness to this he says, "I may refer, in confirmation, to the case of instrumental music . . . if it attains grace perfectly and throughout, but fails to introduce variety in due season or deviates from what is appropriate, the effect is dull satiety. . . ." He then explains why he has used music to illustrate his point:

καὶ οὐκ ἀλλοτρίᾳ κέχρημαι τοῦ πράγματος εἰκόνι· μουσικὴ γάρ τις ἦν καὶ ἡ τῶν πολιτικῶν λόγων ἐπιστήμη τῷ ποσῷ διαλλάττουσα τῆς ἐν ᾠδῇ καὶ ὀργάνοις, οὐχὶ τῷ ποιῷ.[81]

Nor is my illustration foreign to the matter in hand. The science of public oratory is, after all, a sort of musical science, differing from vocal and instrumental music in degree, not in kind.

εἰκόνι denotes, of course, the illustrative comparison, in the form of a condition, that Dionysius has drawn; this sense of εἰκών was the one most often found in pre-Aristotelian literature, in keeping, therefore, with Dionysius' generally "classical" style and vocabulary. Indeed, neither παραβολή nor εἰκασία, the two terms used in *On Style*, appears as a term of comparison in Dionysius.

The impressive treatise *On the Sublime*[82] contains two passages

---

[80] The translation by W. Rhys Roberts, *Dionysius of Halicarnassus On Literary Composition* (London 1910), is used.

[81] Roberts' text.

[82] Goold 174 suggests 12 A.D. as the most likely date for the work. Whether or not such precision is possible, there is general agreement that a date in the first century A.D. is correct (although Grube seems to hedge on this in his *Greek and*

of tantalizing interest. The first, at chapter 32.3, reporting how Aristotle and Theophrastus advised that bold metaphors be softened, has been discussed in connection with Theophrastus and *On Style*. To summarize: both the actual words of softening mentioned by [Longinus], ὡσπερεί and οἱονεί ("as if" and "as it were"), and also his reference to them as words of apology (ὑποτίμησις) indicate that he is attributing to Aristotle and Theophrastus qualifying and parenthetical rather than comparative words. When *On Style*, on the other hand, raises the same theme of softening metaphor and brings forward comparison (εἰκασία) as the foremost means, it looks as though [Longinus'] terms ὡσπερεί and οἱονεί should be taken as comparative words after all.[83] The problem resists final solution and must be left open.

The second passage, like the first, occurs in the section of the treatise that analyzes noble diction (ἡ γενναία φράσις) as a source of sublimity (ὕψος). [Longinus] divides his work into five main sections, each enumerating one source of sublimity: grandeur of thought, inspired passion, employment of figures, noble diction, and grandeur in word arrangement. The third source, employment of figures (ἡ τῶν σχημάτων πλάσις), is the heading under which comparison was discussed in *ad Herennium* and Cicero (and thus probably in Hellenistic treatises); but [Longinus] has no reference at all to comparison under this heading, coming to it

---

Roman Critics and to opt for a much later date by treating [Longinus] in his last chapter). For a full and lucid statement of the various problems of date and authorship, see Roberts, *Longinus On the Sublime* 1–22. Roberts feels that the work was probably written in Alexandria, which would explain its occasionally Hebraic flavor and also the connection of the author with Philo. Goold 177 reverses the sequence and suggests that [Longinus] came from the community of Hellenized Jews that was centered in Alexandria but did his writing at Rome. D. A. Russell, *'Longinus' On the Sublime* (Oxford 1964) xxii–xxx, is more cautious than either Roberts or Goold and specifies neither the date of the treatise nor its place of composition.

[83] This, of course, would strengthen the assumption that a discussion of comparison did occur in Theophrastus.

only within the fourth source, noble diction.[84] In this classification and also in the close connection made between comparison and metaphor he recalls *On Style*, where comparison was treated together with metaphor within the diction appropriate to each style.

Chapter 32 analyzes metaphor as an essential element of noble diction. Chapters 33–36 form something of a digression,[85] in which [Longinus] expresses a preference for the great writer who has a certain number of faults over the trivial writer whose form is perfect. He illustrates this preference by a comparison of Demosthenes with Hyperides and, somewhat differently, of Plato with Lysias. Chapter 37 opens with a summons to return to the subject at hand:

> Ταῖς δὲ μεταφοραῖς γειτνιῶσιν (ἐπανιτέον γὰρ) αἱ παραβο-
> λαὶ καὶ εἰκόνες, ἐκείνῃ μόνον παραλλάττουσαι. . . .

> Closely related to Metaphors (for we must return to our point) are comparisons and similes, differing only in this respect. . . .[86]

Instead of the promised discussion of the two terms of comparison, only a lacuna of two folia in the manuscripts follows;[87] when the text resumes the subject is hyperbole. This is an immeasurable loss in the ancient testimony. Roberts' evaluation of *On the Sublime* is a fair one: "Taken as a whole, it is the most striking single piece of literary criticism produced by any Greek writer posterior

---

[84] The arrangement is certain, as Roberts, *Greek Rhetoric and Literary Criticism* 134, makes clear. T. R. Henn, *Longinus and English Criticism* (Cambridge 1934) 38, is plainly mistaken when he begins a chapter devoted to simile and metaphor with the statement, "Among the five sources of the sublime, Longinus has given the third place to the handling of figures. . . . By 'figures' he appears to mean metaphor and simile." Baldwin, *Ancient Rhetoric and Poetic* 124, commits the same mistake.

[85] As Roberts, *Longinus On the Sublime* 215, notes.

[86] Russell's OCT and Roberts' translation are used.

[87] Such a situation is not uncommon in the work, one third of which is lost through lacunae.

to Aristotle."[88] It is no overstatement to say that the lacuna has probably deprived us of one of the most instructive, and perhaps original, analyses of comparison in ancient rhetoric and criticism.

Despite the lacuna, a few general features of [Longinus'] views can be surmised from the fragment of the chapter that remains. Comparison is tightly bound to metaphor; the author makes no statement, however, that it is a subordinate branch of metaphor. In this respect he may have differed from Aristotle and *On Style.* Two kinds of literary comparison are promised treatment, and the two most traditional terms, παραβολή and εἰκών, are used. Roberts' translation, "comparisons and similes,"[89] cannot be tested in face of the lacuna, but there is no particular reason to think that [Longinus] restricted his understanding of either term to simile alone. Indeed, in the discussion of metaphor in chapter 32, a loose approach to form suggests that [Longinus] is relatively unconcerned about the precise verbal form of both metaphor and comparison. Of the many examples of metaphor, all from Plato's *Timaeus,* several are in form similes:

(1) σφονδύλους τε ὑπεστηρίχθαί φησιν οἷον στρόφιγγας.

(2) καὶ τὴν μὲν τῶν ἐπιθυμιῶν οἴκησιν προσεῖπεν ὡς γυναι-
κωνῖτιν, τὴν τοῦ θυμοῦ δὲ ὥσπερ ἀνδρωνῖτιν.

(3) . . . προβολὴν τῶν ἔξωθεν τὴν σάρκα, οἷον τὰ πιλήματα,
προθέμενοι.

(4) διωχέτευσαν τὸ σῶμα, τέμνοντες ὥσπερ ἐν κήποις ὀχετούς.

(32.5)

(1) The vertebrae, he says, are fixed beneath like pivots.

(2) The seat of the desires he said was like the women's apartments in a house, that of anger like the men's.[90]

---

[88] Roberts, *Longinus On the Sublime* 36. Besides its own virtues, the work belongs to the last great era of Greek literary criticism, and its final chapter, depicting the end of the development of sound eloquence, is correspondingly one of the last sound pieces of criticism by an ancient Greek writer.

[89] Russell xxi gives "Similes" as the title of chapter 37.

[90] To emphasize the simile form, I translate the Greek here somewhat more literally than Roberts' "the seat of the desires he compared to the women's apartments in a house, that of anger to the men's."

(3) . . . putting forward the flesh as a defense against injuries from without, as though it were a hair-cushion.

(4) They irrigated the body, cutting conduits as in gardens.

If [Longinus] meant "simile" by either εἰκών or παραβολή, then all these "simile" examples of metaphor should rather have appeared under one of the terms of comparison. They do not, and it would seem that the fragment of chapter 37 should be regarded simply as the preface to a discussion of two kinds of literary comparison. But it remains unknown in what ways [Longinus] differentiated them from one another and from metaphor.

The Greek writers presented in this chapter form a curious group. Dionysius Thrax really shows only that terms of comparison were not unknown to first-century B.C. grammatical handbooks, and Philodemus does little more than the same thing with respect to an Epicurean rhetorical work. Dionysius of Halicarnassus evinces sparse interest, in the midst of his broad literary concerns, for analysis of comparison. [Demetrius] alone gives considerable attention to comparison, and his views command additional respect in that they are part of a solid work of literary criticism. Finally, the lacuna in [Longinus] represents the greatest *desideratum* in the ancient testimony.

CHAPTER VI

THE SENECAS

Rhetorical bonds between the elder and the younger Seneca are as tenuous as those between the various writers treated in chapter V, and it is equally artificial, and equally convenient, to examine them together. The Senecas illustrate the approach to comparison of educated men, trained and interested in rhetoric though not themselves professional rhetoricians or critics. They are clearly not the only writers of this class who could be considered, but they will serve as models. Their familial ties might suggest that they would use rhetorical terminology in similar ways, but in fact their usage is as distinctly different as is the general character of their writings. The extant work of the elder Seneca consists of famous cases from two types of rhetorical declamation; the work of the younger Seneca is far broader in scope, including letters, tracts, satire, and rhetorical tragedies. One common characteristic is that neither directly analyzes comparisons; in both, use of terms of comparison is more or less casual, arising from more central topics.

The elder Seneca offers few passages of relevance. In the *Controversiae* there are two references to comparison: in both the term used is *comparatio*.[1] *Controversiae* 7.5 treats the case that contains both charge and defense (*accusatio* and *defensio*). Seneca remarks that not all declaimers deliver charge and defense in the same order, and he mentions M. Porcius Latro as favoring the

---

[1] H. Bardon, *Le Vocabulaire de la critique littéraire chez Sénèque le rhéteur* (Paris 1940) 20. There appear to be no instances in the *Suasoriae*.

delivery of the defense first, Arellius Fuscus as favoring the opposite order. He then adds:

> Quidam permiscuerunt accusationem ac defensionem, ut comparationem duorum reorum inirent et crimen, simul reppulissent, statim transferrent; ex quibus fuit Cestius.[2]   (7.5.7)

> Some blend charge and defense, so as to institute a comparison of the two parties and so as to transfer the charge to one at the same time as removing it from the other. Cestius was among these.[3]

Comparatio is used here in the general sense that has been found to be usual. At *Controversiae* 9.6, on the other hand, the term refers to an actual figure of comparison. A stepmother, accused of poisoning someone, implicates her daughter; Seneca recalls the way in which Pompeius Silo proposed to handle the case.

> Silo a parte patris comparationem fecit inter se matris et filiae, et totam hac figura declamavit.   (9.6.14)

> Silo, speaking for the father, made a comparison between the mother and daughter, and argued the whole case by means of this figure.

An extensive passage follows in which the character and motives of mother and daughter are examined in parallel. Silo's *comparatio* is a method of argumentation, assuming here the form of a comparison with parallel description.

Both *imago* and *similitudo* also appear in the *Controversiae*, each on a single occasion[4] but in contexts in which they do not really serve as terms of comparison. *Similitudo* occurs in the prologue of Book I (section 6) in the sense of "copy," "resemblance," as opposed to *veritas*. *Imago* occurs at 1.6.12 and refers to a "pic-

---

[2] Text of A. Kiessling, *Annaei Senecae Oratorum et Rhetorum Sententiae Divisiones Colores* (Leipzig: B. G. Teubner, 1872). Cestius is L. Cestius Pius of Smyrna.

[3] My translation.

[4] Bardon 35, 54.

ture" or "description" drawn by Q. Haterius. Bardon, discussing Seneca's weakening of certain Ciceronian terms, comments on *imago*: "*imago* perd son emploi, connu et précis, de 'comparaison' (εἰκών). . . . Cette signification traditionelle se perd avec Sénèque le Rhéteur. Quintilien la reprendra."[5] He is correct in pointing to the change in Seneca from the figurative use of *imago* frequently found in Cicero, but εἰκών is not the only possible Greek equivalent of *imago*, nor is Quintilian the first to re-establish the precise and figurative use of the term. That effort, as will be seen, belongs to the younger Seneca.

Considerably more passages on comparison occur in the younger Seneca than in the elder. *Imago* is the term most often used; *comparatio*, *collatio*, and *similitudo* appear also.[6] *Comparatio* occurs four times, always in a general, nonfigurative sense of "comparison." A passage from *de Beneficiis* is representative:[7]

. . . ubi in conparatione beneficii praeponderavit iniuria.[8]

(*de Ben.* 6.4.1)

. . . whenever, in balancing the two, the wrong outweighs the benefit.[9]

Collatio also occurs several times in an equally broad sense of "comparison."[10] In addition, it appears once with the meaning

---

[5] *Ibid.*, 81.

[6] A. Pittet, *Vocabulaire philosophique de Sénèque* (Paris 1937), covers A–Com, thus the instances of *collatio* and *comparatio*. The new projected French series of indexes for all the philosophical works has thus far treated only the *ad Marciam de Consolatione* and *de Constantia Sapientis*. For the rest, I have compiled my own list of instances of *imago* and *similitudo*. ThLL is no help on *similitudo*.

[7] See also *de Ira* 3.30.3 and *Epistle* 43.2; 81.15; the last is overlooked by Pittet.

[8] *L. Annaei Senecae de Beneficiis Libri VII, de Clementia Libri II*,[2] ed. C. Hosius (Leipzig: B. G. Teubner, 1914).

[9] J. W. Basore's Loeb translation (Cambridge, Mass., 1928–1935) of the *Moral Essays* is used.

[10] Four times in all, three in a single chapter of the *Naturales Quaestiones* (4.11.2, 11.3, 11.5) and once in the *Epistles* (85.4).

of a logical comparison, or analogy, at *Epistle* 120.4; and, indeed, the transliterated Greek term *analogia* occurs in the same passage as a synonym. This logical use of *collatio* was observed in Cicero's philosophical works.[11] Finally, in *Epistle* 81, the term refers to a figure of comparison. Seneca's topic is *beneficia* (kindnesses), and he states that in balancing kindnesses and wrongs[12] the personal relationship involved may be crucial. To illustrate he offers two comparisons, then uses *collatio* to denote the kind of comparison just drawn:

> "dedisti mihi beneficium in servo, iniuriam fecisti in patre; servasti mihi filium, sed patrem abstulisti." Alia deinceps per quae procedit omnis conlatio. . . .[13]   (81.16)

> Men say: "You conferred a benefit upon me in that matter of the slave, but you did me an injury in the case of my father"; or, "You saved my son, but robbed me of a father." Similarly, he [the good man] will follow up all other matters in which comparisons can be made. . . .[14]

The comparison is argumentative, rather than stylistic, and *collatio* does not appear in Seneca within a stylistic or embellishing framework.

Similitudo, in a general sense of "likeness," "resemblance," is frequent both in Seneca's essays and letters.[15] The most lively instance comes in a passage of *Epistle* 84 in which *imago* is also used nonfiguratively. Seneca explains how reading can aid style, and he employs a rather earthy metaphor: one should digest the separate elements of one's reading in such a way that these ele-

---

[11] See *de Finibus* 4.27.75; above, p. 124.

[12] *In hac conparatione beneficii et iniuriae*. This is one of the four occurrences of *comparatio*, and Seneca here distinguishes it from *collatio* by using *comparatio* to mean the process of balancing or comparing, while *collatio* refers to an actual figure of comparison.

[13] Reynolds' OCT of the *Epistles* is used.

[14] Gummere's Loeb translation of the *Epistles* (London 1917–1925).

[15] For example, *de Providentia* 6.4; *de Clementia* 1.26.4; *Epist.* 12.7; 45.7; 66.8.

ments are blended together and emerge as a single element
bearing the reader's own imprint! In less picturesque language,
he then adds:

> Etiam si cuius in te comparebit similitudo quem admiratio tibi
> altius fixerit, similem esse te volo quomodo filium, non quomodo
> imaginem: imago res mortua est. (84.8)

Even if there shall appear in you a likeness to him who, by reason
of your admiration, has left a deep impress upon you, I would
have you resemble him as a child resembles his father, and not as a
picture resembles its original; for a picture is a lifeless thing.

Four passages present *similitudo* as denoting a figure of comparison. In each case a comparison of more or less detailed parallel
is drawn; in no case is the comparison a simile in form, two of the
passages, indeed, being essentially metaphorical. In *de Tranquillitate Animi*, Annaeus Serenus[16] confesses to Seneca a certain degree
of mental disquiet, but he admits that the disquiet is not violent:

> non esse periculosos hos motus animi nec quicquam tumultuosi
> adferentis scio; ut vera tibi similitudine id, de quo queror, expri-
> mam, non tempestate vexor sed nausea: detrahe ergo quicquid
> hoc est mali et succurre in conspectu terrarum laboranti.[17] (1.17)

I know that these mental disturbances of mine are not dangerous
and give no promise of a storm; to express what I complain of in
apt metaphor, I am distressed, not by a tempest, but by sea-sick-
ness. Do you, then, take from me this trouble, whatever it be, and
rush to the rescue of one who is struggling in full sight of land.

Basore's translation of *similitudine* by "metaphor" reflects the

---

[16] Serenus participates also in *de Constantia Sapientis*. His premature death in
63 A.D. receives a tribute in *Epist.* 63.

[17] *L. Annaei Senecae Opera quae Supersunt*, vol. I, ed. E. Hermes (Leipzig:
B. G. Teubner, 1905), is used for passages from *de Tranquillitate Animi, ad Marciam
de Consolatione*, and *de Vita Beata*.

form of Serenus' figure but passes over its basic purpose of effecting a comparison—the most important meaning conveyed by
similitudo. In the second book of *de Beneficiis* Seneca draws an
extremely long and detailed comparison between throwing a ball
back and forth and giving and receiving a benefit. He introduces his comparison:

> Volo Chrysippi nostri uti similitudine de pilae lusu.   (2.17.3)

> I wish to make use of an illustration that our Chrysippus[18] once
> drew from the playing of ball.

Then he explores several features of successful and unsuccessful
ball games, in each case showing that the analogy to conferring
and receiving benefits is exact.

A very similar, if slightly less extended, comparison occurs in
Epistle 13. Seneca compliments his correspondent Lucilius on his
plucky spirit, then describes a fighter who has often been down
but has never failed to rise and resume the fight. He continues:

> Ergo, ut similitudinem istam prosequar, saepe iam fortuna supra
> te fuit, nec tamen tradidisti te, sed subsiluisti et acrior constitisti.
>
> *(Epist.* 13.3)
> So then, to keep up my figure, Fortune has often in the past got the
> upper hand of you, and yet you have not surrendered, but have
> leaped up and stood your ground still more eagerly.

In this case, *similitudo* denotes not just a detailed comparison but
also one in which the language of the image (boxing) is applied
metaphorically to the subject. The author of *ad Herennium* classified such a comparison as *similitudo apertius dicendi causa* (for the
sake of greater clarity), but for him conciseness (*brevitas*) was a
regular structural feature of this kind of *similitudo*, a feature not
shared by the Senecan passage. Finally, *Epistle* 114, throughout
which Seneca discusses the connection between a man's character

---

[18] The Stoic philosopher.

and his style of speaking, culminates in a lengthy comparison between the soul (*animus*) and a king. The form of the comparison is again metaphorical. Seneca begins, *rex noster est animus* ("the soul is our king"); then, after some description of the soul, he proceeds:

> Quoniam hac similitudine usus sum, perseverabo. Animus noster modo rex est, modo tyrannus: rex cum honesta intuetur . . . ubi vero inpotens, cupidus, delicatus est, transit in nomen detestabile ac dirum et fit tyrannus. (*Epist.* 114.24)

> To persist in my use of this *similitudo* [19]—our soul is at one time a king, at another a tyrant. The king, in that he respects things honourable. . . . But an uncontrolled, passionate, and effeminate soul changes kingship into that most dread and detestable quality—tyranny.

And this king-tyrant image of the soul continues for a good page. Once again *similitudo* has signified a detailed comparison, loose in form, that is used by Seneca seemingly to lend elegant weight to his point; such a purpose appears to be shared by all four figurative instances of *similitudo*.

Imago, Seneca's principal term of comparison, occurs for the most part in the *Epistles*. These passages will be considered first even though the *Epistles* postdate most of the philosophical dialogues.[20] The first passage of consequence is perhaps the most interesting of all; it is also difficult and elusive. In the opening sections of *Epistle* 59, Seneca praises highly the most recent letter from Lucilius. His general approval is summed up in the phrase *habes verba in potestate* [21] ("you have your words under control"). Lucilius has controlled his vocabulary and has fitted it to his

[19] Gummere translates with "simile"; "comparison" or "illustration" would be better.
[20] Pittet x–xi sets out a convenient chronological table of Seneca's philosophical works. The *Epistles* were written from 63–65 A.D.
[21] *Epist.* 59.4.

subject matter, which therefore has also been kept under control, and this in turn indicates that his mind is in good order:

> . . . apparet animum quoque nihil habere supervacui, nihil tumidi.
>
> (*Epist.* 59.5)
>
> . . . your mind, as well as your words, contains nothing super-fluous or bombastic.

The next sentence calls attention to a stylistic trait of Lucilius' letter that might endanger his praiseworthy control of language but in fact, Seneca quickly adds, does not:

> Invenio tamen translationes verborum ut non temerarias ita quae periculum sui fecerint. (59.6)
>
> I do, however, find some metaphors, not, indeed, daring ones, but the kind which have stood the test of use.

The metaphors have caused Seneca initial anxiety but have proved, upon further examination, not to have upset Lucilius' control of language. Seneca now describes at some length a second figure he has found in his friend's letter:

> invenio imagines, quibus si quis nos uti vetat et poetis illas solis iudicat esse concessas, neminem mihi videtur ex antiquis legisse, apud quos nondum captabatur plausibilis oratio: illi, qui simpliciter et demonstrandae rei causa eloquebantur, parabolis [22] referti sunt, quas existimo necessarias, non ex eadem causa qua poetis, sed ut inbecillitatis nostrae adminicula sint, ut et dicentem et audientem in rem praesentem adducant. Sextium [23] ecce cum maxime lego, virum acrem, Graecis verbis, Romanis moribus philosophantem. Movit me imago ab illo posita: ire quadrato agmine exercitum,

[22] That Seneca should here transliterate as a synonym for *imago* παραβολή rather than εἰκών, for which *imago* was the usual equivalent in *ad Herennium* and Cicero, supports what [Demetrius'] use of terms of comparison suggested, namely that during the first century A.D. εἰκών temporarily ceased to be the dominant Greek term.

[23] Q. Sextius, an eclectic philosopher of the Augustan age, who borrowed at once from Stoicism, Platonism, and Pythagorianism.

ubi hostis ab omni parte suspectus est, pugnae paratum. "Idem" inquit "sapiens facere debet: omnis virtutes suas undique expandat, ut ubicumque infesti aliquid orietur, illic parata praesidia sint et ad nutum regentis sine tumultu respondeant." (59.6–7)

I find similes also; of course, if anyone forbids us to use them, maintaining that poets alone have that privilege, he has not, apparently, read any of our ancient prose writers, who had not yet learned to affect a style that should win applause. For those writers, whose eloquence was simple and directed only towards proving their case, are full of comparisons; and I think that these are necessary, not for the same reason which makes them necessary for the poets, but in order that they may serve as props to our feebleness, to bring both speaker and listener face to face with the subject under discussion. For example, I am at this very moment reading Sextius; he is a keen man, and a philosopher who, though he writes in Greek, has the Roman standard of ethics. One of his similes appealed especially to me, that of an army marching in hollow square, in a place where the enemy might be expected to appear from any quarter, ready for battle. "This," said he, "is just what the wise man ought to do; he should have all his fighting qualities deployed on every side, so that wherever the attack threatens, there his supports may be ready to hand and may obey the captain's command without confusion."

Seneca mentions *translatio* (metaphor) and *imago* (a term of comparison) in consecutive sentences. This suggests that he regards them as related figures, a view that would set him apart from the Latin tradition of *ad Herennium* and Cicero and close to Aristotle and *On Style*. Unlike the Greek critics, on the other hand, Seneca clearly does not feel that comparison is subsumed within metaphor. Indeed, he expends so much more effort in dealing with the characteristics of *imago* than *translatio* that, if anything, comparison would seem to be prior in importance. Most probably, however, he regards the two figures as related and equal.

A second point in which Seneca again both recalls and diverges from Aristotle comes in his statement that the effect of the *imagines* of men of the past (the *antiqui*) was to bring both the speaker and the listener into the very presence of the subject being described (*ut et dicentem et audientem in rem praesentem adducant*). In other words, a skillful use of *imagines* should reveal the essence of the subject matter and instruct the listener in the essence. Revelation and instruction are, of course, the very qualities that Aristotle attributed so strongly to metaphor, but to comparison only in certain respects.[24] Seneca discusses the qualities solely with reference to a term of comparison, again changing the Aristotelian emphasis.

A third point, expressing a view in plain opposition to Aristotelian doctrine, lies in Seneca's scorn for those who deny the validity of *imagines* in prose ("if anyone forbids us to use them, maintaining that poets alone have that privilege . . ."). Aristotle did not condemn completely the use of comparisons (εἰκόνες) in prose; he only advocated that they be employed sparingly. Seneca's hypothetical antagonist takes a more extreme position, but the resemblance is sufficient to prompt an initial identification of the antagonist with the Peripatetics of Seneca's day. The roughly contemporary, Peripatetically influenced [Demetrius], however, opposes the categorization of comparison as a poetic figure as heartily as Seneca does, greatly reducing the likelihood of this identification of Seneca's antagonist. An alternative guess might be that one of the rhetorical schools was taking the position Seneca rejects. The two chief schools of the early part of the first century A.D. were those of Apollodorus of Pergamum and Theodorus of Gadara. Apollodorus is said to have sought to limit and restrain speech and, specifically, to do away with the classification of rhetorical figures, returning the term σχῆμα to its original general sense of "form."[25] Theodorus, on the other hand, favored a freer kind of speech. This distantly

---

[24] *Rhet.* 3.10; see above, p. 41.
[25] Quintilian, *Inst. Orat.* 9.1.10ff; see Kroll 1124; Kennedy 335.

suggests that Apollodorus may have advocated restricting comparisons to poetry alone. But Seneca is not normally interested in the technical theories of the rhetorical schools, and identification of his hypothetical antagonist with the school of Apollodorus is as insecure as is identification with the Peripatetics. It is perhaps best to regard Seneca's quarrel with the unnamed opponent as broadly reflecting the dispute over style between the "Asianists" and the "Atticists."[26] The restrictive view of comparison would appear to be an "Atticist" position, while Seneca answers in a somewhat "Asianist" vein.[27]

It would be of interest to know precisely what kind of comparison Sextius' *imago* is. Unfortunately, as Seneca points out, Sextius wrote in Greek (*Graecis verbis . . . philosophantem*), and Seneca's quotation is a translation, perhaps a free one. In addition, he translates only the subject part of Sextius' *imago*; the comparative part is merely paraphrased. At the same time, certain structural features of the *imago* are clear enough, and they display marked differences from the earlier Latin analysis of *imago* in *ad Herennium*.[28] The *imago* is not used for praise or censure. Both subject and comparative parts are developed extensively, whereas in *ad Herennium* only one part of any *imago* is developed. Again—and more the case of *ad Herennium*—the subject part of the *imago* contains metaphor drawn from the comparative part (military terms are applied to the actions recommended for the wise man). In general, then, Seneca's use of *imago*, at least in this opening passage, strikes out in something of a new direction.

Slightly further on in *Epistle* 59, *imago* appears in a broader and more traditional context. Seneca shifts from comparison of the prepared army and the wise man to the subject of folly (*stultitia*) and why we do not resist it successfully. He leads into this with a

---

[26] Norden I 270–300.
[27] Professor Zeph Stewart has brought this possibility to my attention.
[28] 4.49.62.

series of metaphorical thoughts on man's vice-ridden nature, referring at the end to a switch in metaphor that he had made near the beginning:

> Nos multa alligant, multa debilitant. Diu in istis vitiis iacuimus, elui difficile est; non enim inquinati sumus sed infecti. Ne ab alia imagine ad aliam transeamus, hoc quaeram quod saepe mecum dispicio, quid ita nos stultitia tam pertinaciter teneat? (59.9)

> We human beings are fettered and weakened by many vices; we have wallowed in them for a long time, and it is hard for us to be cleansed. We are not merely defiled; we are dyed by them. But, to refrain from passing from one figure to another, I will raise this question, which I often consider in my own heart: why it is that folly holds us with such an insistent grasp?

The "passing from one figure [*imago*] to another" describes the change from a metaphor of fetters to one of dirt and filth, a change Seneca reverses in his last phrase. *Imago* does not denote the metaphor itself, however, but the picture or image used in the metaphor—a common enough sense in *ad Herennium* and in Cicero.

In *Epistle* 72 Seneca exhorts Lucilius not to allow the desire for material goods to impede one's devotion to philosophy. The truth to be remembered, he says, is that man must not demand more from life than he actually receives. Then he adds:

> Solebat Attalus[29] hac imagine uti: "vidisti aliquando canem missa a domino frusta panis aut carnis aperto ore captantem? quidquid excepit protinus integrum devorat et semper ad spem venturi hiat. Idem evenit nobis: quidquid expectantibus fortuna proiecit, id sine ulla voluptate demittimus statim, ad rapinam alterius erecti et attoniti." (72.8)

Attalus used to employ the following *imago*:[30] "Did you ever see

---

[29] A Stoic, Seneca's teacher.
[30] Gummere's "simile," as the form of the *imago* shows, is not quite right; "illustration" would be more accurate.

a dog snapping with wide-open jaws at bits of bread and meat which his master tosses to him? Whatever he catches, he straightway swallows whole, and always opens his jaws in the hope of something more. So it is with ourselves; we stand expectant, and whatever Fortune has thrown to us we forthwith bolt, without any real pleasure, and then stand alert and frantic for something else to snatch."

The structure of this comparative illustration is very close to that in *Epistle* 59. In each case the comparison is an extended one, subject and comparative parts are developed equally, and terms from the comparison are applied metaphorically to the subject ("bolt," "snatch").

Three more instances of *imago* in the *Epistles* conform, with some variation, to the use of the term in *Epistle* 72 and in the main passage of *Epistle* 59. In *Epistle* 74, Seneca indulges in an impressively long comparison between Fortune's fickle favor and a theater dole. So intertwined in the description of Fortune are images of the theater festival, however, that the whole emerges even more as an imagistic picture of Fortune than as an explicit comparison. This can be seen from the opening phrases:

> Hanc enim imaginem animo tuo propone, ludos facere fortunam et in hunc mortalium coetum honores, divitias, gratiam excutere. . . . (74.7)

> Picture now to yourself that Fortune is holding a festival, and is showering down honours, riches, and influence upon this mob of mortals. . . .

In *Epistle* 92 Seneca at one point defends the thesis that a wise man's life despite bodily misfortunes can still be termed happy. An imagined interlocutor interrupts:

> "Frigidum" inquit "aliquid et calidum novimus, inter utrumque tepidum est; sic aliquis beatus est, aliquis miser, aliquis nec beatus nec miser." Volo hanc contra nos positam imaginem excutere.
> (92.21)

"But," someone will say, "we know what is cold and what is hot; a lukewarm temperature lies between. Similarly, A is happy, and B is wretched, and C is neither happy nor wretched." I wish to examine this figure, which is brought into play against us.

Seneca then shows that the illustration of lukewarm temperature is not in fact analogous to a man neither happy nor wretched, and he concludes:

> ergo imago ista dissimilis est. (92.21)

hence your figure offers no analogy.

This argumentative comparison shares with its predecessors the quality of equal development in both parts, but it is considerably less extended and there is no metaphorical transference from comparison to subject.

Finally, toward the end of the long *Epistle* 95 (which Gummere entitles "On the Usefulness of Basic Principles"), Seneca relates some tenets of the philosopher Posidonius, among them the usefulness of illustrating (*descriptio*) each virtue, a practice which, Seneca says, Posidonius called ethology (*ethologia*). He proceeds to quote as an example of *descriptio* the picture in *Georgics* 3.75–85 of the colt of good stock who can be distinguished at an early age from less noble foals. Though he recognizes that Vergil intended his picture to be understood only on the practical level of how to select a fine horse, Seneca chooses to use it as a *descriptio* of a courageous spirit:

> Dum aliud agit, Vergilius noster descripsit virum fortem: ego certe non aliam imaginem magno viro dederim. (95.69)

Vergil's description, though referring to something else, might perfectly well be the portrayal of a brave man; at any rate, I myself should select no other *imago*[31] for a hero.

---

[31] Again Gummere's "simile" is off the mark.

And he then shows how several phrases from the *Georgics* passage could serve to describe the character and spirit of the younger Cato. He thus creates a comparison between Cato and a noble steed; but, as in *Epistle* 74, *imago* denotes more an extended picture of Cato through equine imagery than a straight comparison.

Three relevant instances of *imago* are scattered through the *Moral Essays*. In the early *ad Marciam de Consolatione*[32] Seneca draws a full picture of the uncertainties attending children: will they be eminent or infamous, will they bury their parents or the mournful reverse? He then says:

Ad hanc imaginem agedum totius vitae introitum refer.   (18.1)

Come now, apply this picture to your entrance into life as a whole.

An even fuller picture of the uncertainties that accompany life, extending for perhaps two pages, follows.

The *de Vita Beata* contains the only passage in Seneca in which it is clear that a simile, in fact two similes, are denoted by *imago*. Seneca decries the wish for pleasure at the expense of virtue and argues, by means of a simile, that to hunt great pleasures is like hunting beasts, the mere possession of which is likely to be dangerous to the captor. He moves into a second simile of hunting by means of a transitional sentence:

permanere libet in hac etiamnunc huius rei imagine. . . .   (14.3)

I wish to dwell still further upon this comparison. . . .

In both similes, terms of hunting are applied metaphorically to the subject of pleasure.

Lastly, *imago* appears in *de Beneficiis*, as in *Epistle* 59, in collocation with *translatio*. At one point in the fourth book of the tract Seneca explains to an interlocutor in what sense he feels justified

---

[32] Written ca. 40 A.D.

in calling a benefit a loan (*creditum*), though he will agree that a loan is not to be desired for itself, whereas a benefit is:

> "Dicitis" inquit "beneficium creditum insolubile esse, creditum autem non est res per se expetenda." Cum creditum dicimus, imagine et translatione utimur. . . . Ad haec verba demonstrandae rei causa descendimus; cum dico creditum, intellegitur tamquam creditum. (4.12.1)

> "You say," someone retorts, "a benefit is a loan that cannot be repaid; but a loan is not something that is desirable in itself." When I use the term "loan," I resort to a figure, a metaphor. . . . We resort to such terms for the purpose of making something clear; when I say a "loan," a quasi-loan is understood.

Basore's translation leaves the passage somewhat obscure. He makes *imagine* a most unusual synonym of *translatione* ("I resort to a figure, a metaphor"), although the Latin separates the terms (*imagine et translatione*); and his rendering of *tamquam creditum* by "quasi-loan" is unclear. It would seem more natural to take *imagine et translatione* as the common juxtaposition of "comparison and metaphor," with *tamquam creditum* exemplifying— in the form of a simile—the former. The final phrase would mean, "When I say 'loan,' 'just like a loan' is understood." Seneca states in the previous sentence that such figures (as comparison and metaphor) are used to clarify, and this view parallels his argument in *Epistle* 59 that *imagines* are fitting in prose and serve to illustrate the essence of the subject matter. When the passage is interpreted in this way, *imago* and *translatio* assume a traditional paired sense, and it becomes possible to note an approach to comparison that appears elsewhere in Seneca.

Seneca has for the moment established *imago* as the principal Latin term of comparison, in sharp contrast to *ad Herennium* and Cicero, where *similitudo* was dominant. His choice of terminology will recur in a later imperial tutor, Fronto; but Quintilian returns in this matter, as in so many others, to Cicero. *Imago* refers most often to the kind of comparison designated in earlier authors, and at times in Seneca himself, by *similitudo*: a comparison that is extended and develops both parts equally. In addition, Seneca is particularly prone to comparisons in which there is imagistic transference from comparative to subject part. This seems to be an extension of the sense of *imago* as "picture," and certain of the passages considered have been at least as pictorial as they have been comparative. In two further points, Seneca does not continue what were characteristic features of comparison in *ad Herennium* and Cicero. The word *simile* does not occur as a term of comparison but only as an adjective. And nowhere does the collocation of historical example (*exemplum*) and a term (or terms) of comparison appear.[33] In these several ways, Seneca illustrates the somewhat different approach to comparison of a nontechnical writer as compared with professional rhetoricians. In common with the rhetoricians and critics treated thus far, however, he is not aware of simile as an independent figure of comparison.

[33] *Exemplum* does appear quite commonly by itself, however, and in one curious instance (*de Ben.* 2.32.2) is used to refer to a simile, not at all historical, between returning a ball and returning a benefit—exactly the kind of comparison that is termed *similitudo* earlier in the book (2.17.3); see above, p. 166.

CHAPTER VII

QUINTILIAN

It can fairly be said that Quintilian offers the most complete and perceptive discussion of comparison in antiquity. The difficulties and obscurities that mark his work make it all too clear, however, that this is a judgment not so much in praise of Quintilian as in regret at the general brevity and elusiveness of the other ancient discussions. In this chapter passages dealing with comparison will be treated more or less as they appear in the *Institutio Oratoria*; there will not be an examination of instances of one term, then another. *Similitudo, simile, imago, comparatio,* and *collatio* are all used, but it is soon apparent that, as in Cicero, *similitudo* is the basic term of comparison.[1] There are two principal, and relatively lengthy, analyses of comparison in the *Institutio*, one in Book V, the other in Book VIII. But three earlier and much briefer passages, together with certain other related passages, should be examined first.

The first chapter of Book III opens with the programmatic statement that the book will deal with the origins and constituent parts of oratory at greater length than has been done by any previous writer on the subject. The topic, Quintilian says, is of great and recognized importance. It will afford little pleasure to a reader, however, since it consists almost entirely of a bare recital of precepts, whereas other parts of the *Institutio* present opportunities for embellishment that will attract students to the work

[1] E. Bonnell, *Lexicon Quintilianeum* (Leipzig 1834), vol. VI of G. L. Spalding, *M. Fabii Quintiliani De Institutione Oratoria Libri Duodecim* (Leipzig 1798–1834), is an invaluable aid.

by making it more enjoyable to read.[2] Lucretius expressed the same principle, Quintilian continues, in a noted *similitudo*:

qua ratione se Lucretius dicit praecepta philosophiae carmine esse complexum; namque hac, ut est notum, similitudine utitur:

> "ac veluti pueris absinthia taetra medentes
> cum dare conantur, prius oras pocula circum
> aspirant mellis dulci flavoque liquore"[3]

et quae secuntur.[4] (3.1.4)

Lucretius has the same object in mind when he states that he has set forth his philosophical system in verse; for you will remember the well-known simile which he uses:

> "And as physicians when they seek to give
> A draught of bitter wormwood to a child,
> First smear along the edge that rims the cup
> The liquid sweets of honey, golden-hued,"

and the rest.[5]

Little can be said about this instance of *similitudo* except that it refers to a simile that in its original context is constructed with equal and parallel development of subject and comparative parts.

Similitudo appears again later in Book III in a familiar context. In chapter 9 Quintilian begins his discussion of judicial oratory. He gives the five common parts of a judicial speech[6] and adds that certain authorities (wrongly, in his opinion) include division, proposition, and digression.[7] Of digression (*excessus*) he says that

---

[2] 3.1.1–3.

[3] This simile occurs twice in Lucretius, at 1.936–938 and 4.11–13. In both instances the Lucretian simile reads *contingunt* for Quintilian's *aspirant*, and Lucretius 1.936 reads *sed*, 4.11 *nam*, for Quintilian's *ac*.

[4] The text of L. Radermacher, *M. Fabii Quintiliani Institutionis Oratoriae Libri XII²*, addn. and corr. by V. Buchheit (Leipzig 1959), is used throughout.

[5] H. E. Butler's Loeb Library translation (London 1920–1922) is used unless otherwise noted.

[6] *Prooemium, narratio, probatio, refutatio, peroratio.*

[7] *Partitio, propositio, excessus.*

if it is outside the judicial case (*causa*) it is not a part of it, and if it is within the *causa* it is an aid or embellishment[8] and therefore again not part of the case. If everything in a case were part of it, then

> cur non argumentum, similitudo, locus communis, affectus, exempla partes vocentur ? (3.9.4)

> why not call argument, comparison, commonplace, pathos, illustration parts of the case?

The collocation, or in this case near-collocation, of a term of comparison and *exemplum* (historical example or illustration) was seen first in Aristotle's παραβολή and παράδειγμα and then frequently in *ad Herennium* and Cicero, but it was absent from [Demetrius] and the younger Seneca. In the present passage, Quintilian treats the two terms as embellishments in oratory, an approach unlike Aristotle's but similar to *ad Herennium*'s. His coupling of the two terms here is slightly extenuated since one does not immediately follow the other. Elsewhere in the *Institutio* the terms do appear consecutively: these passages will now be examined, along with others such as the above in which *similitudo* and *exemplum* are part of a group but not precisely juxtaposed.

At 9.2.2 *similitudo* and *exemplum* occur consecutively in the midst of a group of terms; but this is to be ascribed, at least in part, not to Quintilian's own decision but to his immediate source, *de Oratore*. The first chapter of Book IX discusses figures and tropes generally.[9] Part of the chapter is an extensive quotation of *de Oratore* 3.52.201–54.208, in which Cicero briefly defines a great number of figures of thought. Among them:

> tum duo illa, quae maxime movent, similitudo et exemplum.[10]
> (9.1.31; *de Orat.* 3.53.205)

---

[8] *Adiutorium vel ornamentum.*
[9] This discussion will be of interest again later; see below, p. 186.
[10] See above, p. 100.

Comparisons and examples may be introduced, both of them most effective methods.

In chapter 2 Quintilian goes on to state that his own list of figures of thought will be less extensive than Cicero's and will include only such means of expression as are not in straightforward speech (*illo simplici modo indicandi*). All such common modes of expression are essential components of an oration, he says, but need not be treated as figures of thought. A list of them follows, including in sequence *similitudo* and *exemplum*. The list gives no analysis of either term but simply illustrates Quintilian's recognition of the traditional coupling, at the same time that he differs from Cicero's classification of the pair.

Another direct juxtaposition is at 5.13.23–24, in a chapter dealing with refutation. Quintilian remarks in section 23 that since most accusations are based on similarities (*similibus*) to past deeds that have been judged chargeable, the chief duty of the defense is to point out whatever in the alleged similarity is in fact dissimilar (*dissimile*) to the actual case.[11] This is easily done when the prosecution draws *similitudines* from beasts or from lifeless objects, whereas *exempla* used to support a charge must be disputed variously:

> illas vero similitudines, quae ducuntur ex mutis animalibus aut inanimis, facile est eludere. exempla rerum varie tractanda sunt, si nocebunt: quae si vetera erunt, fabulosa dicere licebit, si indubia, maxime quidem dissimilia. (5.13.23–24)

As to parallels drawn from dumb animals or inanimate objects, they are easy to make light of. Examples drawn from facts, if damaging to our case, must be treated in various ways: if they are ancient history, we may call them legendary, while if they are undoubted, we must lay stress on their extreme dissimilarity.

[11] This paraphrase, which takes note of what is said earlier in the chapter, enlarges somewhat on Quintilian's immediate words.

Here both *similitudo* and *exemplum* are classified under *simile*, which bears the nonfigurative sense of "resemblance," "similarity." The particular type of *similitudo* specified ("drawn from dumb animals or inanimate objects") can also be observed in the first main discussion of *similitudo*,[12] which occurs two chapters before the present passage. Indeed, the use of the term in the present passage may help supply a correct addendum to the slightly earlier one.

One further instance in which Quintilian lists *similitudo* and *exemplum* in close, but not direct, collocation comes at 10.1.49 and forms part of his unbounded praise of Homer as the model of all oratorical excellence. Books I, II, and IX of the *Iliad* have already been held up as exemplars of legal pleading and counsel in general,[13] and the opening verses of both Homeric epics have been represented as ideal oratorical *prooemia*.[14] Part of section 49 continues:

> iam similitudines, amplificationes, exempla, digressus, signa rerum et argumenta cetera quaeque probandi ac refutandi sunt ita multa, ut. . . .

> Then again his comparisons, amplifications, illustrations, digressions, indications of fact, and all other arguments of proof and refutation are so numerous that. . . .[15]

As in the other collocations of *similitudo* and *exemplum*, so here no illustration of them is given, though it is natural to assume that *similitudines* refers to the Homeric similes.

On another point, Radermacher's text is obscure. Does *et argumenta cetera quaeque probandi ac refutandi* ("and all other argument of proof and refutation") refer back to and include the

---

[12] 5.11.23; see below, pp. 198–200.

[13] 10.1.47.

[14] 10.1.48.

[15] My translation of Radermacher's text. Butler follows the preferable emendation *et argumenta ceteraque genera* defended below.

previous terms, which then would also be elements of proof and refutation, or is the phrase to be taken independently? *Argumenta* (arguments, inferences) are in rhetoric usually distinct from *signa* (indications, signs), and this would suggest the independence of the phrase. On the other hand, what is to be done then with *cetera* (other)? It seems best to deviate from Radermacher and to follow the reading of Halm, Meister, and Peterson: *signa rerum et argumenta ceteraque genera probandi ac refutandi*[16] (indications of fact, inferential arguments, and the other methods of proof and refutation). In this reading there is no obscurity over *cetera*; it looks back to the whole list of terms, including *similitudo* and *exemplum*, which thus are among the kinds of proof and refutation. A complexity remains, however. Such a classification of a term of comparison and historical example is certainly not novel. Aristotle placed παραβολή and παράδειγμα under the category of κοιναί πίστεις (general proofs), and we have already seen a similar classification in Quintilian himself, at 5.13.23–24. But he makes quite another sort of classification, too. In his comments on the long passage quoted from *de Oratore*,[17] Quintilian says that *similitudo* and *exemplum* are such common modes of expression that they should not be particularized even so much as to call them figures of thought. Again, in the passage at 3.9.4 discussed above, the two terms are said to be similar to digression in that while they may be in a case they are not part of a case but merely ornaments to it. *Similitudo* and *exemplum*, then, may occur in any section of a *causa*, including not just proof and refutation but also

---

[16] This reading is an emendation of J. Caesar, "Zu Quintilian," *Philologus* 13 (1858) 757. All the manuscripts save one read *ceteraque quae*, which forces *sunt* to be taken with *quae* and leaves the main sentence without a verb. It was on this basis that Caesar emended. The one ms. that reads otherwise is *Vat. lat.* 1762 (*V*), whose reading, *cetera quaeque*, Radermacher adopts with resultant ambiguity. Radermacher's choice may have derived from an overeagerness to make use of the *V* ms., which came to light largely through his efforts in 1905 (see vol. I x of his edition) and which he was the first to incorporate in a text of Quintilian.

[17] 9.1.31 and 9.2.2.

exordium, statement of facts, and peroration. In other words, it seems impossible to specify under what heading Quintilian feels that the two terms primarily belong. In part they are ingredients of oratorical proof; in part they are potential ornaments in every element of oratory. These dual sides are difficult to reconcile, but they are exactly parallel to the dual nature Quintilian assigns to *similitudo* in his two main analyses of the term. He should be regarded, therefore, in the above passages as consciously maintaining disparate classifications of *similitudo* and *exemplum* rather than as eclectically and unconsciously reporting divergent theories.[18]

Having looked at the several collocations in Quintilian of *similitudo* and *exemplum*, one can return to the passages on comparison that occur before the first main discussion at 5.11. The third of these is at 4.1.70.[19] The whole chapter deals with the various problems of the exordium, or proem. At section 63 Quintilian raises the question of the applicability of apostrophe in the exordium, and he maintains, against certain *scriptores artium*,[20] that the figure is applicable if it can be shown to add spirit and force to the exordium. References to speeches of Demosthenes, Cicero, and Sallust[21] follow in which Quintilian specifies instances not only of apostrophe but of prosopopoeia, historical example (*exemplum*), and partition that are used advantageously in exordia.[22] He then adds:

> non tamen haec, quia possunt bene aliquando fieri, passim facienda sunt, sed quotiens praeceptum vicerit ratio: quo modo et similitudine, dum brevi, et translatione atque aliis tropis, quae omnia cauti illi ac diligentes prohibent, utemur interim. . . .   (4.1.70)

[18] This is not to say that Quintilian's views in general were not eclectic. They certainly were; see Kroll 1105.

[19] The first two were at 3.1.4 and 3.9.4, the latter leading into the digression on the further collocations of *similitudo* and *exemplum*.

[20] 4.1.65.

[21] Actually to a speech against Cicero falsely attributed to Sallust.

[22] 4.1.66–69.

Still such artifices, although they may be employed at times to good effect, are not to be indulged in indiscriminately, but only when there is strong reason for breaking the rule. The same remark applies to simile (which must however be brief), metaphor and other tropes, all of which are forbidden by our cautious and pedantic teachers of rhetoric, but which we shall none the less occasionally employ.

This is the first coupling in Quintilian of metaphor and a term of comparison. Just as in the several collocations of *similitudo* and *exemplum*, so here no illustrations of either *similitudo* or *translatio* are given, which hampers analysis, but certain points deserve comment.

First, it is clear that, although *exemplum* appears in section 69, just before the passage quoted, and is separated from *similitudine* by only one rhetorical term (partition), *similitudo* and *translatio* are the terms being coupled, not *exemplum* and *similitudo*.[23] Secondly, Quintilian differs in terminology from Seneca who paired *imago*, his principal term of comparison, with *translatio*. Thirdly, as in Seneca's *Epistle* 59, so Quintilian refers here to certain persons who forbid the use of comparison. The situation is less extreme, though, than in Seneca. Quintilian says of those who hold opposing views to his that they forbid not only comparison but also metaphor and other tropes, but he does not imply that theirs is a comprehensive disapproval. His concern in the present passage is with the use of tropes in the exordium, and he is merely indicating that "our cautious and pedantic teachers of rhetoric" forbid this particular use of tropes, not all uses in every part of a speech. Seneca's opponent, on the other hand, prohibited use of *imago* in prose altogether.[24]

The fourth, and most complex, point of interest is the classifica-

[23] Indeed, wherever in Quintilian *similitudo* and *exemplum* are coupled it is always in that order, never reversed as would be the case here.

[24] Despite this difference, it is tempting to think that Seneca's indefinite opponent (*quis*) and Quintilian's *cauti illi ac diligentes* belong to a single school of conservative "Atticists."

tion of *similitudo*. Quintilian certainly treats the term here as one of the ornaments of an exordium. Of two previous classifications of the term as an ornament, one (at 3.9.4) said no more than that *similitudo* and *exemplum* were ornaments to a *causa*; the other (at 9.2.2) said that *similitudo* and *exemplum*, while too common to be regarded as figures of thought, nevertheless can be used figuratively (*admittunt autem . . . figuras*, 9.2.5). But in the present passage Quintilian talks of *similitudo*, *translatio*, and "other tropes," not "other figures of thought." Is he saying that *similitudo* when coupled with *exemplum* is, if anything, a figure of thought but that the same term when coupled with *translatio* is, quite differently, a trope? Or are *tropus* and *figura* synonymous? The latter, if true, would present a sharp contradiction to other sections of the *Institutio*. Chapter 1 of Book IX is devoted in part to the specific task of defining and separating tropes and figures, and chapters 2 and 3 detail a number of *figurae*, while chapter 6 of Book VIII does the same for *tropi*. Thus Quintilian feels the two to be quite distinct, at least in general. In 8.6 *translatio* is discussed extensively as a trope. *Similitudo* is also mentioned, not specifically as a trope but as a term that includes *translatio*.[25]

The problem cannot be solved with any finality. Quintilian appears to distinguish between the classifications of *similitudo/exemplum* and *similitudo/translatio*, but it remains unclear exactly what he feels the difference is between these two categories of *similitudo* as an ornament. In the present passage, *dum brevi* ("which must however be brief") might be thought to furnish a clue, but in fact it does not because it refers primarily to the general theme of brevity Quintilian has been stressing throughout the chapter as an essential characteristic of all exordia. The phrase does not mean that only a *brevis similitudo* will be a *tropus* but rather that only a *brevis similitudo* will be used in an exordium. A

[25] See below, p. 230.

compromise remedy to the problem would be to assume that Quintilian simply is careless in his terminology and, while not consciously regarding *figura* and *tropus* as synonymous, nevertheless slips into applying both terms to *similitudo*. It is true that a distinction between tropes and figures was never drawn very consistently in ancient criticism and rhetoric,[26] and Quintilian could be an illustration of this fact. Elsewhere in the *Institutio*, however, he seems at such pains to separate *figura* and *tropus* that one hesitates to believe he has suddenly lapsed in this single case. Without pressing the matter too hard, therefore, it may be stated that Quintilian purposefully includes the collocation of *similitudo* and *translatio* among *tropi* and the collocation of *similitudo* and *exemplum* (if any classification is possible) among the *figurae sententiarum*.[27]

Quintilian's first extended discussion of comparison comes at 5.11.1–31. He has opened 5.9 thus:

> Omnis igitur probatio artificialis constat aut signis aut argumentis aut exemplis. . . .

> Every artificial proof consists either of indications, arguments or examples. . . .

The chapter deals with the first category of proof, *signa* (indications, signs); chapter 10 moves on to *argumenta* of all sorts.[28] The beginning of chapter 11 suggests that Quintilian intends only to pair *similitudo* and *exemplum* once again, but he soon goes a good deal further:

> Tertium genus ex iis, quae extrinsecus adducuntur in causam, Graeci vocant παράδειγμα, quo nomine et generaliter usi sunt in

[26] Kroll 1110.

[27] Quintilian creates a somewhat parallel situation at 9.1.7, where he says that irony at times should be classified a trope, at times a figure.

[28] Including, at 5.10.87, arguments that are *adposita vel comparativa* (apposite or comparative), that is, arguments proving the lesser from the greater, the greater from the lesser, or equals from equals.

omni similium adpositione et specialiter in iis, quae rerum gestarum auctoritate nituntur. nostri fere similitudinem vocare maluerunt, quod ab illis ⟨proprie⟩[29] παραβολή dicitur, hoc alterum exemplum, quamquam et hoc simile et illud exemplum.

The third kind of proof, which is drawn into the service of the case from without, is styled a παράδειγμα by the Greeks, who apply the term to all comparisons of like with like, but more especially to historical parallels. Roman writers have for the most part preferred to give the name of comparison to that which the Greeks style ⟨strictly⟩[30] παραβολή, while they translate παράδειγμα by example, although this latter involves comparison, while the former is of the nature of an example.

Two points merit comment. The *Graeci* to whom Quintilian refers are clearly Aristotle and the Aristotelian tradition. *Rhetoric* 2.20 presented the same hierarchy of παράδειγμα as a general term incorporating both historical example (παράδειγμα in a narrow sense) and fictional comparison (παραβολή). Secondly, Quintilian's *nostri* ("Roman writers") does not include Seneca. He explicitly gives *similitudo* as the usual Latin equivalent of παραβολή, while Seneca used *imago* as a synonym for the transliterated *parabola*.

Thus far Quintilian is mainly reporting the terminology of other Greek and Latin critics. His own views begin to appear in the concluding phrase of the passage, *quamquam et hoc simile et illud exemplum* ("although this latter involves comparison, while the former is of the nature of an example"). The phrase indicates a divergence from the common Roman differentiation of *similitudo* and *exemplum*, and Quintilian proceeds to explain a bit more:

nos, quo facilius propositum explicemus, utrumque παράδειγμα esse credamus et ipsi appellemus exemplum.   (5.11.2)

---

[29] Radermacher's addition.
[30] My translation of Radermacher's *proprie*; Butler does not include the addition.

For my own part, I prefer with a view to making my purpose easier of apprehension to regard both as παραδείγματα and to call them examples.

Quintilian is returning, in other words, to the Aristotelian hierarchy that made both fictional comparison (παραβολή) and historical example (παράδειγμα) elements of παράδειγμα in a broad sense of rhetorical proof. In the same way he proposes to use *exemplum* both as a broad kind of proof and in a narrower sense of historical example. In its more limited meaning the term can be coupled with *similitudo*, and, Quintilian continues, Cicero refers to this limited meaning when he speaks of *exemplum* and his own equivalent of *similitudo*, *collatio*:

> nec vereor ne videar repugnare Ciceroni, quamquam conlationem separat ab exemplo. nam idem omnem argumentationem dividit in duas partes, inductionem et ratiocinationem, ut plerique Graecorum in παραδείγματα et ἐπιχειρήματα, dixeruntque παράδειγμα ῥητορικὴν ἐπαγωγήν.[31]   (5.11.2)

Nor am I afraid of being thought to disagree with Cicero, although he does separate comparison from example. For he divides all arguments into two classes, induction and ratiocination, just as most Greeks divide it into παραιδείγματα and ἐπιχειρήματα, explaining παράδειγμα as a rhetorical induction.

Cicero's major term for a whole species of argument is *inductio*, the equivalent (in the terminology of logic) to Quintilian's rhetorical *exemplum* in its broad sense, and the Ciceronian and Quintilianic words are, in turn, parallel to Aristotle's logical ἐπαγωγή and rhetorical παράδειγμα. Cicero thus only uses

---

[31] The Ciceronian reference is to *de Inv.* 1.30.49, where Cicero actually speaks not only of *collatio* and *exemplum* but also of *imago* as separate divisions of *comparabile*; Quintilian omits mention of Cicero's tripartite division. That the phrase *plerique Graecorum* again refers to Aristotle and the Aristotelians can be seen from the equation of παράδειγμα and ῥητορικὴ ἐπαγωγή at *Rhet.* 2.20.1393a27. See Solmsen, *AJP* 62 (1941) 39, for the originality of Aristotle's equation.

exemplum in its narrow sense of historical example, distinct from comparison. Quintilian at the moment is using *exemplum* as a general kind of proof (Cicero's *inductio*), but he also recognizes the stricter application of *exemplum* and so does not consider himself at odds with Cicero's terminology.

One more indication that in these opening comments on *exemplum* Quintilian has set himself in the Aristotelian tradition comes in the next sentence:

> nam illa, qua plurimum est Socrates usus, hanc habuit viam.
>
> (5.11.3)
>
> The method of argument chiefly used by Socrates was of this nature.

Socrates' method was in logical terminology ἐπαγωγή (inductive comparison), in rhetorical terminology παράδειγμα. Aristotle says something very similar: he states that the Socratic method is by παραβολή,[32] but he regards παραβολή as an element of παράδειγμα. Thus, for Aristotle the Socratic method is by a type of παράδειγμα, and Quintilian deviates only slightly in saying that Socrates chiefly used παράδειγμα or ῥητορικὴ ἐπαγωγή.[33]

---

[32] *Rhet.* 2.20.1393b4.

[33] The foregoing analysis of the opening sentences of chapter 11 differs considerably from that of Cousin I 286ff, in particular from two of his statements. His paraphrase of Quintilian's second and third sentences (*nostri fere . . . appellemus exemplum*) reads: "Les Latins se servent du mot *similitudo*, qui correspond à παραβολή et du mot *exemplum*, qui traduit παράδειγμα. Quintilien préfère le dernier terme: *exemplum* et *similitudo* lui paraissent cependant répondre à παράδειγμα." This interpretation makes Quintilian seem very straightforward, but overlooks the complicating final phrase *et ipsi appellemus exemplum* by which Quintilian indicates that he intends to include both *similitudo* and *exemplum* under a larger rubric of *exemplum*. Cousin does not recognize, in other words, that Quintilian proposes two different levels of meaning for *exemplum*, just as Aristotle's παράδειγμα has two different levels. A little further on Cousin remarks that "Quintilien, comme on l'a vu plus haut, fait d'*exemplum* et de *similitudo* des synonymes de παράδειγμα." This appears to be an overly literal interpretation

The next two sections of the chapter give examples of the Socratic method of *inductio*, and it is only within section 5 that Quintilian returns to the subject of comparison:

> Omnia igitur ex hoc genere sumpta necesse est aut similia esse aut dissimilia aut contraria. similitudo[34] adsumitur interim et ad orationis ornatum. sed illa, cum res exiget: nunc ea, quae ad probationem pertinent, exsequar.

> All arguments of this kind, therefore, must be from things like or unlike or contrary. Comparisons[35] are, it is true, sometimes employed for the embellishment of the speech as well, but I will deal with them in their proper place; at present I shall pursue what relates to proof.[36]

"All arguments of this kind" refers to the type of proof just illustrated by the Socratic method, namely *inductio* or, in its wide sense, *exemplum*. Quintilian's next sentence, stating that *similitudo* is appropriate to embellishment as well as to proof and that in time the embellishing *similitudo* will also be treated, expresses a dual classification of *similitudo* that has already been noticed in the

---

of Quintilian's *utrumque* παράδειγμα *esse credamus*. The phrase is in fact somewhat elliptical, as J. S. Watson, *Quintilian's Institutes of Oratory* (London 1856) I 362, shows in his translation: ". . . let me include both [i.e., *exemplum* and *similitudo*] under the word παράδειγμα." It is only the two levels of *exemplum* that Quintilian equates with the two levels of παράδειγμα. *Similitudo* is separate and indeed comes *under* παράδειγμα in its broad sense of rhetorical proof. Cousin also holds that Quintilian essentially follows Cicero in the whole chapter; but it is rather the Aristotelian tradition to which he adheres, even opposing Cicero in a few places. In this connection P. Teichert, *De Fontibus Quintiliani Rhetoricis* (Brunsberg 1884) 3, argues that most of the traces of Aristotle in Quintilian appear in Books II, III, and V, fewer traces in IV, VIII, and IX.

34 Much that follows is based on this word, which in fact is Regius' conjecture for the mss. *dissimilitudo*; but there is absolutely no doubt about the correctness of the emendation.

35 Butler translates *similitudo* narrowly by "similes."

36 The final clause is translated inaccurately by Butler as "at present I am concerned with the use of similitude in proof." Quintilian merely says that he is returning to the general topic of proof.

different headings under which *similitudo* and *exemplum* are paired. The classification is an important one. Quintilian's promise is fulfilled at 8.3.72–81, which deals with *similitudo* not as an element of *probatio* but of *ornatus*, and for the first time in (extant) ancient criticism these two purposes of comparison are clearly proposed as elements of a single term, with each purpose analyzed under a separate rubric of oratory. In *ad Herennium*,[37] it will be recalled, two of the four purposes of *similitudo* were *ornandi causa* and *probandi causa*, embellishment and proof. But the author, far from regarding the two purposes as belonging to different parts of oratory, classified both under *similitudo* as an embellishing figure of thought.

Quintilian is the first critic to distinguish these two purposes of comparison and yet to see that they are facets of a central idea of comparison and, while he is treating one of them, to show that he is aware of the other. Aristotle is here again to some degree his precursor. In the *Rhetoric* παραβολή denotes fictional comparison as an element of παράδειγμα, one of the common proofs; εἰκών denotes comparison as an embellishment of style. Aristotle clearly has a sense of two purposes inherent in rhetorical comparison. But his use of two terms suggests that the two purposes form entirely distinct realms of comparison, and he makes no reference to εἰκών in his analysis of παραβολή, or *vice versa*. In contrast, Quintilian's use of the one term *similitudo* indicates that the comparisons of proof and of embellishment are, while independent, parts of a single concept of comparison, and this indication is reinforced by his reference in the present passage to the *similitudo* of embellishment and by the reference to the *similitudo* of proof that will be found in his discussion of the embellishing *similitudo*. What Quintilian and Aristotle recognize in common is that there is a kind of comparison to be analyzed under the rubric of proof and a kind to be analyzed under the rubric of stylistic embellishment.

[37] *Ad Her.* 4.45.59.

The above passage from section 5 calls attention to the *similitudo* of embellishment, then returns to the subject at hand, proof (*nunc ea, quae ad probationem pertinent, exsequar*). The following sections take up what Quintilian calls the strongest aid to proof, *exemplum*:

> potentissimum autem est inter ea, quae sunt huius generis, quod proprie vocamus exemplum, id est rei gestae aut ut gestae utilis ad persuadendum id, quod intenderis, commemoratio. (5.11.6)

> The most important of proofs of this class is that which is most properly styled example, that is to say the adducing of some past action real or assumed which may serve to persuade the audience of the truth of the point which we are trying to make.

Quintilian has switched from his use of *exemplum* as a broad rhetorical term equivalent to the logical *inductio* to what in the opening sections of the chapter he put forward as the common view of the term, namely an example drawing on historical authority. Not only is this switch indicated by the definition of *exemplum* but also by the first phrase ("the most important of proofs of this class . . ."). He discusses various aspects of *exemplum* through section 21. Then section 22 begins: *Proximas exemplo vires habet similitudo* ("Next to example, comparison is of the greatest effect").[38] Only if Quintilian has been using *exemplum* in its common, limited sense is this statement possible. In the broad meaning of *exemplum* as equivalent to *inductio, similitudo* could not be said to be second to it in efficacy—*similitudo* would have to be defined as *part* of *exemplum*, just as historical example itself would be *part* of this broad sense of *exemplum*.[39]

Quintilian proceeds to an analysis of *exemplum* along the lines set down in section 5 by subclassifying *exempla* into those of

---

[38] Watson's translation. Butler's "simile has a force not unlike that of example" is much less accurate.

[39] Thus the meaning of *proprie* in the passage is not so much "properly," but rather is nearer to the primary sense of the word, "particularly," "specially," almost "narrowly."

things like, unlike, and contrary. He cites first an *exemplum* expressing likeness:

> simile est: "iure occisus est Saturninus sicut Gracchi". (5.11.6)

> We argue from the like when we say, "Saturninus was justly killed, as were the Gracchi".

This is followed by one expressing unlikeness and one expressing contrariety. The example of likeness (*simile*), despite its simile form, is not intended as an instance of *similitudo* but simply as one of three possible kinds of *exemplum*. Quintilian scrupulously differentiates between *simile* and *similitudo* throughout the whole chapter. In the analysis of *exemplum*, *similitudo* is used only in the sentence already discussed: *similitudo adsumitur interim et ad orationis ornatum* ("comparisons are, it is true, sometimes employed for the embellishment of the speech as well"). Otherwise, only forms of *simile* appear, referring to historical examples of likeness.[40]

In fact, Quintilian's comment on *similitudo* seems increasingly to be uneasily situated, since neither what comes before nor what comes after in any way demands it. The first sentence of section 5, *omnia igitur . . . contraria* ("all arguments of this kind, therefore . . . contrary"), is a general, programmatic statement of three ways to approach *exemplum* in its broad sense as a major kind of proof. In the succeeding sections Quintilian treats the best type of this kind of proof, namely *exemplum*, in the narrow sense of historical example, and the first part of his analysis consists of instances of the three approaches just mentioned—like, unlike, and contrary. This sequence is altogether natural; the comment *similitudo adsumitur . . . exsequar*, on the other hand, occurs unnaturally. It has nothing to do directly with the sections on his-

---

[40] As would be expected, the *exemplum* expressing *simile* does not appear regularly in the form of a simile. Examples at 5.11.8 and 5.11.11 are respectively conditional and declarative in form.

torical example that follow, nor does it explain the first sentence;[41] it simply refers to a second subordinate type of *exemplum* in its broad sense.

The solution may well lie in regarding section 5 as having been written originally without the comment on *similitudo*. When Quintilian came in chapter 3 of Book VIII to treat the *similitudo* of embellishment and referred back to his discussion of the *similitudo* of proof[42] he may have decided to include a cross reference in the earlier book as well, placing it, somewhat awkwardly and without much thought, near the beginning of his examination of the different elements of *exemplum* as a major kind of proof, among which would be the *similitudo* of proof. The brief comment on the *similitudo* of embellishment would therefore constitute a later insert by Quintilian.[43]

The analysis of historical example continues through section 21. Section 22 begins a new part of chapter 11 that runs through section 31. The subject is *similitudo*, a second subordinate type of *exemplum* in its broad sense. Though considerable difficulties emerge, section 22 is straightforward and in accord with the earlier part of the chapter:

[41] It might be thought to explain further *similia* (like) in the first sentence, but, as has already been noted, *simile* and *similitudo* are not used synonymously anywhere in the chapter.

[42] 8.3.72; below, p. 215.

[43] The use of the first person in *exsequar* excludes the possibility that the comment derives from a marginal scholiastic note. The comment would have been situated most aesthetically just before the beginning of the actual discussion of *similitudo* in section 22: if it were to have stood originally just before the phrase *proximas exemplo vires habet similitudo*, which opens section 22, Quintilian's thoughts on *similitudo* as a kind of proof would be prefaced, fittingly enough, by a comment expressing his realization that this is not the only type of *similitudo* with which he will deal in his work. This "aesthetic" solution, however, requires that a transfer of the comment from an original position just before section 22 to its present position in section 5 somehow be assumed. Such a transfer is probably too violent to be considered, and one is left with the more pragmatic explanation of the comment as a rather hasty later addition to section 5.

Proximas exemplo vires habet similitudo, praecipueque illa, quae ducitur citra ullam tralationum mixturam ex rebus paene paribus: "ut qui accipere in campo consuerunt, iis candidatis, quorum nummos suppressos esse putant, inimicissimi solent esse: sic eius modi iudices infesti tum reo venerant."[44]

Next to example, comparison is of the greatest effect,[45] more especially when drawn from things nearly equal without any admixture of metaphor, as in the following case: "Just as those who have been accustomed to receive bribes in the Campus Martius are specially hostile to those whom they suspect of having withheld the money, so in the present case the judges came into court with a strong prejudice against the accused."

Quintilian's argument is lucid and sensible. He has now taken up another aid to proof, *similitudo*, and he states that it can be of considerable effect, particularly if no metaphor is included and if the *similitudo* treats things that are almost equal. His example, in form a simile, makes both points clear. The mob that comes to the elections hostile to the candidate whom they consider to have withheld all doles is exactly the same as judges who enter the court hostile to the defendant from whom they suppose no bribes will be forthcoming.[46] No details in either situation contradicts a detail in the other. In addition, both parts of the *similitudo* are drawn from a similar background, Roman public life. By "without any admixture of metaphor" Quintilian means that there is no metaphorical term in either part of the *similitudo* to distract the listener from Cicero's point. For instance, the simple verb *venerant* (came) is used, whereas such a metaphorical verb as *repserant* (crept) would evoke a fittingly baleful serpent picture but might also obscure the main point by attracting attention to the metaphorical image.

[44] Cicero, *pro Cluentio* 27.75.

[45] Again, Watson's translation rather than Butler's is used for this opening phrase.

[46] This last detail is supplied by the surrounding context in Cicero's speech.

Quintilian's view that a nonmetaphorical *similitudo* will best serve as an aid to proof forms an interesting contrast with Aristotle's effort[47] to present the finest sort of εἰκών—an element of style, not proof—as one that closely resembles a proportional metaphor. Indirectly, Quintilian seems once again to be standing in the Aristotelian tradition. It may even be possible that he is actually following a Peripatetic source that took the implication of Aristotle's connection between the stylistic εἰκών and metaphor and spelled out Quintillian's own reverse point, namely that a comparison aiming at proof rather than ornament should ideally contain no metaphorical element.

Thus far, all is clear enough. The next sections are considerably more difficult. What emerges basically is that sections 23–25 are a lengthy digression from Quintilian's own *similitudo* of proof as outlined in section 22, to which he briefly but significantly returns in section 26. Section 23 opens:

> nam παραβολή, quam Cicero conlationem vocat, longius res quae comparentur repetere solet.

> For παραβολή, which Cicero translates by "comparison," is often apt to compare things whose resemblance is far less obvious.

Why does Quintilian shift to the Greek term παραβολή, and what is its relation to the *similitudo* of proof he has just defined and illustrated? It is helpful to recall the beginning of the chapter: Quintilian argued that the common—and Ciceronian—view of *similitudo* and *exemplum* was that the terms were equivalent to the Greek παραβολή and παράδειγμα and also separate from each other. Cicero differed only in his use of *collatio* rather than *similitudo*. In Quintilian's own view, on the other hand, *similitudo* and *exemplum* were contained within the wider meaning of *exemplum* as the rhetorical equivalent of *inductio*. Thus, by employing παραβολή (and the explanatory connective *nam*) here,

---

[47] *Rhet.* 3.10–11.

Quintilian refers to a Greek usage followed by the majority of Latin writers with the term *similitudo* (and by Cicero with *collatio*), but not precisely equivalent to his own *similitudo* of proof. And in turning to this more common *similitudo* of proof he avoids confusion by not immediately reusing the term *similitudo*, substituting in its stead παραβολή, the Greek equivalent of the common *similitudo* of proof.

The difference between Quintilian's own *similitudo* of proof and the common παραβολή/*similitudo* is that the latter is drawn from more disparate subjects (*longius*) and is thus less effective as proof. Quintilian proceeds to illustrate these features of παρα-βολή/*similitudo*:[48]

> nec hominum modo inter se opera similia spectantur, ut Cicero pro Murena facit: "quod si e portu solventibus, qui iam in portum ex alto invehuntur, praecipere summo studio solent et tempestatum rationem et praedonum et locorum, quod natura adfert, ut iis faveamus, qui eadem pericula, quibus nos perfuncti sumus, ingrediantur: quo tandem me animo esse oportet, prope iam ex magna iactatione terram videntem, in hunc, cui video maximas tempestates esse subeundas?"[49] sed et a mutis atque etiam inanimis interim ⟨simile⟩[50] huius modi ducitur. (5.11.23)

> Nor does it merely compare the actions of men as Cicero does in the *pro Murena*: "But if those who have just come into harbour from the high seas are in the habit of showing the greatest solicitude in warning those who are on the point of leaving port of the state of the weather, the likelihood of falling in with pirates, and the nature of the coasts which they are like to visit (for it is a natural instinct that we should take a kindly interest in those who

[48] It might be thought that the points of difference between Quintilian's *similitudo* and the common *similitudo* would be illustrated indirectly by examples of *collatio* in Cicero, but such hopes are in vain. Quintilian's reference is to the use of *collatio* at *de Inv.* 1.30.49, where the term is paired with *exemplum*, but no example is included.

[49] *Pro Murena* 2.4.

[50] Halm's supplement; but see text below.

are about to face the dangers from which we have just escaped), what think you should be my attitude who am now in sight of land after a mighty tossing on the sea, towards this man who, as I clearly see, has to face the wildest weather?" On the contrary, similitudes[51] of this kind are sometimes drawn from dumb animals and inanimate objects.

Quintilian might have barely accepted the lengthy conditional comparison from the *pro Murena* within his own interpretation of *similitudo*, but he certainly would have regarded it as far from an ideal representative. The two situations compared are fairly *pares* (equal) in that they are both drawn from human activities; but, whereas Quintilian's own *similitudo* compared two aspects of Roman public life, this common παραβολή/*similitudo* compares Cicero's attitude as he approaches Murena's case to that of sailors finally reaching port and commiserating with those who are about to face the dangers of the open sea. A second, and more unequivocal, fact is that the example contains metaphor in its subject part. Cicero continues the sea-and-sailor image and applies it metaphorically to his own and Murena's situations (for example, "now in sight of land after a mighty tossing on the sea"), rather than presenting this part of the comparison simply. The result is that the whole comparison, by Quintilian's standard, is weakened as an aid to proof.

Two elements, then, disparate subject matter and metaphorical imagery, set the common παραβολή/*similitudo* apart from Quintilian's *similitudo*. The first element would seem to be the criterion by which Quintilian refuses to praise the other kinds of παραβολή/*similitudo*, mentioned at the end of the passage, that compare human activities to animals and inanimate objects. Each part of any such comparison would be so different in subject from the other part that the comparison as a whole would be altogether "unequal" and would contribute little toward the proving of particular points.

[51] Watson's word "similitudes" is better than Butler's "similes."

Radermacher's text is unsure. He follows Halm's addition of *simile*, but the reading is unlikely. As has been pointed out, *simile* is not used anywhere else in the chapter as a term of comparison but always carries the meaning of "likeness" or, adjectivally, "that which is like." The negative argument is reinforced by a positive one: a better supplement lies at hand. At 5.13.23–24, a passage noted earlier as one of the collocations of *similitudo* and *exemplum*, occurs the phrase:

> illas vero similitudines, quae ducuntur ex mutis animalibus aut inanimis. . . .

> As to *similitudines* drawn from dumb animals or inanimate objects. . . .

The wording plainly recalls that of the present passage:

> sed et a mutis atque etiam inanimis interim * * * huius modi ducitur.

> On the contrary, * * * of this kind are sometimes drawn from dumb animals and inanimate objects.

The necessary supplement, therefore, is surely *similitudo*.[52] This will not subvert the earlier suggestion that Quintilian uses παραβολή at the beginning of section 23 in order to avoid reusing *similitudo* in a different sense from that of section 22. Having avoided the term, for clarity, at the beginning of the section, he can use it easily at the end. His own *similitudo* and the common παραβολή/*similitudo*, though they differ in effectiveness, are nonetheless both *similitudines* of proof.

Section 23 has turned from Quintilian's own *similitudo* to what he considers the common *similitudo* of proof. The latter part of

---

[52] Or, perhaps, *similitudines huius modi ducuntur*. I am indebted to Professor Stewart for pointing out the similarity between the phrases in chapters 13 and 11; I had been uneasy over Halm's *simile* but thought that perhaps παραβολή should replace it.

section 24 and section 25 will provide more examples of the common *similitudo* of proof. The first part of section 24, however, digresses from what is already something of a digression and comments briefly on another rhetorical term:

> et quoniam similium alia facies in alia ratione, admonendum est, rarius esse in oratione illud genus, quod εἰκόνα Graeci vocant, quo exprimitur rerum aut personarum imago, ut Cassius:[53]
>
> "quis istam faciem planipedis[54] senis torquens?"
>
> quam id, quo probabilius fit quod intendimus.

Further, since similar objects often take on a different appearance when viewed from a different angle, I feel that I ought to point out that the kind of comparison which the Greeks call εἰκών, and which expresses the appearance of things and persons (as for instance in the line of Cassius—

> "Who is he making that contorted face of an old, barefooted dancer?")[55]

should be more sparingly used in oratory than those comparisons which help to prove our point.

Quintilian's comment is in the nature of a footnote ("I feel that I ought to point out") to his main topic of *similitudines* of proof. He remarks that different kinds of likenesses will have various aspects in various situations. The kind of likeness called εἰκών, by which things or people are pictured, differs from the kind by which a point becomes more credible (*probabilius*), and therefore εἰκών is used sparingly.

The reason for the inferiority of εἰκών to *similitudo* (either Quintilian's or the common παραβολή/*similitudo*) as an aid to proof is indicated by the example. The personal description is

---

[53] Probably C. Cassius Parmensis, a poet and dramatist of the second half of the first century B.C.

[54] Regius' emendation for the mss. *lanipedi*.

[55] My translation. Butler does not follow Regius' emendation.

metaphorical, making the εἰκών straightway less serviceable for proof than Quintilian's own *similitudo*. It is harder to detect what distinguishes the εἰκών from the common *similitudo*, but it would seem to be the lack of any real comparison in the εἰκών. A descriptive likeness is expressed but no specific comparison of two situations occurs, in contrast both to the example of the common *similitudo* in section 23 and to those that will be treated shortly in sections 24 and 25.

It should be noted here that the examination of *similitudo* in Book VIII will show that Quintilian is not presenting in this example of εἰκών the only type of stylistic figure "which expresses the appearance of things and persons." At 8.3.72 a definition of *similitudo* as an aid to embellishment is given that contains language very like the present definition of εἰκών.[56] In addition, it will be seen that most examples of the embellishing *similitudo* do make a specific comparison, not simply a descriptive likeness. Quintilian, therefore, although he does not state the connection directly, appears to be using εἰκών in the present passage to designate one type of the *similitudo* that will be treated eventually as a stylistic embellishment rather than as an aid to proof. Furthermore, his allegiance to the Aristotelian tradition displays itself again: in section 23 he has used παραβολή to denote a kind of comparison of proof (exactly Aristotle's use of the term), and here in section 24 he uses εἰκών to describe a kind of stylistic embellishment (again Aristotle's use of the term).

One further point. Quintilian states that εἰκών is to be employed more sparingly (*rarius*) than *similitudines* of proof. But more sparingly in what? The received text, followed by all editors, *in oratione* (in oratory), is at the least curious; a better reading may well be *in probatione* (in proof). Quintilian's whole work is on oratory—it is the *Institutio Oratoria*. It seems unlikely, in this footnote on a subdivision (the common παραβολή/simili-

[56] See below, p. 216; the similar words are *ad exprimendam rerum imaginem*, recalling the phrase here, *quo exprimitur rerum aut personarum imago*.

tudo) of a subdivision (Quintilian's own *similitudo*) of a subdivision (*exemplum* in its broad sense) of the topic of proof, that
Quintilian would make a statement applicable beyond the realm
of proof to all oratory. By contrast, *in probatione* restricts the footnote on εἰκών to the immediate major subject of proof. It warns
against frequent use of εἰκών as an aid to proof but does not ex-
clude the possibility that εἰκών might be suitably used in some
other part of oratory. And, as has been noted, a suitable part does
arise in the discussion in Book VIII of comparison as a stylistic
embellishment. Thus, the comprehensive phrase *in oratione* is not
only unlikely but also somewhat inaccurate; *in probatione* suffers
neither handicap.

Having finished his note on εἰκών, Quintilian returns to the
common παραβολή/*similitudo* and gives additional examples. The
last point made about the common *similitudo* was that it could be
drawn "from dumb animals and inanimate objects," and the
comparative parts of these additional examples put Quintilian's
point into practice: they are images of the soil, bees and ants, the
body, horses, and stones.

> ut, si animum dicas excolendum, similitudine utaris terrae, quae
> neglecta sentes ac dumos, culta fructus creat: aut, si ad curam rei
> publicae horteris, ostendas, apes etiam formicasque, non modo
> muta, sed etiam parva animalia, in commune tamen laborare. ex
> hoc genere dictum illud est Ciceronis: "ut corpora nostra sine
> mente, ita civitas sine lege suis partibus, ut nervis ac sanguine et
> membris, uti non potest".[57] sed ut hac corporis humani pro
> Cluentio, ita pro Cornelio equorum,[58] pro Archia[59] saxorum
> quoque usus est similitudine.   (5.11.24–25)

For instance, if you wish to argue that the mind requires cultivation, you would use a comparison drawn from the soil, which if

[57] *Pro Cluentio* 53.146.
[58] The precise reference is unknown since the *pro Cornelio* is lost.
[59] *Pro Archia* 8.19.

neglected produces thorns and thickets, but if cultivated will bear fruit; or if you are exhorting someone to enter the service of the state, you will point out that bees and ants, though not merely dumb animals, but tiny insects, still toil for the common weal. Of this kind is the saying of Cicero: "As our bodies can make no use of their members without a mind to direct them, so the state can make no use of its component parts, which may be compared to the sinews, blood and limbs, unless it is directed by law." And just as he draws this simile in the *pro Cluentio* from the analogy of the human body, so in the *pro Cornelio* he draws a simile from horses, and in the *pro Archia* from stones.

The deficiencies of the common παραβολή/*similitudo* as an aid to proof are clearly on view in these examples. There is obvious imparity between the subject parts (development of the mind, service to the state, and—in the *pro Archia* passage—the poet's art) and the comparative parts, which are drawn "from dumb animals and inanimate objects." In addition, metaphor is present in certain of the examples. A farming term, *excolendum* ("requires cultivation"), is applied to the development of the mind; similarly, in the *pro Cluentio* passage, the terms "sinews, blood, and limbs" apply literally to the body image and metaphorically to the subject of a state without laws. Of the two examples whose exact wording either is given or is known, the *pro Cluentio* passage has the form of a simile, the *pro Archia* passage does not. The reference in the latter is to that part of the famous defense of literature in which Cicero, first with a statement, then with a question, appeals to the jury not to be moved less by the words of poets than stones, wildernesses, and savage beasts are moved by voice and song. Quintilian is not alluding casually to a little-known passage. He quotes the same passage, accurately, in the discussion of *similitudo* in Book VIII.[60] This fact, coupled with the conditional form of the first example of the common παραβολή/

---

[60] 8.3.75; see below, p. 218.

similitudo in section 23, indicates that Quintilian regards the common *similitudo* as adhering to no set form.

At the beginning of section 26, Quintilian returns briefly to his own *similitudo* of proof in order to make a contrast with the examples of the common παραβολή/*similitudo* just given:

> illa, ut dixi, propiora: "ut remiges sine gubernatore, sic milites sine imperatore nihil valere".⁶¹   (5.11.26)

> Those [*similitudines*], as I have said, are closer, "as rowers without a pilot, so soldiers without a general are useless."⁶²

Propiora (closer) stands in clear contrast to *longius* (more disparate), which at the beginning of section 23 described the common *similitudo* of proof, and indicates that Quintilian is referring to his own more restricted, and more effective, *similitudo* of proof.⁶³ His whole treatment of *similitudines* of proof from sections 22 to 26 thus assumes a chiasmus: A (the special *similitudo*, section 22), B (the common *similitudo*, section 23), C (the footnote on εἰκών, section 24), B (the common *similitudo*, sections 24–25), A (the special *similitudo*, section 26). In the present passage, the example fulfills all the requirements set down by Quintilian in section 22 as desirable for his special *similitudo* of proof. There is no metaphorical admixture; the two parts of the comparison are "equal" in their parallel structure; and the subjects, rowers without a pilot and soldiers without a general, are also completely "equal" in that both refer to the same human condition of underlings without a leader. The form of the example is a simile, as was true also for Quintilian's earlier example of his special *similitudo*. Never-

⁶¹ Source unknown.

⁶² My translation, for the reason given in the following note.

⁶³ Translators have not understood this sequence. Spalding II 325 refers *illa, ut dixi, propiora* not back to section 22 but to the common *similitudo* of section 23. Watson, *Institutes of Oratory* I 368, translates: "Such as the following are, as I said, more ready to present themselves" (and he refers to Spalding's inaccurate note). Butler translates: "As I have already said, the following type of simile comes more readily to hand." Each fails to see the precise significance of *propiora*.

theless, he so clearly expresses interest only in the subject matter and metaphorical imagery, that is, the content, of his *similitudo* of proof that it seems fair not to ascribe any final significance to the common simile form of his two examples. In content his own *similitudo* of proof is severely limited; in form it probably can enjoy as much freedom as the common παραβολή/*similitudo*.

The positive part of Quintilian's discussion of the *similitudo* of proof ends with this brief second mention of his own special *similitudo*. The remaining sections, 26–31, set out features that Quintilian feels are not good for or germane to *similitudines* of proof. Faulty *similitudines* are taken up first:

> solent[64] tamen fallere similitudinum species, ideoque adhibendum est eis iudicium. neque enim ut navis utilior nova quam vetus, sic amicitia, vel, ut laudanda quae pecuniam suam pluribus largitur, ita quae formam. verba sunt in his similia vetustatis et largitionis, vis quidem longe diversa pecuniae et pudicitiae ⟨navis et amicitiae⟩,[65] itaque in hoc genere maxime quaeritur, an simile sit quod infertur.　　　　　　　　　　　　　　　　　　　　(5.11.26–27)

But the appearance of comparisons is apt to mislead us, and judgment is accordingly to be employed in the use of them; for we must not say that "as a new ship is more serviceable than an old one, so it is with friendship;" nor that, "as the woman is to be

[64] Since a whole new portion of the discussion of *similitudines* of proof begins at this point, Radermacher's text would be improved by a paragraph division as in Watson's translation.

[65] Radermacher attributes this addendum, which fills out the sense, to Spalding, but indicates that Spalding wishes to put the phrase before *pecuniae*. To the contrary, Spalding wishes the phrase to be placed exactly where Radermacher has put it, and he credits Gesner (1738 edition) as the first to sense the need for some addition. In fact, it *would* be better to place, as in Halm's 1868 edition, *navis et amicitiae* (the subjects of the first false *similitudo*) before *pecuniae et pudicitiae* (the subjects of the second false *similitudo*). As it stands, the logical addition is positioned illogically. Meister (1853) goes the other way, makes no addition, and deletes *pecuniae et pudicitiae*, so that only *vis quidem longe diversa* is left, but this seems excessive pruning. I am grateful to Mr. M. Winterbottom for correspondence on this crux and on other points in the present chapter.

commended who is liberal of her money to many, so also she who is liberal of her beauty." The allusions to age and liberality in these examples have a similarity; but their force is quite different, when applied to money and chastity, ships and friendship. Therefore in this type of proof the question is especially important whether what is adduced for comparison is similar.

By means of two (faulty) similes, Quintilian illustrates his warning that the presence or absence of similarity in a comparison must be judged carefully. The terms *similitudo* and *simile* are as strictly distinguished here as elsewhere in the chapter, *simile* meaning "similar" or "similarity," *similitudo* being the technical term for a comparison of proof.[66]

The remainder of section 27 and sections 28–29 refer to the Socratic method of interrogation in order to illustrate further the dangers of errant comparisons. The connection is indirect. Socratic questioning was not by *similitudo* but by ῥητορικὴ ἐπαγωγή (or *inductio*), as Quintilian has already remarked in section 3. But such questions often led the hapless victim into a flawed comparison, expressed or implied, and this is the connection with *similitudo* that Quintilian makes use of. Thus the wife of Xenophon, at the end of a series of questions, was once led by Aspasia into a position from which her next statement would have had to be, had she not defaulted by blushing: "Yes, I said I would prefer my neighbor's better gold and better ornaments to my own; now I must say that I would prefer her better husband to my own."[67] Quintilian's point is that Xenophon's wife had answered Aspasia's earlier questions from a covetous point of view and that therefore her final comparison must also be a covetous one (and imperfect as well, since the wish to exchange

---

[66] Butler is far from precise in distinguishing the two terms; hence the translation of the above passage is a combination of Watson's and my own.

[67] Quintilian's source for this piece of Socratic interrogation by Aspasia is *de Inv.* 1.31.51, where *inductio* is the topic under discussion. Cicero attributes the story to Aeschines Socraticus.

husbands did not really exist). He concludes by showing how Xenophon's wife could have answered in a manner becoming to a wife, thus creating a fitting *similitudo*:

> at, si respondisset, malle se aurum suum tale esse, quale illud esset, potuisset pudice respondere, malle se virum suum talem esse, qualis melior esset. (5.11.29)

> If on the other hand she had replied that she would prefer her ornaments to be of the same quality as those of her neighbour, she might have answered without putting herself to the blush that she would prefer her husband to be like him who was his superior in virtue.

This then is a *similitudo*, indirectly stated, which by careful *iudicium* (judgment) expresses what is really meant to be *simile* (similar).

Having spent four sections (26–29) on faulty *similitudines*, Quintilian proceeds to what is unessential in analyzing a *similitudo* of proof. He lists subdivisions of *similitudo* others have made that he regards as inconsequential, and his attitude toward these subdividers is expressed in the first and last sentences of the passage:

> Scio quosdam inani diligentia per minutissimas ista partis secuisse. . . . sed quid haec ad praesens propositum magnopere pertineant, non reperio. (5.11.30,31)

> I am aware that some writers have shown pedantic zeal in making a minute classification. . . . But I cannot see that such distinctions have any real bearing on the subject under discussion.

It is somewhat strange that Quintilian should scoff at this "minute classification," since it turns out essentially to be divisions of *similitudo* into *simile* (what is like), *dissimile* (what is unlike), and *contrarium* (what is contrary), and in section 5 he himself has said of *exemplum* in its broad sense (*similitudo* being a part of this type of *exemplum*) that "all arguments of this kind, therefore, must be

from things like or unlike or contrary."[68] The answer seems two-fold: Quintilian feels he has elucidated the *similitudo* of proof sufficiently and has no need for further, and less meaningful, categories. In addition, at least for his own *similitudo* of proof, the divisions of *simile*, *dissimile*, and *contrarium* are not really applicable. *Dissimile* and *contrarium* clearly conflict with his injunction in section 22 for comparisons of "things nearly equal"; and even in the subdivision of *simile* Quintilian reports that the "some writers" set up a category of *aliquid minus simile, ut simia homini* ("lesser similitude, such as that of a monkey to a man"), a category that may thus include comparison of "dumb animals" to humans and would be far from exemplary for Quintilian's own *similitudo* of proof.

It is impossible to identify securely the *quidam* ("some writers") whose minute divisions Quintilian rebukes. Several verbal affinities can be noted with different passages in Cicero, particularly from *de Inventione*.[69] Upon examination, however, Quintilian appears to be drawing upon the same kind of Hellenistic rhetorical categories as Cicero did rather than upon Cicero himself. Furthermore, Quintilian does not hesitate to refer to Cicero by name elsewhere even when disagreeing with him.[70] Though Cicero is possibly included in "some writers," it seems that the primary reference is to unnamed recent or contemporary critics.

With this criticism of unessential subdivisions of *similitudo*, Quintilian brings to a somewhat negative conclusion his analysis of the *similitudo* of proof. The next sections of chapter 11 continue discussion of *simile*, *dissimile*, and *contrarium*, but in a context in which Quintilian feels that such distinctions *are* applicable—in arguments of points of law. In section 34 it might be thought that Quintilian is commenting further on comparisons of proof:

---

[68] Above, p. 191.
[69] See especially *de Inv.* 1.28.42; also *Top.* 3.15, 11.46; *de Orat.* 2.40.168.
[70] For example, 3.2.4; 3.3.6; 4.2.64.

Analogian quidam a simili separaverunt, nos eam subiectam huic generi putamus. nam ut unum ad decem, est ad decem centum simile certe: est et, ut hostis, sic malus civis.

Some have separated analogy from similitude; I consider it comprehended in similitude. For when we say, As one is to ten, so are ten to a hundred, there is a similitude, as much as there is when we say, As is an enemy, so is a bad citizen.[71]

Two brief similes are adduced, but the use of the term *simile* rather than *similitudo* creates an initial suspicion that Quintilian is simply presenting analogy as part of the argument of likeness; the next sentences corroborate the suspicion by commenting first on the greater range of *simile* than *analogia*, and then continuing with remarks and examples of *dissimile* and *contrarium*.

Quintilian's first major discussion of comparison has contained careful analysis and considerable understanding of comparison as an aid to proof. His second extended discussion is in Book VIII, but in between a few sections in chapter 3 of Book VI need comment. The topic of the whole chapter is the ability to excite laughter in a judge or an audience. Sections 53–56 deal generally with jests on names, which Quintilian regards as something less than the best kind of humor. Even Cicero's famous banter over the name of Verres is not praised, and the single play on a name that Quintilian does consider happy seems rather flat:

. . . ut pro Caecina Cicero in testem Sex. Clodium Phormionem: "nec minus niger", inquit, "nec minus confidens quam est ille Terentianus Phormio".[72]   (6.3.56)

. . . when Cicero in the *pro Caecina* says of the witness Sextus Clodius Phormio, "He was not less black or less bold than the Phormio of Terence."

[71] Watson's translation.
[72] *Pro Caecina* 10.27. Butler notes that the reference probably is not to Phormio's natural color but to his stage makeup.

Section 57 moves on to what Quintilian regards as a better and livelier type of jest, that which is drawn from the particular force of things:

> Acriora igitur sunt et elegantiora quae trahuntur ex vi rerum. in iis maxime valet similitudo, si tamen ad aliquid inferius levi-usque referatur: qualia veteres illi iocabantur, qui Lentulum "Spintherem" et Scipionem "Serapionem"[73] esse dixerunt. sed ea non ab hominibus modo petitur, verum etiam ab animalibus, ut nobis pueris Iunius Bassus, homo in primis dicax, "asinus albus"[74] vocabatur, et Sarmentus * * *[75] sicut P. Blaesius Iulium, hominem nigrum et macrum et pandum, "fibulam ferream" dixit. (6.3.57–58)

We may note therefore that jests which turn on the meaning of things are at once more pointed and more elegant. In such cases resemblances between things produce the best effects, more especially if we refer to something of an inferior or more trivial nature, as in the jests of which our forefathers were so fond, when they called Lentulus Spinther and Scipio Serapio. But such jests may be drawn not merely from the names of men, but from animals as well; for example when I was a boy, Junius Bassus, one of the wittiest of men, was nicknamed the white ass. And Sarmentus * * * for example Publius Blessius called a certain Julius, who was dark, lean and bent, the iron buckle.

Despite Butler's "resemblances between things," *similitudo* is better taken as "comparison" or "figures of comparison." Several comparisons are expressed, in the form of metaphorical

---

[73] Valerius Maximus 9.14.3–4 explains Lentulus' epithet as deriving from his resemblance to a bad actor named Spinther, and Scipio's from his resemblance to a dealer in sacrificial animals named Serapio.

[74] The precise point of the epithet is in doubt but lies perhaps in the fact that Junius brays constantly but is a white (man).

[75] Radermacher's asterisks. He rightly supposes a lacuna here; for his conjecture, see text below.

epithets.[76] A more conventional statement of comparison probably stood in the lacuna. It has been masterfully filled by Radermacher,[77] who found an indication of what it should contain from Horace, *Satires* 1.5.56–57:

> prior Sarmentus: "equi te[78]
> esse feri similem dico. . . ."

And first Sarmentus says, "I claim you are like a unicorn. . . ."

From this he conjectured *et Sarmentus ⟨Messium Cicirrum equo fero comparavit⟩*,[79] "and Sarmentus ⟨compared Messius Cicirrus to a unicorn⟩." He noticed further that Quintilian had drawn his first examples from human beings ("they called Lentulus Spinther and Scipio Serapio"), his next examples from animals ("Junius Bassus . . . was nicknamed the white ass" and now "and Sarmentus ⟨compared Messius Cicirrus to a unicorn⟩"), and his final example from inanimate life ("Blessius called a certain Julius . . . the iron buckle"). This sequence reminded him of Quintilian's phrase on the common παραβολή/*similitudo* at 5.11.23, "nor does it merely compare the actions of men . . . [but is] sometimes drawn from dumb animals and inanimate objects" (*sed et a mutis atque etiam inanimis . . . ducitur*), and he therefore completed the conjecture, *et Sarmentus ⟨Messium Cicirrum equo fero comparavit. ducitur et ab inanimis⟩ sicut P. Blaesius . . .* ("the comparison may also be drawn from inanimate objects: for example Publius Blessius . . ."). The resemblance to 5.11.23 surely exists

---

[76] All these apparently represent another of the infrequent Latin recollections of the Greek Old Comedy game of εἰκάζειν-ἀντεικάζειν (comparison-retorting comparison). For an earlier Latin instance, see Cicero, *de Orat.* 2.66.265–266 (above, chap. IV n. 39).

[77] What follows is an expansion of what is implied in Radermacher's critical note.

[78] The *te*, as Horace's surrounding verses show, is Messius Cicirrus.

[79] The Horatian passage might rather suggest a reading, *et Sarmentus ⟨Messium Cicirrum equi feri similem esse dixit⟩*.

and connects the present use of *similitudo* with the earlier clearly figurative sense of the term.

Quintilian's next comment, while difficult, again gives to *similitudo* a figurative meaning, not just a general sense of "resemblance":

adhibetur autem similitudo interim palam, interim inseri[80] solet parabolae: cuius est generis illud Augusti, qui militi libellum timide porrigenti: "noli", inquit, "tamquam assem elephanto des". (6.3.59)

Such comparisons[81] may be put to the service of wit either openly or allusively. Of the latter type is the remark of Augustus, made to a soldier who showed signs of timidity in presenting a petition, "Don't hold it out as if you were giving a penny to an elephant."

The difficulty of the passage lies in the precise significance of *parabolae* ("allusively"). Quintilian appears to be employing the term quite differently from his use of παραβολή in 5.11.23 as a synonym for the common *similitudo* of proof. Here, *parabola* is a subordinate characteristic of the *similitudo* of jest. Some such *similitudines* are expressed openly ("they called Lentulus Spinther," for example), some by *parabola*, and the comparison that follows is allusive and inferential. Such a meaning for *parabola* is odd indeed. It might be argued that the transliterated *parabola* can bear a quite separate sense from the Greek παραβολή, but at 8.3.77[82] *parabola* will occur in a very analogous sense to that of παραβολή at 5.11.23. The exact nature of the *similitudo* of jest stated by *parabola* remains vague.[83]

---

[80] Regius' emendation of the mss. *serio* or *inserio*.

[81] Butler once again translates by "resemblances."

[82] See below, p. 221.

[83] In fact, as Regius' emendation shows, the text here is vexed and the trouble may well extend to *parabolae*. The next mention of *similitudo* supplies a possible emendation; see the next paragraph and note.

The chapter goes on in the next sections to a different classification of humor, but a classification of a familiar type, that of *simile, dissimile,* and *contrarium.* As in 5.11, so here *simile* is not a synonym for *similitudo.* The terms are not quite so clearly separated as they were in the earlier book, however, and within the analysis of *simile* there is a brief return to the *similitudo* of humor. In section 62 Quintilian remarks:

> iungitur amphiboliae similitudo,[84] ut a Gabba, qui pilam negligenter petenti: "sic", inquit, "petis, tamquam Caesaris candidatus". nam illud "petis" ambiguum est, securitas similis.

> Comparison[85] and ambiguity may be used in conjunction: Gabba for example said to a man who stood very much at his ease when playing ball, "You stand as if you were one of Caesar's candidates." The ambiguity lies in the word *stand*, while the indifference shown by the player supplies the resemblance.

Both *similitudo* (the example of which is an ambiguous, jesting simile) and a brief note in section 61 on the *translatio* of humor come within the larger category of humor depending on *simile* (likeness, resemblance). The proximate mention of *translatio* and *similitudo* brings metaphor and a term of comparison into collocation, as at 4.1.70,[86] but there is no ensuing discussion that might develop the connection further.[87]

---

[84] This connection of *similitudo* with *amphibolia* (ambiguity), accompanied by an example rather similar to the example of the *similitudo* stated by *parabola*, suggests that in section 59 an easier sense would arise through reading . . . *interim inseri solet amphiboliae* ("such comparisons may be put to the service of wit either openly or through ambiguity").

[85] Butler continues to translate *similitudo*, too broadly, as "resemblance," which is the proper meaning, as he himself indicates, of *similis* at the end of the passage.

[86] See above, p. 185.

[87] Neither Butler nor Watson thinks that *translatio* is being used by Quintilian in the sense of "metaphor." They both translate by "application." But two examples that follow are both metaphorical likenesses, and the figurative use of the term appears likely.

Quintilian's second major analysis of comparison is presented in chapter 3 of Book VIII. The chapter is devoted wholly to the subject of embellishment or ornament (*ornatus*) in oratory. One of the excellences of embellishment is vivid illustration (ἐνάργεια or *repraesentatio*), which commands attention more than mere clarity (*perspicuitas*) can.[88] Quintilian spends several sections on this form of embellishment, concluding with the statement that there is no higher excellence in oratory and that it is far from unattainable if only we look to and follow nature.[89]

Another of the excellences of *ornatus*, closely related to ἐνάργεια but aiming particularly at the illumination of things, is *similitudo*. Quintilian's first sentences on this division of embellishment show him fully conscious of its relation to the *similitudo* of proof:

> Praeclare vero ad inferendam rebus lucem repertae sunt similitudines: quarum aliae sunt, quae probationis gratia inter argumenta ponuntur, aliae ad exprimendam rerum imaginem[90] compositae, quod est huius loci proprium:
>
> inde lupi ceu
raptores atra in nebula[91]
>
> et
>
> avi similis, quae circum litora, circum
piscosos scopulos humilis volat aequora iuxta.[92]
>
> (8.3.72)

The invention of *similitudines*[93] has also provided an admirable means of illuminating our descriptions. Some of these are designed

---

[88] 8.3.61.

[89] 8.3.71.

[90] *Imago* is used here not as a term of comparison but in a nonfigurative sense of "picture," "likeness."

[91] *Aeneid* 2.355–356.

[92] *Ibid.* 4.254–255.

[93] Butler regularly translates *similitudo* throughout these sections by "simile." As will be seen, this is misleading; I regularly substitute the Latin term. Occasionally other minor changes are made from Butler's translations.

for insertion among our arguments to help our proof, while others are devised to make our pictures yet more vivid; it is with this latter class that I am now specially concerned. The following are good examples:—

> "Thence like fierce wolves beneath the cloud of night,"

or

> "Like the bird that flies
> Around the shore and the fish-haunted reef,
> Skimming the deep."

Quintilian explicitly associates his present kind of *similitudo* with the *similitudo* of proof while characterizing the two as different in purpose. Less explicitly, he portrays the *similitudo* of embellishment as similar in descriptive purpose to εἰκών, as the term was defined at 5.11.24. The verbally analogous phrases are: for εἰκών, *quo exprimitur rerum aut personarum imago*; for *similitudo, aliae ad exprimendam rerum imaginem compositae*. Quintilian's position seems to be that, broadly speaking, he is now taking up treatment of the figure that would be termed εἰκών by the Greeks. The equivalence remains an implied one, however, and is by no means total. Quintilian at no point in the sections on the *similitudo* of embellishment uses the term εἰκών; he only recalls its definition in the language of the definition of *similitudo*. Furthermore, at 5.11.24 εἰκών is, in its sphere of applicability, set quite apart from the *similitudo* of proof. On the other hand, in the discussion of the embellishing *similitudo* Quintilian will at times appear to regard it as bordering upon and almost interchangeable with the *similitudo* of proof—a situation that in 5.11.24 does not seem possible between εἰκών and the *similitudo* of proof.

Having made an opening definition of the *similitudo* of embellishment and illustrated it with two Vergilian similes, Quintilian plunges into more detailed analysis:

quo in genere id est praecipue custodiendum, ne id, quod similitudinis gratia adscivimus, aut obscurum sit aut ignotum: debet enim quod inlustrandae alterius rei gratia adsumitur, ipsum esse clarius eo, quod inluminat. quare poetis quidem permittamus sane eius modi exempla:

> qualis, ubi hibernam Lyciam Xanthique fluenta
> deserit aut Delum maternam invisit, Apollo.[94]

non idem oratorem decebit, ut occultis aperta demonstret.

(8.3.73–74)

In employing this form of ornament we must be especially careful that the matter chosen for our *similitudo* is neither obscure nor unfamiliar: for anything that is selected for the purpose of illuminating something else must itself be clearer than that which it is designed to illustrate. Therefore while we may permit poets to employ such *similitudines* as:—

> "As when Apollo wintry Lycia leaves,
> And Xanthus' streams, or visits Delos' isle,
> His mother's home,"

it would be quite unsuitable for an orator to illustrate something quite plain by such obscure allusions.

This is the first statement in ancient criticism that in oratory the comparative part of a comparison should be clearer than the subject part. It is impossible to say, of course, whether Quintilian is being truly original or is following some unknown predecessor. Most of the *Institutio* is, in one way or another, derivative. Still, the possibility should be left open that the present remark arises wholly from his own reflection. A second point is that Quintilian does here what he will also do elsewhere in his discussion of the *similitudo* of *ornatus*: he breaks a comparison into its two parts, subject and comparative, and for lack of another word he uses the term of the whole comparison (*similitudo*) for the comparative part only. It will be seen in section 77 that difficulty arises when he wishes to refer in the same phrase both to the whole comparison and to its comparative part.

[94] *Aeneid* 4.143–144.

Thirdly, Quintilian is already beginning to vacillate in his separation of the practical and stylistic sides of oratory. If the purpose of an embellishing *similitudo* is vivid illumination it should make no difference whether the comparative part is plain or obscure, so long as a certain brilliant atmosphere is created. Indeed, earlier, in his treatment of ἐνάργεια (8.3.61), he has said that vivid description does even more for style than mere clarity can. The same should hold true for a vivid *similitudo* of embellishment, and it should not be necessary to require the comparative part to be *clarius* (clearer) than the subject part. But the practical side of Quintilian's overall understanding of *similitudo* as an element of prose oratory has come to the fore, and in this passage he partially unites the *similitudines* of embellishment and proof by unexpectedly limiting the structural range of the embellishing *similitudo* in oratory, if not in poetry.

If the above passage lessened the distance between *similitudines* of proof and embellishment by limiting the scope of the latter, Quintilian's next remarks appear to strive for the same end by expanding the ornamental character of the former. The result is somewhat ambiguous:

> sed illud quoque, de quo in argumentis diximus, similitudinis genus ornat orationem facitque sublimem, floridam, iucundam, mirabilem. nam quo quaeque longius petita est, hoc plus adfert novitatis atque inexpectata magis est. illa volgaria videri possunt et utilia tantum ad conciliandum fidem: "ut terram cultu, sic animum disciplinis meliorem uberioremque fieri",[95] et "ut medici abalienata morbis membra praecidant, ita turpes ac perniciosos, etiam si nobis sanguine cohaereant, amputandos".[96] iam sublimius illud pro Archia:[97] "saxa atque solitudines voci respondent, bestiae saepe inmanes cantu flectuntur atque consistunt" et cetera.
>
> (8.3.74–75)

[95] Source unknown.
[96] Source unknown.
[97] *Pro Archia* 8.19.

But even the type of *similitudo* which I discussed in connection with arguments is an ornament to oratory, and serves to make it sublime, rich, attractive or striking, as the case may be. For the more remote the *similitudo* is from the subject to which it is applied, the greater will be the impression of novelty and the unexpected which it produces. The following type may be regarded as commonplace and useful only as helping to create an impression of sincerity: "As the soil is improved and rendered more fertile by culture, so is the mind by education," or "As physicians amputate mortified limbs, so must we lop away foul and dangerous criminals, even though they be bound to us by ties of blood." Far finer is the following from Cicero's defence of Archias: "Rock and deserts reply to the voice of man, savage beasts are oft-times tamed by the power of music and stay their onslaught," and the rest.

To what part of 5.11 does "the type of *similitudo* which I discussed in connexion with arguments" refer? It is easy to assume, as Butler does in a note, that Quintilian has in mind 5.11.22, namely his own *similitudo* of proof. Surely better, however, is to refer the phrase to the analysis of the common παραβολή/*similitudo* in 5.11.23–25; both the language and the examples of the present passage lead to this conclusion. Quintilian says: "For the more remote (*longius*) the *similitudo* is. . . ." The same word was used in 5.11.23 as the key to distinguishing between the παραβολή/*similitudo* and Quintilian's special *similitudo*; it meant that the two parts of the comparison were not "equal" and that there might be an admixture of metaphor. All three examples here illustrate both traits: they compare mute or inanimate objects (the soil, diseased limbs, stones and beasts) to active human qualities (the mind, wicked people, a jury). In addition, they all contain metaphor: the application of "more fertile" to the mind, of "lop away" to criminals, and (less strongly) of "reply" to rocks and deserts. Furthermore, the first of the examples is almost identical to a παραβολή/*similitudo* indirectly reported in 5.11.24:

"if you wish to argue that the mind requires cultivation, you would use a comparison drawn from the soil . . ." and the last example is precisely the same passage from *pro Archia* that was alluded to at 5.11.25.

Strictly speaking, these examples do not illustrate the *similitudo* of embellishment but the *similitudo* of proof which "is an ornament to oratory" (*ornat orationem*). But clearly this very characteristic serves to make them at the same time examples of proof *and* embellishment. The lines between the two have for the moment virtually disappeared. This is stressed in the next section: Quintilian moves on to the topic of faulty *similitudines* of embellishment without indicating in any way that he has done with ornamental *similitudines* of proof and is returning to embellishment. He can do this without confusion only because in a real sense the examples cover both areas.

Quintilian proceeds to lament the use of faulty embellishing *similitudines* by certain declaimers of the day:

> quod quidem genus a quibusdam declamatoria maxime licentia corruptum est: nam et falsis utuntur, nec illa iis, quibus similia videri volunt, adplicant. quorum utrumque in his est, quae me iuvene ubique cantari solebant: "magnorum fluminum navigabiles fontes sunt", et "generosioris arboris statim planta cum fructu est."[98]　　　　　　　　　　　　　　　　　　　　　(8.3.76)

This type of *similitudo* has, however, sadly degenerated in the hands of some of our declaimers owing to the license of the schools. For they adopt false comparisons, and even then do not apply them as they should to the subjects to which they wish them to provide a parallel. Both these faults are exemplified in two *similitudines* which were on the lips of everyone when I was a young man, "Even the sources of mighty rivers are navigable," and "The truly generous tree bears fruit while it is yet a sapling."

[98] Sources of these two faulty *similitudines* unknown.

Just as he dealt with imperfect *similitudines* of proof in 5.11.27–29, so now Quintilian comes to the corresponding embellishing *similitudines*. He censures not only their falseness but also their incorrect application. It is not true to say either that the very springs of great rivers are navigable or that fruit appears even on the young shoot of a superior tree. Conversely, "navigable" and "fruit" have been applied wrongly, since the spring of a river is not after all similar to something navigable nor is a young shoot similar to something with fruit. Nevertheless, despite their flaws the examples are still descriptive in nature; they attempt to express the appearance of things (the *rerum imaginem* of section 72); and in their freely metaphorical form they recall both the form and character of εἰκών in 5.11.24. In a word, they are still definitely *similitudines* of embellishment.

Quintilian now approaches his last important piece of analysis of the embellishing *similitudo*. The particular element to be analyzed is both preceded and succeeded by tantalizing statements of certain other elements whose significance is never treated in any detail. Section 77 begins with the first of these:

> in omni autem parabole aut praecedit similitudo, res sequitur, aut praecedit res et similitudo sequitur.

> In every comparison the *similitudo* either precedes or follows the subject which it illustrates.

It is here that Quintilian faces the difficulty, mentioned in connection with sections 73–74, of having to refer in the same phrase both to the whole of a comparison and also just to the comparative part. The latter, being the indispensable unit of a comparison, is described by *similitudo*; the former receives an alternate term, *parabole*. The precise reason for Quintilian's choice of the term must be left unsettled. There is little in common between its present use and the only other appearance of the transliterated term, at 6.3.59.[99] It has more affinity with the use of παραβολή

[99] See above, p. 213.

at 5.11.23, which also denoted a certain kind of whole comparison, though one of proof.[100] But, at least in part, Quintilian reaches for an additional term of comparison without having coordinated its use and meaning throughout the *Institutio*.

A few lines after the above passage, in section 78, Quintilian illustrates the two possible sequences of subject and comparative parts. For the order *similitudo*/subject he reuses *Aeneid* 2.355–356, which earlier formed his initial example of an embellishing *similitudo*. For the order subject/*similitudo* he uses *Georgics* 1.512–514. The illustrations are interesting but insufficient. What is really called for is some statement of the difference, if any, that results from the use of one order or the other: for example, is one more fitting than the other in a *similitudo* of embellishment? There is no such statement, indicating perhaps that Quintilian sees no difference; but if this is so, it seems somewhat profitless to have presented the two orders so explicitly. More probably he has a definite distinction in mind but simply does not expand on it. The whole analysis of the embellishing *similitudo* is marked by brevity, and not every statement is amplified adequately. The last feature to be mentioned, in section 81, will display the same unsatisfactory character.

Between his statement of the two orders of the embellishing *similitudo* and his examples of them, Quintilian begins to describe what he considers the finest relation between subject and comparative parts. He prefaces the description with a brief mention of still a third possible order:

> sed interim libera et separata est, interim, quod longe optimum est, cum re, cuius est imago, conectitur, conlatione invicem respondente, quod facit redditio contraria, quae ἀνταπόδοσις dicitur.
>
> (8.3.77)

---

[100] In other words, the Greek term and one transliterated instance stand allied to some degree against the other transliterated instance. This seems illogical, but it may easily be due to the transmission of the text. Perhaps Quintilian himself used the Greek term in all three passages, but only one survived the copyists.

But sometimes it is free and detached, and sometimes, a far better arrangement, is attached to the subject which it illustrates, the correspondence between the resemblances being exact, an effect produced by reciprocal representation, which the Greeks style ἀνταπόδοσις.

"Free and detached" would seem to refer back to the kind of order displayed by the faulty *similitudines* in section 76. They were flat descriptive statements ("even the sources of mighty rivers are navigable"), and there was no indication of the subject to which they were the comparative part. Thus, the *similitudo* was "detached" from the subject (*res*). This division shows in turn that there, also, Quintilian was using *similitudo* in its sense of the "comparative part" of an embellishing *similitudo*.

The main portion of the above passage describes with a flurry of terms a certain relation between *similitudo* and subject that creates what is called *redditio contraria* or ἀνταπόδοσις. Not only these but also other technical terms occur. *Imago*, as in the opening definition of the embellishing *similitudo*, does not denote a figure but means simply "image," "illustration." *Collatio*, which Quintilian mentioned at 5.11.23 as Cicero's term for a *similitudo* of proof, is used here not as any sort of rival figure of comparison to *similitudo*, but rather quite independently to describe the way in which a *similitudo* of *redditio contraria* works. Its broad meaning is "comparison"[101] and its phrase may be rendered "with comparative details answering each other" or, with Butler, "the correspondence between the resemblances being exact." *Redditio contraria* and ἀνταπόδοσις are striking terms. The former seems to be found only in the present passage, the latter (until the late

---

[101] At 7.7.2, *collatio* again appears in a general sense of "comparison." Specifically, it denotes a setting of two things side by side, whether they are like or unlike, for the purpose of comparison but without any attempt to create a figure of comparison. It will be seen (below, pp. 231–234) that this is also the regular meaning of *comparatio* in the *Institutio*.

technical treatises) only in *On Style*,[102] where it occurs in sections 23 and 250, referring in each case to a correspondence between the various elements of contrasting or antithetical clauses. Quintilian gives the term a similar sense but connects it with embellishing comparisons.[103]

Two questions are appropriate: did Quintilian know of the term ἀνταπόδοσις from *On Style*, and is *redditio contraria* his own translation? Though uncertainty must linger, the likelihood of both possibilities is good. The first point may serve as yet another indication of an early empire date for *On Style*. The second would appear to credit Quintilian with a minor innovation in rhetorical terminology. The actual kind of comparison he is describing, on the other hand, was recognized as a distinctive type as early as *ad Herennium*, where it formed the fourth class of embellishing *similitudines*.[104]

After Quintilian gives his examples, mentioned above, of the orders *similitudo*/subject and subject/*similitudo*, he returns to the comparison containing ἀνταπόδοσις. His first sentence makes it very clear that this type of comparison does not involve any specific sequence of subject and comparative parts, for he says of the two examples just given:

sed hae sunt sine antapodosi.   (8.3.79)

There is, however, no *antapodosis* in these.

[102] See above, p. 139. There are several instances of the term in the late treatises. The verb ἀνταποδιδόναι, it will be recalled, appears early, in Aristotle's *Rhetoric* 3.4.1407a16 (above, p. 45).

[103] The definition given the term by Ernesti 25 is somewhat inaccurate: "Hinc ἀνταπόδοσις dicitur in comparatione et similitudine, *redditio*, h. e. altera illius pars, quae particulis *ita, sic* insignitur. De qua vid. Quintil. VIII 3.78 sqq." It is not just the presence of the subject part of a comparison that creates ἀνταπόδοσις, but the detailed correspondence between subject and comparative parts.

[104] *Ad Her.* 4.47.60; above, p. 73. The fact that neither *redditio contraria* nor ἀνταπόδοσις appears in *ad Herennium* is an *argumentum ex silentio*, but a good one, for early empire introduction of both terms into the rhetorical vocabulary. But, ἀνταπόδοσις occurs in a nonrhetorical sense as early as Aristotle.

He then redescribes the fine effect of *redditio contraria*, points out that Vergil exemplifies it outstandingly but that he will draw from oratory, and quotes a simile from *pro Murena*:

> redditio autem illa rem utramque, quam comparat, velut subicit oculis et pariter ostendit. cuius praeclara apud Vergilium multa reperio exempla, sed oratoriis potius utendum est. dicit Cicero pro Murena:[105] "ut aiunt in Graecis artificibus eos auloedos esse, qui citharoedi fieri non potuerint: sic nos videmus, qui oratores evadere non potuerint, eos ad iuris studium devenire." (8.3.79)

Such reciprocal representation places both subjects of comparison before our very eyes, displaying them side by side. Virgil provides many remarkable examples, but it will be better for me to quote from oratory. In the *pro Murena* Cicero says, "As among Greek musicians (for so they say), only those turn flute-players that cannot play the lyre, so here at Rome we see that those who cannot acquire the art of oratory betake themselves to the study of the law."

What Quintilian means by "reciprocal representation" is easily seen in the corresponding details of the *pro Murena* passage. This is the case also in a second example, again from *pro Murena*, which Quintilian prefaces with a significant remark:

> illud pro eodem iam paene poetico spiritu, sed tamen cum sua redditione, quod est ad ornatum accommodatius: "nam ut tempestates saepe certo aliquo caeli signo commoventur, saepe inproviso nulla ex certa ratione obscura aliqua ex causa concitantur: sic in hac comitiorum tempestate populari saepe intellegas, quo signo commota sit, saepe ita obscura est, ut sine causa excitata videatur."[106] (8.3.80)

There is also another *similitudo* in the same speech, which is almost worthy of a poet, but in virtue of its reciprocal representation is

---

[105] *Pro Murena* 13.29.
[106] *Ibid.*, 17.36.

better adapted for ornament: "For as tempests are generally preceded by some premonitory signs in the heaven, but often, on the other hand, break forth for some obscure reason without any warning whatsoever, so in the tempests which sway the people at our Roman elections we are not seldom in a position to discern their origin, and yet, on the other hand, it is frequently so obscure that the storm seems to have burst without any apparent cause."

Once again, as in section 73, Quintilian appears to place structural limits on an embellishing *similitudo* in oratory, and again his comments effectually unite *similitudines* of embellishment and proof. The *pro Murena* simile is almost poetic, he says, but the presence of *redditio contraria* makes it suited for oratorical ornament. The poetic aspect would seem to arise from the boldness of comparing meteorological phenomena to the emotional workings of the *comitia* and from the metaphorical application of "tempests" and "storm" to human tumult. But these "poetic" elements that, when combined with *redditio contraria*, produce a splendid embellishing *similitudo* are exactly what marked the common *similitudo* of proof—disparate subject matter and metaphorical admixture.

Thus, Quintilian comes near suggesting that the *similitudo* of embellishment is at its finest when it is most similar to a *similitudo* of proof. There is a curiously double nature to his whole discussion. The opening definition of the embellishing *similitudo* clearly seeks to distinguish its nature from the *similitudo* of proof. This distinction is furthered by ambiguity in the application of the term *similitudo*. At the beginning of the analysis, *similitudo* appears to refer to the whole of a comparison; but it refers increasingly only to the comparative part as opposed to the subject part, and in section 77 Quintilian goes so far as to apply another term, *parabole*, to the whole comparison. The emphasis on the comparative part of an embellishing *similitudo* is also demonstrated by the examples. Until he comes to those containing *redditio contraria*, with two exceptions he quotes only comparative parts of comparisons. The exceptions are the two examples in section 75 which are *utilia tantum ad conciliandum fidem* ("useful only as helping to create an impression of sincerity"), but these, as noted earlier, are just as much examples of *similitudines* of proof. These two and the two containing *redditio contraria*, the four examples closest to *similitudines* of proof (in which a consistent resemblance throughout the comparison is important), quote both subject and comparative parts. All the other, more pointedly embellishing *similitudines*, in which the actual descriptive comparison is central, present just that part; and the term itself virtually means "comparative part of a comparison." On the one hand, Quintilian establishes these very definite differences between *similitudines* of proof and embellishment; on the other, the embellishing *similitudo* praised most highly is that which possesses *redditio contraria* and which, as a result, approaches becoming a *similitudo* of proof. It is a strange twist that the culminating *similitudo* of embellishment is the one most analogous to a *similitudo* of proof, but it is another indication of Quintilian's basically practical, rather than stylistic, bias throughout the *Institutio*.

Quintilian appends a last comment to his discussion that is as disappointingly incomplete as are his remarks on the possible orders of a comparison. Section 81 states:

> sunt et illae breves: "vagi per silvas ritu ferarum",[107] et illud Ciceronis in Clodium:[108] "quo ex iudicio velut ex incendio nudus effugit." quibus similia possunt cuicumque etiam ex cotidiano sermone succurrere.

> We find also shorter ones, such as "Wandering like wild beasts through the woods," or the passage from Cicero's speech against Clodius: "He fled from the court like a man escaping naked from

[107] Source unknown.
[108] The speech is lost.

a fire." Similar examples from everyday speech will occur to everyone.

Illae breves ("shorter ones") might be taken to refer to short *similitudines* of *redditio contraria*, but the absence from the examples of any structure of detailed correspondence makes it certain that the words refer instead to brief embellishing *similitudines* in general. For the second time—the first being in *On Style*—an explicit distinction is drawn between shorter and longer comparisons.[109] The author of *On Style* regarded this distinction as momentous enough to warrant different terms, εἰκασία and παραβολή, for the two types. Quintilian supplies no noun to *illae breves*, but his whole approach to comparison has been unitarian, and *similitudines* is surely the noun to be understood. Apart from this we are eager, in vain, for further analysis beyond the mere fact that there are short *similitudines* that are easily called up from daily speech. Nothing more is offered, and again the overall brevity of Quintilian's discussion of the *similitudo* of embellishment (a bare two and a half pages of text) seems the reason. All his comments vary in sparseness rather than thoroughness.

In Quintilian's second main treatment of comparison, the majority of examples are cast in the form of similes; but, as with the *similitudo* of proof, so here the indications are strong that there is no particular restriction on the form of an embellishing *similitudo*. Certain of the examples (for example, that from the *pro Archia* and the two that are faulty in application) are broadly comparative in their form; in addition, as in Book V, there is simply no hint in Quintilian's text of interest in verbal form.[110]

---

[109] This shared point may form an argument for dating *On Style* relatively close to the *Institutio*.

[110] Thus, not only Butler in his Loeb translation but also J. W. H. Atkins, *Literary Criticism in Antiquity* (Cambridge, Eng., 1934) II 270, seems restrictive in his repeated use of "simile" to describe Quintilian's remarks on *similitudo* in 8.3.72–81. "Embellishing comparison" would be better.

All this seems negated in chapter 6 of Book VIII, where a final important mention of *similitudo* occurs. The term is connected with metaphor. The same connection has been met at 4.1.70 and 6.3.61–62,[111] but not in the two major discussions of *similitudo*. Chapter 6 deals with tropes, and an analysis of metaphor as a trope occupies sections 4–18. Quintilian pauses in the middle for a general reflection:

> in totum autem metaphora brevior est similitudo eoque distat, quod illa comparatur rei, quam volumus exprimere, haec pro ipsa re dicitur. comparatio est, cum dico fecisse quid hominem "ut leonem", translatio, cum dico de homine "leo est".   (8.6.8–9)

On the whole metaphor is a shorter form of simile, while there is this further difference, that in the latter we compare some object to the thing which we wish to describe, whereas in the former this object is actually substituted for the thing. It is a comparison when I say that a man did something *like a lion*, it is a metaphor when I say of him, *He is a lion*.

The most striking point is that Quintilian says *similitudo/comparatio* differs from *metaphora/translatio* only by the addition of an introductory word of comparison, apparently defining simile. Other implications of the passage should, however, be glanced at before this is discussed more fully.

Quintilian's examples plainly stand in the Aristotelian tradition. Part of Aristotle's opening definition of εἰκών ran: "When the poet says of Achilles that he 'leapt on the foe as a lion,' this is an εἰκών; when he says of him 'the lion leapt,' it is a metaphor."[112] Though Quintilian's wording is not identical, the similarity is unmistakable.[113] At the same time, the first phrase of the passage opposes and reverses Aristotle. Quintilian starts his discussion of

---

111 See above, pp. 185 and 214.

112 *Rhet.* 3.4.1406b21–22.

113 The allegiance is even more noteworthy if Teichert 28 is correct in asserting that this particular example does not occur in other writers.

metaphor in section 4 with extravagant praise of it as both the most common and the most beautiful of all tropes and as so pleasing and elegant that it will shine forth even in the most distinguished speech. Thus far, his views coincide with Aristotle's own fervent belief in the value of metaphor. But when Aristotle, within his analysis of metaphor, came to treat εἰκών, he distinctly and repeatedly relegated it to a position of subordination to metaphor. Quintilian's statement is quite definitely on the other side: *in totum autem metaphora brevior est similitudo* ("on the whole metaphor is a shorter form of *similitudo*"). He does not say *brevior est quam similitudo* or *brevior est similitudine* ("shorter *than similitudo*"), which would put metaphor and *similitudo* on an equal footing. Thus, no matter how glorious and important a trope metaphor is, it still fits within the larger category of *similitudo*. Quintilian does not state whether he is discussing more a *similitudo* of proof or one of embellishment. Metaphors that are purely ornamental are illustrated in the section immediately preceding, so that one might guess that Quintilian has in mind the embellishing *similitudo*; but it is most probable that the term refers widely to both proof and ornament.

We have already seen one reversal of the Aristotelian hierarchy in the vexed passage at *de Oratore* 3.39.157.[114] It suffices here to repeat that Quintilian's sentences more reasonably support the authenticity than the spuriousness of the Ciceronian passage. If Aristotle and Quintilian are the two most important figures of antiquity for ideas of comparison, with the author of *On Style* and Cicero occupying the second rank, an interesting division emerges between the view of the major Greek critics that metaphor incorporates comparison and the view of the Latin critics that comparison incorporates metaphor.

Not one but two terms of comparison are used in the present passage, *similitudo* and *comparatio*. Two terms for metaphor are

---

[114] See above, pp. 106–111, for a study of the passage including the relevance of Quintilian's present comments.

also used, the transliterated *metaphora* and the Latin *translatio*. The latter are certainly synonymous and cause no difficulty, but what of the first pair? They are being used synonymously, and they appear to define simile. And yet both in the two major discussions, and in the isolated appearances, of *similitudo* the term clearly has involved more than the circumscribed figure of a simile. If, then, it is just simile that Quintilian proposes to define, *comparatio* must be the term that essentially *means* "simile" and that has drawn *similitudo* here into the same meaning. In this case, two facts should be verifiable: that *similitudo* and *comparatio* are not in general used synonymously in the *Institutio* (if they are, *comparatio* will straightway mean something broader than simile) and that *comparatio* consistently denotes simile. Although the first of these can indeed be verified, the second cannot.

A general indication of the first is that *comparatio* does not appear in either main treatment of *similitudo*. Even more, there are several passages in which the terms do appear jointly but are clearly distinct; one comes further on in 8.6. At section 67 Quintilian turns to the trope of hyperbole, mentioning several ways of expressing it.[115] Two that occur in sequence are:

> aut res per similitudinem attollimus:
> > credas innare revulsas Cycladas,[116]
>
> aut per comparationem, ut
> > fulminis ocior alis.[117]   (8.6.68–69)

Again, we may exalt our theme by the use of *similitudo*, as in the phrase:

> > "Thou wouldst have deemed
> > That Cyclad isles uprooted swam the deep."

---

[115] Schenkeveld 85 points out a close similarity between Quintilian's headings and those found in *On Style*'s discussion of hyperbole at section 124.

[116] *Aeneid* 8.691.

[117] *Ibid.*, 5.319.

Or we may produce the same result by introducing a *comparatio*, as in the phrase:

"Swifter than the levin's wings."

Here, neither example is a simile. The *similitudo* would seem to fit the category of a descriptive comparison that is "free and detached"[118] from its subject; the *comparatio* is a comparison of degree.[119]

Another passage comes at 8.5.5. The chapter deals with *sententiae* (striking thoughts). Quintilian says in section 5 that some writers have distinguished ten types of *sententiae*, and he specifies five:

per interrogationem, per comparationem, infitiationem, similitudinem, admirationem et cetera huius modi.

interrogation, comparison, denial, similarity, admiration, and the like.

The two terms are certainly separate. No example of *similitudo* is given, but one of *comparatio* comes in section 19:

"placet hoc ergo, leges, diligentissimae pudoris custodes, decimas uxoribus dari, quartas meretricibus?"

"Is it your pleasure, then, ye laws, the faithful guardians of chastity, that wives should receive a tithe and harlots a quarter?"

In this question, the tenth part of an estate to which, by the *lex Julia et Papia Poppaea*, childless wives were entitled is compared to the fourth part bequeathed to some prostitutes. The two situations are set side by side (it does not matter whether there is any similarity between them) and left to be compared.

A third example may be found in 6.3, where Quintilian treats

[118] 8.3.77, *libera et separata*.
[119] On occasion, as at 1.5.45, Quintilian uses *comparatio* to denote "the comparative" as opposed to "the superlative."

not only *similitudo* but also *comparatio* as an element of humor: at section 66 *comparatio* is included at the end of a list of modes of argument (*loci argumentorum*) that can be used for humor.

It is manifest that *similitudo* and *comparatio* are independent terms in Quintilian. The special meaning of *comparatio* (the second point to be considered) is indicated in the above passage at 8.5.19, and a few further instances can be adduced. At 3.8.34, Quintilian remarks:

> ita fere omnis suasoria nihil est aliud quam comparatio. . . .

> Consequently as a rule all deliberative speeches are based simply on comparison. . . .

He goes on to say that the *comparatio* in every topic is between its advantages and disadvantages. The two are to be set side by side and judged; *comparatio* designates the act of comparing, not a figure of comparison.

At the beginning of 9.2 (one of Quintilian's chapters on figures), *similitudo* and *exemplum*, it will be recalled,[120] are listed among the elements of speech too common to be called figures. In section 100 Quintilian turns to *comparatio*, classifies it as a figure[121]—though he remains uncommitted as to whether it is a figure of thought or of diction—and gives an example from *pro Murena*:

> "vigilas tu de nocte, ut tuis consultoribus respondeas, ille, ut eo, quo contendit, mature cum exercitu perveniat: te gallorum, illum bucinarum cantus exsuscitat"[122] et cetera.   (9.2.100)

> "You pass wakeful nights that you may be able to reply to your clients; he that he and his army may arrive betimes at their destination. You are roused by cockcrow, he by the bugle's reveillé," and so on.

[120] See above, p. 181.
[121] The mss. actually say it is not a figure, *comparationem equidem video figuram non esse*, but Madvig's *nunc* or Halm's *quoque* clearly should replace the mss. *non*.
[122] *Pro Murena* 9.22.

Here the lawyer and the soldier are placed side by side for comparison, their dissimilarity rather than their similarity forming the basis of the *comparatio*.

Finally, at 8.4.9–10 *comparatio* signifies the way to express amplification of something by elevating a lower object. Two examples from Cicero are produced, the first from *Philippics* 2.25.63:

"si hoc tibi inter cenam et in illis inmanibus poculis tuis accidisset, quis non turpe duceret? in coetu vero populi Romani."

"If this had befallen you at the dinner-table in the midst of your amazing potations, who would not have thought it unseemly? But it occurred at an assembly of the Roman people."

and the second from *in Catilinam* 1.7.17:

"servi mehercule mei si me isto pacto metuerent, ut te metuunt omnes cives tui, domum meam relinquendam putarem."

"In truth, if my slaves feared me as all your fellow-citizens fear you, I should think it wise to leave my house."

In both conditional sentences two situations are again placed together and compared. No equation or basic resemblance need exist between them.

All the above passages have the insistent cumulative effect of demonstrating that although *similitudo* and *comparatio* are for Quintilian quite distinct terms, *comparatio* itself, far from denoting simile, does not even describe a figure of comparison so much as the nonfigurative act of comparison. The solution to the apparent definition of simile at 8.6.8–9 now lies readily at hand and is analogous to the illusory definition of simile in Aristotle's *Rhetoric*. There is no need to circumscribe *similitudo* and *comparatio* unduly; it is the process of comparison, either figurative or nonfigurative,[123] that Quintilian means by the two terms in 8.6.8–9. Any kind of comparison will always be more extensive than metaphor, and so Quintilian is able to say, as a general dictum, *metaphora brevior est similitudo* ("metaphor is a shortened form of comparison"). The simile that serves as an example of *similitudo/comparatio* stems from tradition and convenience. Aristotle's Homeric lion supplied Quintilian with traditional examples of metaphor and comparison, and at the same time with most convenient ones, since the easiest way to illustrate the difference between the two figures is by the single addition of an introductory word of comparison. Quintilian would, of course, include the resulting simile within the realm of comparison, but it is abundantly clear that simile is not the *prescribed* form for *similitudo, comparatio*, or indeed any of his terms of comparison.

With this particular problem set at rest, Quintilian's principal ideas of comparison can be summarized. The passages at 4.1.70, 6.3.61–62, and 8.6.8–9 form significant exceptions, but in general Quintilian belongs to those non-Aristotelian critics who do not link metaphor and comparison. When he connects them at 8.6.8–9, he opposes the Aristotelian tradition and designates comparison as the major, metaphor as the secondary figure. Comparison and historical example, by contrast, are frequently joined, with neither subordinate to the other. Quintilian delineates two main spheres of comparison, proof and embellishment, with one term, *similitudo*, serving for both spheres. Indeed, this is essentially the only term by which he denotes a figure of comparison. Within the comparison of proof he distinguishes between a special and highly effective kind and one that is common and less effective. Within the comparison of embellishment, he separates a short from a longer comparison; he introduces novel terminology; he

---

123 Schenkeveld 89 also argues against thinking that Quintilian defines simile in this passage; but he goes too far in the other direction, saying that not even comparison in general is being discussed, but the nonfigurative qualities of "likeness" and "similarity."

makes a noteworthy exhortation for greater clarity in the comparative part than in the subject part of a comparison; he continually stresses the comparative part as the essential component of an embellishing comparison. These several perceptions, and more, mark Quintilian's analysis of comparison as the most intricate and suggestive that we own from antiquity.

CHAPTER VIII

AFTER QUINTILIAN

Plutarch, Fronto, Late Technical Treatises

The purpose of this chapter is more to round off than to advance. As indicated in the preface, the present study terminates at the point where rhetorical criticism ceases to be even remotely literary and becomes purely technical. The metamorphosis is complete by the end of the second century A.D. Quintilian, much earlier, is in fact the last major critic who approaches his subject broadly; but two literary figures of the end of the first century and the first part of the second make interesting use of terms of comparison in figurative contexts that may be instanced as the latest testimony on ancient theories of comparison before the technical age of the Second Sophistic gains total sway.

The first figure, Plutarch, scatters terms of comparison through his many writings.[1] Nowhere does an actual discussion of comparison occur, but the passages serve to illustrate the continuing use and interpretation of the different terms. Several are employed: at times they refer to simile, but their whole sphere of meaning is clearly broader.

As a term of comparison, παραβολή occurs only at *de Recta Ratione Audiendi* 40e[2] and carries a nonfigurative sense of the act of comparison. Plutarch remarks that after one listens to a lecture it is useful to compose a speech of one's own and compare it with

---

[1] Heavy reliance has been placed on D. Wyttenbach, *Lexicon Plutarcheum* (Leipzig 1843), for the various instances.

[2] Apart from the spurious and late *de Vita et Poesi Homeri*.

what has been heard.[3] At 40f he goes on to say that disdainful arrogance is cut short by such comparisons, and here he uses the term ἀντιπαραβολή—which appears in Plutarch only in this passage.[4]

Plutarch's most common term of comparison is εἰκών; indeed, the same is true of all Greek critics except [Demetrius]. If the rhetorical instances of εἰκών are taken as they appear in order in the *Moralia* (there will also be one instance from the *Lives*), Plutarch's understanding of the term emerges clearly. In the *Consolatio ad Apollonium* 104f,[5] εἰκών designates the imagery of leaves as used to depict human existence. Plutarch has just quoted the famous simile of *Iliad* 6.146ff, οἵη περ φύλλων γενεή, τοίη δὲ καὶ ἀνδρῶν ("as is the generation of leaves, so also that of mortals"). He comments:

ταύτῃ δ' ὅτι καλῶς ἐχρήσατο τῇ εἰκόνι τοῦ ἀνθρωπείου βίου δῆλον ἐξ ὧν ἐν ἄλλῳ τόπῳ φησὶν οὕτω. . . .

That he [Homer] has admirably made use of this image of human life is clear from what he says in another place, in these words. . . .

A second Homeric simile follows (*Iliad* 21.463ff) that compares human beings to leaves. The precise reference of τῇ εἰκόνι ("this image") is not to the whole of the two similes but to the leaf imagery of each. In *de Defectu Oraculorum* 430c, on the other hand, εἰκών does refer to the whole of a simile. The central speaker of the dialogue, Lamprias, in expounding certain of Plato's physical doctrines from the *Timaeus*, in particular the condition of the elements before the organization of the universe, says of Plato:

[3] The exact phrase containing παραβολή is: χρήσιμον δὲ πρὸς τοῦτο καὶ τὸ τῆς παραβολῆς ("to this end the process of comparison is useful"). The text is *Plutarchi Chaeronensis Moralia*, ed. G. N. Bernardakis (Leipzig: B. G. Teubner, 1888–1896). The Loeb translations are used throughout.

[4] See above, p. 29, for the earlier use of this rare term in Aristotle's *Rhetoric*.

[5] The work is perhaps spurious, but if so it was probably written by some contemporary and can thus still illustrate the use of terms of comparison in about 100 A.D.

ἔτι δὲ μᾶλλον εἰκόνι τὸ συμβαῖνον ἐνδείκνυται. . . .

What takes place he describes more clearly by a simile. . . .

He then quotes part of the simile in *Timaeus* 52e that compares the elements in their primitive condition to grain being shaken and winnowed.[6]

Thus far, εἰκών has designated a part or the whole of a simile. Other instances in Plutarch are of a different character. In *Quaestiones Convivales* 2.3.636f the proposition is debated whether the egg or the bird came first. Firmus has just given a series of arguments for the primacy of the egg, and Senecio, who argues the other side, opens with a rebuke:

> Ταῦτα τοῦ Φίρμου διεξιόντος, ὁ Σενεκίων ἔφη τὴν τελευταίαν τῶν εἰκόνων αὐτῷ πρώτην ἀντιπίπτειν.

When Firmus had gone through these points, Senecio said that his last comparison stood in opposition to his first.[7]

The two εἰκόνες to which Senecio refers are, respectively, a conditional comparison (if small things are the principles of great things, then it is likely that the egg came before the bird[8]) and a general comparative illustration (almost nothing has a beginning except from an egg—birds, fish, lizards, snakes; therefore it is quite correct in the rites of Dionysus to dedicate an egg as a symbol of that which begets everything else[9]).

At *An Seni Respublica Gerenda Sit* 785e, Plutarch laments the

---

[6] Another very analogous passage comes in *de Genio Socratis* 575b. Archedamus opens the dialogue by telling Caphisias of a description, given him by a painter, of people who look at paintings; the description, Archedamus says, was expressed in an εἰκών (ἐν εἰκόνι λελεγμένον), and a simile follows.

[7] My own translation. No Loeb volume yet exists for the first six books of the *Quaestiones Convivales*.

[8] *Quaestiones Convivales* 2.3.636a–b (a close paraphrase, not a precise translation).

[9] *Ibid.*, 636a; again a close paraphrase.

custom of urging statesmen in their old age to give themselves up to self-indulgence while calling it rest, and he comments scornfully:

οὐκ οἶδα ποτέρᾳ δυεῖν εἰκόνων αἰσχρῶν πρέπειν δόξει μᾶλλον ὁ βίος αὐτοῦ.

I do not know which of two disgraceful pictures his [the old statesman's] life will seem to resemble more closely.

Two descriptive pictures follow, one of sailors deserting their ship and devoting themselves to sexual excesses,[10] the other of Heracles in Omphale's palace giving up his lion's skin and donning a yellow robe while being fanned by Omphale's maids.

In *Bruta Ratione Uti* 988d, Gryllus belabors Odysseus with having no more courage than do wild beasts. He reminds him that poets praise great warriors with such epithets as "lionhearted," adding that this actually indicates less courage in the warriors than in the beasts, since epithets are usually exaggerations. He then gives two more examples:

ἀλλ᾽ ὥσπερ οἶμαι τοὺς ταχεῖς "ποδηνέμους" καὶ τοὺς καλούς "θεοειδεῖς" ὑπερβαλλόμενοι ταῖς εἰκόσιν ὀνομάζουσιν, οὕτω τῶν δεινῶν μάχεσθαι πρὸς τὰ κρείττονα ποιοῦνται τὰς ἀφομοιώσεις.

But, I imagine, just as when those who are swift are called "windfooted" and those who are handsome are called "godlike," there is exaggeration in the imagery; just so the poets bring in a higher ideal when they compare mighty warriors to something else.

ταῖς εἰκόσιν refers to the two epithets but *means* "descriptive imagery" or "descriptive comparison." It is clear that this is Plutarch's general understanding of εἰκών, and as such it can apply equally well to similes and epithets. Another term,

[10] In general theme this picture goes at least as far back as Plato's sailor image, which is also termed an εἰκών, in *Republic* VI. See above, p. 15.

ἀφομοίωσις, makes its sole appearance in Plutarch here and carries a broad sense of "comparison." Neither in Plutarch nor elsewhere in ancient rhetoric is the word a recurring term of comparison.[11]

A final figurative instance of εἰκών comes in the *Lives*. At *Alexander* 65, Plutarch discusses Alexander's dealings with philosophers, particularly Calanus. He introduces one of Calanus' pieces of advice:

Τοῦτον δὲ λέγεται καὶ τὸ παράδειγμα τῆς ἀρχῆς τῷ Ἀλεξάνδρῳ προθέσθαι.[12]

It was Calanus, as we are told, who laid before Alexander the famous illustration of government.

The tale is then recounted that Calanus placed a withered hide before Alexander, showing that only when he stepped in the middle would it remain stationary. Plutarch adds:

Ἐβούλετο δὲ ἡ εἰκὼν ἔνδειξις εἶναι τοῦ τὰ μέσα δεῖν μάλιστα τῆς ἀρχῆς πιέζειν καὶ μὴ μακρὰν ἀποπλανᾶσθαι τὸν Ἀλέξανδρον.

The similitude was designed to show that Alexander ought to put most constraint upon the middle of his empire and not wander far away from it.

The use of εἰκών to designate an illustrative comparison is perfectly predictable. More irregular is the synonymous use of παράδειγμα. Juxtaposition of παράδειγμα and εἰκών would normally indicate a context dealing with historical example and comparison; here, however, the "example" of the withered hide is not at all historical, and παράδειγμα carries a more general sense than usual.

[11] ὁμοίωσις also appears once in Plutarch, at *Quomodo Adulator ab Amico Internoscatur* 53c, but in a nonrhetorical sense of "imitation."
[12] The text is *Plutarchi Vitae Parallelae*, ed. C. Sintenis (Leipzig: B. G. Teubner, 1853–1884).

One additional term, which has appeared before only in *On Style*, occurs also in Plutarch: εἰκασία. It is used twice, once to refer to a simile. In *Themistocles* 29 Plutarch reports, from among the great Athenian's many experiences at the Persian court during his exile, that the King once asked him his opinion of Greek affairs but was put off by a Themistoclean simile which made the point that, as in the embroidery of tapestries, he, too, needed time to prepare such an opinion. Plutarch then says:

’Επεὶ δὲ, ἡσθέντος τοῦ βασιλέως τῇ εἰκασίᾳ καὶ λαμβάνειν κελεύσαντος. . . .

The King at once showed his pleasure at this comparison by bidding him take time. . . .

In *Amatorius* 765e, on the other hand, εἰκασία refers to a description of the birth and parentage of Eros in a fragment of Alcaeus[13] and bears a sense of "imagistic picture." No explicit comparison is made in the Alcaeus fragment, and the use of εἰκασία here is thus similar to certain descriptive passages in *On Style*.[14]

Plutarch's overall use of terms of comparison does not break new ground, but a few variations are discernible. εἰκών possesses exactly the frequency and range of application we would expect; but a much rarer term, εἰκασία, reappears; even rarer terms, ἀντιπαραβολή and ἀφομοίωσις, each grace a solitary passage; παραβολή in its lone appearance is less of a figure than usual; and παράδειγμα is used without historical reference. These idiosyncrasies suggest a free approach to terminology that would be particularly natural for a writer not professionally involved in rhetoric.[15]

---

[13] Alcaeus, frag. 327 (ed. Lobel/Page).

[14] *On Style* 172; see above, p. 152.

[15] It is of note that in the spurious *de Vita et Poesi Homeri*, which belongs to the age of the late technical treatises, terms of comparison are used somewhat differently since they regularly refer to Homeric similes.

The second post-Quintilianic figure to be considered, Marcus Cornelius Fronto, is very close in background and chronology to the age of the Second Sophistic and the late technical treatises. Born around 100 A.D. in the Roman colony of Cirta in Numidia, he was of a Roman family, but it is likely that his schooling was primarily in Greek letters and literature and that he acquired knowledge of Roman literature only later.[16] He was a contemporary of Herodes Atticus and only slightly earlier than Aelius Aristides, both figures of the Second Sophistic. Most of his extant work is in Latin, but he does not really continue the Roman rhetorical tradition; and it is a mark of the Second Sophistic that Greek and Roman rhetoric, which remained fairly distinguishable up to this point, now become virtually one.[17] Nevertheless, Fronto's correspondence, which is all that remains of his work, is sufficiently literary and nontechnical in nature that his views of comparison may be accepted as belonging more to "classical" rhetoric than to the age of the technical handbooks.

Two terms, εἰκών and *imago*, are used repeatedly (and synonymously) and are discussed at some length in three of Fronto's letters and in one from Marcus Aurelius to him. These discussions have been taken as presenting εἰκών and *imago* in the sense of "simile,"[18] but a careful look shows the case to be rather that Fronto employs the terms essentially, and quite traditionally, in the meaning of "imagistic description." The four letters will be reviewed here in their approximate chronological order as arranged by Haines.

The earliest is a letter from Marcus Aurelius to his teacher, written probably in 139 A.D. After expressing anxiety over Fronto's health, Marcus says he has nearly completed all ten

---

[16] C. R. Haines, *Marcus Cornelius Fronto* (London 1919–1920) I xxiii. Haines's Loeb translations are used.

[17] Clarke 131.

[18] For instance, Haines I xxxv: "Similes, or εἰκόνες, formed an important part of Fronto's oratorical armoury"; and Clarke, 134: "Fronto made much use of such exercises as the composition of maxims (*gnomae*) and similes (εἰκόνες)."

εἰκόνες that Fronto had set him. Only one continues to be troublesome, and he asks Fronto's aid. He outlines the topic:

> Est autem quod in insula Aenaria intus lacus est: in eo lacu alia insula est, et ea quoque inhabitatur. Ἔνθ' ἐμὴν δ' εἰκόνα ποιοῦμεν.[19]　　　　　　　　　(*ad M. Caesarem* 3.7)

It is the one of the inland lake in the island Aenaria; in that lake there is another island, it, too, inhabited. From this we draw my simile.

Marcus' letter stops here, but Fronto responds to his plea in expansive detail. He begins by referring to Marcus' predicament and then indicates a solution:

> Imaginem, quam te quaerere ais, meque tibi socium ad quaerendum et optionem sumis, num moleste feres, si in tuo atque in tui patris sinu id futurum quaeram?　　　　　(*ad M. Caes.* 3.8)

As to the simile, which you say you are puzzling over and for which you call me in as your ally and adjutant in finding the clue, you will not take it amiss, will you, if I look for the clue to that fancy within your breast and your father's breast?

He will look for the εἰκών/*imago* in the hearts of Marcus and his father, Antoninus Pius. An extensive simile follows, an abbreviated paraphrase of which would be: as that island Aenaria in the sea is exposed to all dangers but protects the inner lake island (and that lake island still receives all the benefits of the main island such as habitation and sea breezes), so Marcus' father bears all the troubles of the state and protects Marcus from them while still admitting him to all the pleasures of imperial power.

After the elaborate simile Fronto remarks:

> Igitur hac imagine multimodis uti potes ubi patri tuo gratias ages, in qua oratione locupletissimum et copiosissimum te esse oportet.

[19] The text is that of M. P. J. Van Den Hout, *M. Cornelii Frontonis Epistulae* (Leiden 1954).

Accordingly you can use this simile in a variety of ways, when you return thanks to your father,[20] on which occasion you should be most full and copious.

What is the exact connotation of *hac imagine*? Haines's "this simile" suggests that several times in his speech of thanks Marcus is to use the simile Fronto has just drawn, but the remainder of the letter raises doubts. A few sentences later Fronto says he will not give any more examples, but will relate to Marcus general principles for making εἰκόνες; after urging Marcus to send on any that he composes, Fronto states:

> Iam primum quidem illud scis, εἰκόνα ei rei adsumi ut aut ornet quid aut deturpet aut aequiperet aut deminuat aut ampliet aut ex minus credibili credibile efficiat. Ubi nihil eorum usus erit, locus εἰκόνος non erit.

> Now, in the first place, you are aware that an εἰκών[21] is used for the purpose of setting off a thing or discrediting it, or comparing, or depreciating, or amplifying it, or of making credible what is scarcely credible. Where nothing of the kind is required, there will be no room for an εἰκών.

Fronto's understanding of εἰκών begins to come clear in this passage. It is used for certain effects on "a thing" (*quid*). The "a thing" is the subject at hand, such as Antoninus' paternal care. εἰκών, then, denotes the imagistic description of the subject. It has all the various purposes enumerated by Fronto and will assume various forms. It can certainly be joined with the subject as a simile but need not be. Thus, the earlier phrase *hac imagine multimodis uti potes* ("you can use this *imago* in a variety of ways") means that the image of an island containing a lake with an island can be used in many ways to describe Antoninus' laudable attitude toward Marcus. Fronto has arranged one such description;

---

[20] Marcus' thanks would be for having been made Caesar in 139 A.D.

[21] The meaning of the terms is still being established; therefore I write the terms themselves rather than Haines's "simile."

Marcus can arrange others for the same purpose of "setting off" Antoninus' paternal care.

Immediately after the above passage, Fronto shifts his comments to the method of choosing those characteristics of the subject to be mirrored in the *imago*. He unambiguously separates *imago* from the subject treated:

> Postea ubi rei propositae imaginem scribes, ut, si pingeres, insignia animadverteres eius rei cuius imaginem pingeres, item in scribendo facies.

> Hereafter when you compose an *imago* for a subject in hand, just as, if you were a painter, you would notice the characteristics of the object you were painting, so must you do in writing.

The different characteristics are then listed in Greek:

> τὰ ὁμογενῆ, τὰ ὁμοειδῆ, τὰ ὅλα, τὰ μέρη, τὰ ἴδια, τὰ διάφορα, τὰ ἀντικείμενα, τὰ ἑπόμενα καὶ παρακολουθοῦντα, τὰ ὀνόματα, τὰ συμβεβηκότα, τὰ στοιχεῖα.

> the likenesses of kind, the likenesses of form, the whole, the parts, the individual traits, the differences, the contraries, the consequences and the resultants, the names, the accidents, the elements.

Fronto states that out of all these possibilities his own εἰκών/ *imago* made use of one of τὰ συμβεβηκότα ("the accidents," that is, the contingent attributes) of his subject, namely the characteristics of security and enjoyment. He tells Marcus that it is now up to him to handle the topic of an island with a lake and inner island in fitting ways by means of the advice just proffered. The letter concludes with a promise to investigate the whole art of εἰκόνες more fully at some future date.

The third letter of interest is one written in Greek by Fronto to Marcus Aurelius' mother, Domitia Lucilla, in 143 A.D. It is not a weighty letter: no serious news is conveyed, no important topic broached. Fronto writes because he has not done so in some time, and the letter consists of several apologies for his tardiness (he has been writing a speech for the emperor), with miscellaneous remarks on εἰκόνες separating the apologies.

Fronto begins humbly by saying that concern over the emperor's speech prevented him from thinking of anything else and that in this respect he is like a hyena whose neck can be stretched forward but not to either side. Having drawn this simile he proceeds to two more pictures, one of snakes who dart straight forward but not to the side, and the other of spears and arrows that hit their target when hurled straight and not bent to the side by the wind or the gods. He then remarks:

> Ταύτας μὲν δὴ τρεῖς εἰκόνας ἐμαυτῷ προσείκασα, τὰς μὲν δύο
> ἀγρίας καὶ θηριώδεις, τὴν τῆς ὑαίνης καὶ τὴν τῶν ὄφεων, τρίτην
> δὲ τὴν τῶν βελῶν καὶ αὐτὴν ἀπάνθρωπον οὖσαν καὶ ἄμουσον.
>
> (ad M. Caes. 1.10; Epistulae Graecae 1)

These three εἰκόνες, then, have I applied to myself, two of them fierce and savage, that of the hyena and that of the snake, and a third drawn from missiles, it, too, non-human and harsh.

"These three εἰκόνες" does not refer to three similes but to the imagistic descriptions Fronto has created, one of which has been incorporated in a simile, the other two expressed independently and in declarative form. He goes on to a fourth and a fifth εἰκών depicting his singlemindedness. The fourth portrays the best wind as one that blows from the stern; the fifth describes the best line as a straight line. Of the latter εἰκών he says that it is not only inanimate (ἄψυχος), like the spear picture, but even incorporeal (ἀσώματος).

Fronto next asks rhetorically what kind of εἰκών is persuasive and supplies his own answer:

> Τίς ἂν οὖν εἰκὼν εὑρεθείη πιθανή; μάλιστα μὲν ἀνθρωπίνη,
> ἄμεινον δὲ εἰ καὶ μουσική. εἰ δ' αὖ καὶ φιλίας ἢ ἔρωτος αὐτῇ
> μετείη, μᾶλλον ἂν ἔτι ἡ εἰκὼν ἐοίκοι.

What εἰκών, then, can be found convincing? One above all that is human, better still if it be also cultured; and if it partake, too, of friendship and love, the εἰκών would be all the more a similitude.

"Human" (ἀνθρωπίνη) would seem to contrast with an εἰκών that is inanimate and incorporeal—a reminder of Quintilian's *similitudo* of proof, which is less effective and convincing when it draws its comparative part from mute and inanimate objects.[22] Fronto follows with a description of Orpheus turning to look back instead of keeping his gaze straight ahead. The Orpheus picture includes "friendship and love" and to this extent is "convincing" (πιθανή). But in dealing with the world of the dead it is not "human" and in this respect is not persuasive, as Fronto recognizes:

καὶ γὰρ αὕτη τις ἀπίθανος ἡ τοῦ Ὀρφέως εἰκὼν ἐξ ᾅδου ἀνι-μημένη.

For this, too, is somewhat unconvincing, this εἰκών of Orpheus fetched up from Hades.

Fronto now shifts from the topic of εἰκόνες to apologies to Domitia, but after a few sentences he inserts the remark:

ἀλλὰ γὰρ τέχνωσις τῶν εἰκόνων ἐπεισρεῖ καὶ ἐπιφύεται.

But, indeed, the craftmanship of εἰκόνες is an insinuating thing and grows on us.

And he presents yet another imagistic description that has occurred to him, playing on the nonfigurative meaning of εἰκών by saying that it is particularly apt to call this an εἰκών because it derives from painting. His description is a lengthy one of himself approaching his encomium of the emperor with all the care that Protogenes took in his eleven-year project of painting the Ialysus.

---

[22] Quintilian 5.11.23-24; see above, pp. 199-204.

Fronto stresses that he has included praise of the emperor's son also, and thus in effect has painted a double Ialysus. He adds that Marcus is Domitia's son as Hephaestus is Hera's, and notes:

ἀπέστω δὲ τὸ τῶν ποδῶν ταύτης τῆς τοῦ Ἡφαίστου εἰκόνος.

But let there be no "halting" in this εἰκών from Hephaestus.

Fronto wants to keep any suggested analogy of Hephaestus' lameness out of the comparison, but once again it is not the whole comparison to which εἰκών refers. Lameness is a feature only of the illustrative image of Hephaestus.

After making a further play on the double meaning, figurative and nonfigurative, of εἰκών, Fronto concludes the letter by asking Domitia to forgive any barbarisms the letter may contain and to look only for the meaning of each word. Anacharsis the Scythian, he says, did not write perfect Attic but was commended for his thoughts. In much the same way, he himself, also a barbarian, may be permitted to browse (νέμεσθαι) in Attic Greek and to bleat (βληχᾶσθαι) barbarisms. Having issued this last spate of images, he closes abruptly (and perhaps none too soon):

οὐκοῦν παύσομαι μηδὲν ἕτερον γράφων ἀλλὰ εἰκόνας.

So will I make an end of writing nothing but εἰκόνες.

The letter is replete with imagistic descriptions, mostly of Fronto's undeviating devotion to his encomiastic labors. A few of these are combined with subjects to make whole comparisons, in simile form. But the concluding sentence, and the entire letter, uses εἰκών in the first instance to signify descriptive pictures, not complete comparisons.

The fourth and final letter, again from Fronto to Marcus Aurelius, was written between 145 and 147 A.D. There is a single passage on εἰκών/*imago*. Marcus has written Fronto of the serious (eventually fatal) illness of his infant daughter, Faustina.[23] Fronto

---

[23] *Ad M. Caes.* 4.11.

replies that when he first opened the letter he thought Marcus was describing his own illness, and that on learning it was Faustina's he was still concerned but somehow felt easier. He attributes his sense of relief to the human tendency to be shocked most at the very first news of something. Then he prefaces the εἰκών/*imago* with which he will describe his experience with this observation:

> Ego, qui a meo magistro et parente Athenodoto ad exempla et imagines quasdam rerum, quas ille εἰκόνας appellabat, apte animo conprehendundas adcommodandasque mediocriter institutus sum, hanc huiusce rei imaginem repperisse videor, cur meus translatus metus levior sit mihi visus.   (*ad M. Caes.* 4.12)

> Tolerably well trained as I was by my master and parent Athenodotus in the nice apprehension by the mind and application of illustrations and, as it were, similes of things, which he called εἰκόνας,[24] I think I have hit upon the following simile of this kind, to explain the fact that the transference of my fear seemed an alleviation of it.

This is the only collocation in Fronto of historical illustration or example (*exempla*) and a term of comparison (*imagines*). There is no elaboration, but the mere juxtaposition is sufficient to show awareness, in a largely nontechnical writer, of the traditional rhetorical coupling. His *imago* follows:

> simile solere evenire onus grave umero gestantibus, cum illud onus in sinistrum ab dextro umero transtulere, quamquam nihil de pondere, deminutum sit, tamen ut oneris translatio videatur etiam et elevatio.

> much the same thing happens to those who, carrying a heavy weight on their shoulder, transfer it from the right shoulder to the left, so that, though the burden remains as it was, yet the transference of the pressure seems even a relief.

[24] This is Haines's own use of the Greek term, not my substitute for his translation.

In these passages Fronto's understanding of εἰκών/*imago* is perhaps even clearer than before. He speaks of the "*imagines* of things," and his *imago* forms only the comparative part of his intended comparison between the shifted burden and the shifted attribution of illness. Despite Haines's constant use of "simile," for Fronto both terms plainly denote "imagistic description." Fronto is absolutely consistent in his own application of εἰκών/*imago*, but his view is a slight modification of the common rhetorical use of the terms. In such critics as Aristotle and in *ad Herennium* and *On Style*, both εἰκών and *imago* could easily refer to a whole comparison as well as to imagistic description. Fronto, keenly aware (as his verbal byplay shows) of the general meaning "picture, portrait, likeness, image" of the terms, carries over the general meaning quite pointedly into the rhetorical, figurative meaning and does not extend their application beyond the actual imagistic portion of a comparison.

The nature of analyses of comparison in the late technical treatises and the extent to which they differ in character and aim from the rhetorical works that preceded them can be indicated with precision. No matter how much technical material has arisen in the treatises examined thus far, most of them were composed, at least partially, as literature. The same cannot be said of the large mass of technical treatises issuing from the late second, third, fourth, and fifth centuries A.D.: they are handbooks, compendia of different rubrics of rhetoric with brief discussion of each rubric. The traditional major divisions of rhetoric are often ignored in favor of long lists of figures and tropes, and many of the handbooks purport to be no more than *de Tropis* or Περὶ σχημάτων (*On Figures*). They make no literary pretensions; they do not claim to search for the ideal orator or to speak with authority on earlier writers of prose and poetry. There is, then, an essential difference in motive and method between them and even such highly "professional" earlier works as Aristotle's *Rhetoric* or *ad Herennium*.

The number of these late treatises, almost all of which contain sections on comparison, is great. If one adds the copious commentary on comparison and simile in the Homeric scholia,[25] the resulting corpus is of considerable size. No attempt will be made to select typical observations from the whole corpus. Rather, the comments on comparison in a single handbook, Trypho's Περὶ τρόπων (*On Tropes*), will serve to illustrate the pattern of the other treatises. Trypho's work is selected on several grounds: it is representative in that more late treatises survive in Greek than in Latin; its format is typical; in addition, its attribution to the first-century B.C. grammarian Trypho has been argued as incorrect,[26] and it seems appropriate to look at it within its rightful period.

The handbook is some fifteen pages long,[27] a fairly standard size for those treatises that discuss no more than tropes or figures. A definition of φράσις (diction) as consisting of κυριολογία (literal expression) and τρόποι (tropes) opens the treatise. Next, the first of two major divisions of τρόποι is defined as οἱ γενικω-

---

[25] Separating out the chronological strata of the Homeric scholia is, of course, a special and complex problem. At least some of the scholiastic comments on Homeric similes may go back to the Alexandrian critics and thus provide testimony on comparison in what otherwise is the lacuna of the Hellenistic centuries. R. Schlunk, "Vergil and the Homeric Scholia," *AJP* 88 (1967) 33–45, takes Vergil's adaptation in Book XII of the Iliadic breaking of the truce and notes that in several places Vergil departs from Homer precisely where the scholiasts criticize Homer. Similar reflections of the scholia can perhaps be traced in many passages; indeed, M. Coffey, "Vergil and the Tradition of the Ancient Epic Simile" (address to Vergil Society of London, 1960) remarks, as quoted by Schlunk: "The scholia frequently comment on the lowliness of the subject matter of some of the similes of the *Iliad*. It is possible that theories of decorum affected Apollonius' practice, and so in turn, that of Vergil." See also A. Clausing, *Kritik und Exegese der homerischen Gleichnisse in Altertum* (Parchim 1913). But much work needs to be done before a confident assertion can be made that in general the scholia on the Homeric similes are pieces of Alexandrian criticism. The terminology employed and the types of comment made are so analogous to those in the late treatises that it seems most natural to associate them principally with late antiquity.

[26] See above, pp. xi and 137.

[27] L. Spengel, *Rhetores Graeci* III (Leipzig 1856) 191–206.

τάτην ἐμφαίνοντες στάσιν (those which display a generic structure), and Trypho lists fourteen of these, including metaphor.
Each is described and illustrated, which occupies about eight
pages. Trypho then says: "These are the tropes which go beyond
the normal use of grammar; the remainder are ones of diction
(φράσις) and number twenty-seven." A typical sort of handbook
volte-face is evident here. Having opened the treatise by presenting
τρόποι as one of two main classes of φράσις, Trypho now without a murmur offers φράσις as the second of two main types of
τρόποι. His list begins: ὑπερβολή (hyperbole), ἔμφασις (emphasis), ἐνέργεια (activity), παρασιώπησις (passing over in
silence), ὁμοίωσις, εἰκών, παράδειγμα, παραβολή, and so on.
After he names the twenty-seven "tropes of diction," he defines
and illustrates each one in turn under an individual heading. But
only twenty-four receive headings; the three that do not are
εἰκών, παράδειγμα, and παραβολή—despite their presence in
the original list they are subsequently treated within the heading
of ὁμοίωσις. Inconsistencies of this kind are frequent in the handbooks. Trypho's section on ὁμοίωσις begins:

Ὁμοίωσίς ἐστι ῥῆσις, καθ' ἣν ἕτερον ἑτέρῳ παραβάλλομεν,
εἴδη δὲ αὐτῆς εἰσι τρία, εἰκών, παράδειγμα, παραβολή.

Ὁμοίωσις is a form of speech in which we compare one thing
to another. Its forms are three, εἰκών, παράδειγμα, παραβολή.

The first subdivision, εἰκών, is then defined as λόγος ἐναργῶς
ἐξομοιοῦν πειρώμενος (an expression attempting to liken visibly);
Trypho states that this can be accomplished by comparing whole
with whole, part with part, size with size, form with form, and
color with color. Homeric similes illustrate each category, the
example for comparisons of whole with whole, for instance, being
the phrase περίφρων Πηνελόπεια, Ἀρτέμιδι ἰκέλη[28] (prudent
Penelope, like to Artemis). In each case, as Trypho's definition

---

[28] The phrase occurs both at *Odyssey* 17.36–37 and 19.53–54.

indicates, the point of the comparison is some kind of physical, visible likeness.

The second subdivision, παράδειγμα, is described:

> παράδειγμά ἐστι τοῦ προγεγονότος πράγματος παρένθεσις καθ᾽ ὁμοιότητα τῶν ὑποκειμένων πρὸς παραίνεσιν προτροπῆς ἢ ἀποτροπῆς ἕνεκεν.

> παράδειγμα is the insertion of an event of the past by reason of its likeness to the subject in order to give counsel of encouragement or discouragement.

This otherwise straightforward definition of historical example sets itself apart a little by the special purpose invoked. Two Homeric passages supply an example of encouragement (Orestes as a precedent for Telemachus to slay those who disgrace his father's halls)[29] and one of discouragement (the fate of Lycurgus as a precedent for not opposing the gods).[30] Trypho closes his remarks on παράδειγμα by distinguishing it from παραβολή:

> διαφέρει δὲ παράδειγμα παραβολῆς, ὅτι τὸ μὲν παράδειγμα ἀπὸ γεγονότων πραγμάτων παραλαμβάνεται, ἡ δὲ παραβολὴ ἐξ ἀορίστων καὶ ἐνδεχομένων γενέσθαι.

> Historical example differs from παραβολή in that it is drawn from actual past events, while παραβολή comes from what is indeterminate and possible.

After two sudden paragraphs on κόμμα (short clauses) and χαρακτῆρες ῥητορικοί (rhetorical styles), which are obviously misplaced and are bracketed by Spengel, Trypho presents παραβολή:

> Παραβολή ἐστι λόγος διὰ παραθέσεως ὁμοίου πράγματος τὸ ὑποκείμενον μετ᾽ ἐνεργείας παριστάνων.

[29] *Od.* 1.298–300.
[30] *Il.* 6.130–131.

Παραβολή is an expression setting forth with activity the subject by placing beside it a like matter.

As with εἰκών, there are several ways of structuring παραβολή. Emotion may be placed beside emotion, disposition beside disposition, nature beside nature, deed beside deed. Four Homeric similes constitute the examples, the famous "as is the generation of leaves, so also that of mortals"[31] forming the illustration of nature placed beside like nature. These examples, however, are not followed by any further comments on παραβολή, and the whole section on ὁμοίωσις comes to an abrupt conclusion.

The dry, classifying spirit of Trypho's analysis is immediately evident. As for his approach, the grouping of two terms of comparison and historical example is standard in the late treatises. Also normal is the complete separation of metaphor and comparison. All examples are from poetry and indeed from Homer, a common situation in the Greek handbooks; in the Latin treatises Vergil supplies most examples. The examples are not peculiar to Trypho; several are used to illustrate equivalent divisions of εἰκών, παράδειγμα, and παραβολή in Herodian and Polybius Sardianus, the two third-century rhetoricians with whom Trypho is most closely united. At the same time, Trypho, like every late rhetorician, strives for differences of detail from every other rhetorician,[32] and thus there are definite variations in organization and classification among Trypho, Herodian, and Polybius. Each example of εἰκών and παραβολή that Trypho uses is a simile or part of one, again a regular feature of the late treatises. But there are several reasons not to take this as an indication that Trypho intends to denote strictly "simile" by any of his terms. Reliance on Homer for examples of comparison foreordains the form of the examples, since Homer casts virtually every comparison as a simile. More importantly, the situation is again closely analogous

[31] *Il.* 6.146.
[32] Kroll 1137; Clarke 140.

to that in *On Style*. Each example of two terms is a simile. If form were at the heart of Trypho's analysis, there would be no need for more than one term; use of two shows that Trypho is classifying on the basis of something other than form. And indeed, his approach is clear enough. ὁμοίωσις is the main heading and must mean "comparison" in a broad sense, as its definition states ("a form of speech in which we compare one thing to another"). Its component elements are: εἰκών, which describes any comparison of objects visibly or physically alike; παράδειγμα, which is comparison involving historical precedent and whose examples are in no way similes; and παραβολή, whose examples *are* similes but which is said to differ from παράδειγμα not in form but in lack of historical definiteness, and which compares similar objects for the purpose of vividness and action. The boundaries of παραβολή are not so easily seen as those of εἰκών and παράδειγμα, but in any case Trypho does not suggest a limit on its form.

This preliminary glance at the corpus of the late treatises, it may be suggested, reveals the same basic interest in the nature, purpose, and content, rather than the form, of comparison that has been observed throughout the ancient testimony.[33]

[33] In time, as mentioned in the preface, it is hoped that a full study of the late handbooks and scholia will be forthcoming.

CHAPTER IX

CONCLUSION

Each of the preceding chapters has produced certain conclusions regarding ancient theories of comparison; it is now possible to formulate a general summary and briefly remark on the nature of the testimony.

The ancient critics are interested essentially in purpose and method. The two central purposes that they assign to comparison are proof and embellishment; and these dual aims are present in the work of nearly every critic who deals with the whole of rhetoric, including Aristotle, the author of *ad Herennium*, Cicero, and Quintilian. The methods of comparison discussed are almost as various as the number of critics. Description, contrast, vividness, negation, parallel, sequence, brevity, length—these and more appear, though recognition of any difference between a brief and a lengthy comparison is surprisingly infrequent.

Comparison is rarely discussed as an isolated component of rhetoric. Its traditional partners are metaphor and historical example, and throughout the ancient testimony it is paired now with one, now with the other. In general, but not invariably, Greek critics choose the collocation of comparison and metaphor, Latin critics that of comparison (often two terms of comparison) and historical example. When comparison and metaphor are paired, a recurring question is which of the two is a subordinate branch of the other. Again a broad Greek-Latin division results: the supremacy of metaphor is affirmed by most Greek critics, the supremacy of comparison by certain Latin critics. As an element of stylistic embellishment, comparison is usually classified as a figure of thought and on this ground is often distinguished from metaphor, which is normally designated a figure of diction. But these classifications are sometimes blurred. The ancient critics fluctuate between regarding comparisons in oratory and poetry as essentially similar and as sharply distinct. On occasion both views seem to exist simultaneously, and a critic will illustrate types of oratorical comparison with examples from poetry in one place while firmly distinguishing between comparisons fit for oratory and those fit for poetry in another. There is no attempt, however, to represent actual comparisons from poetry by one term and comparisons from prose by another. Finally, the critics indiscriminately apply the various terms to all forms of comparison, and in no treatise does a shift in use from one term to another necessarily involve a shift from one form to another. Thus, of the four major terms of comparison—εἰκών, παραβολή, *imago*, and *similitudo*—no one of them refers appreciably more to a particular form of comparison, such as simile, than do the other three. The testimony seems to dictate that we regard none of them—nor the less frequently used terms—as consciously signifying the idea of simile.

Ancient and modern views of comparison may be balanced in two different areas. The question of the primacy of metaphor or comparison has probably not yet been solved. One scholar,[1] while noting that most modern critics agree with the Latin inclination toward comparison, argues that the question should not even be put: metaphor and comparison, he suggests, are generically distinct. Metaphor is a treatment of language and implies more, while comparison is a treatment of thought and expresses more. This may well be a sound approach, but it is certainly not exclusively modern. As has been indicated, a considerable portion of the ancient testimony also separates metaphor and comparison by the similar criterion that metaphor is a figure of diction,

[1] Stanford 28ff.

comparison a figure of thought. In this area ancient and modern views seem equally diverse.

By contrast, a real distinction between ancient and modern ideas can be made in a second area. Modern usage regards simile as a unique figure of comparison; the corpus of ancient criticism does not. We separate simile from other kinds of comparison on the basis of form. It has no purpose peculiarly its own; it is not restricted to either prose or poetry; it has no mandatory length or brevity; it may or may not display parallel development of its subject and comparative parts. Its form alone has been the sufficient ground for application of an independent term. The ancients approach simile and comparison quite otherwise: in purpose, in sphere and method of use, and in content simile differs not at all from other figures of comparison. And, the ancients seem to reason, if two terms of comparison are to be used within a single analysis, let them denote important distinctions of purpose and method, not variations of form. What the truly significant separable elements of comparison are may be left without final judgment. But one might hesitate to maintain that in this area ancient critical acumen has been superseded.

SELECT BIBLIOGRAPHY

Abbott, K. M., W. A. Oldfather, and H. V. Canter. *Index Verborum In Ciceronis Rhetorica*. Urbana: University of Illinois Press, 1964.

Adler, A. *Suidae Lexicon*. 5 vols. Leipzig: B. G. Teubner, 1928–1938.

Anderson, W. D. "Notes on the Simile in Homer and his Successors," *Classical Journal* 53 (1957) 81–87.

Arbusow, L. *Colores Rhetorici*. Göttingen: Vanderhoeck & Ruprecht, 1948.

Ast, D. F. *Lexicon Platonicum*. 3 vols., 2nd ed. Berlin: H. Barsdorf, 1908.

Atkins, J. W. H. *Literary Criticism in Antiquity*. 2 vols. Cambridge: Cambridge University Press, 1934.

Baldwin, C. S. *Ancient Rhetoric and Poetic*. New York: Macmillan, 1924.

Bardon, H. *Le Vocabulaire de la critique littéraire chez Sénèque le rhéteur*. Paris: Société d'édition "Les Belles-lettres," 1940.

Barwick, K. "Remmius Palaemon und die römische Ars Grammatica," *Philologus* supp. 15, pt. 2 (1922) 1–272.

Basore, J. W. *Seneca, Moral Essays*. 3 vols. Loeb Classical Library. Cambridge, Mass.: Harvard University Press, 1928–1935.

Bonitz, H. *Index Aristotelicus*, vol. V of *Aristotelis Opera*, ed. I. Bekker. Berlin: G. Reimer, 1870.

Bonnell, E. *Lexicon Quintilianeum*, vol. VI of G. L. Spalding, *M. Fabii Quintiliani* .... Leipzig: F. C. G. Vogelius, 1834.

Buchheit, V. *Untersuchungen zur Theorie des Genos Epideiktikon von Gorgias bis Aristoteles*. Munich: M. Hueber, 1960.

Butler, H. E. *The Institutio Oratoria of Quintilian*. 4 vols. Loeb Classical Library. London: William Heinemann, 1920–1922.

Caesar, J. "Zu Quintilian," *Philologus* 13 (1858) 756–759.

Calboli, G. *Cornificiana, 2: l'autore e la tendenza politica della Rhetorica ad Herennium*. Bologna: Accademia delle Scienze, 1965.

Caplan, H. [*Cicero*] *Ad C. Herennium de Ratione Dicendi* (*Rhetorica ad Herennium*). Loeb Classical Library. Cambridge, Mass.: Harvard University Press, 1954.

Clark, D. L. *Rhetoric and Poetry in the Renaissance*. New York: Russell & Russell, 1922.

Select Bibliography

Clark, D. L. *Rhetoric in Greco-Roman Education.* New York: Columbia University Press, 1957.

Clarke, M. L. *Rhetoric at Rome.* 2nd ed. London: L. Cohen & West, 1965.

Clausing, A. *Kritik und Exegese der homerischen Gleichnisse in Altertum.* Parchim: Freise, 1913.

Cohn, L. "Dionysius," no. 134, *RE* 5 (1903) cols. 977–983.

Cope, E. M. *An Introduction to Aristotle's Rhetoric.* London and Cambridge: Macmillan, 1867.

———— *The Rhetoric of Aristotle.* 3 vols., rev. ed. J. E. Sandys. Cambridge: Cambridge University Press, 1877.

Cousin, J. *Etudes sur Quintilien.* 2 vols. Paris: Boivin, 1936.

D'Alton, J. F. *Roman Literary Theory and Criticism.* London and New York: Longmans, Green, 1931.

Dodds, E. R. *Plato, Gorgias.* Oxford: Clarendon Press, 1959.

Douglas, A. E. "*Clausulae* in the *Rhetorica ad Herennium* as Evidence of its Date," *Classical Quarterly,* n.s. 10 (1960) 65–78.

Ernesti, J. *Lexicon Technologiae Graecorum Rhetoricae.* Leipzig: C. Fritsch, 1795.

Forster, E. S. *De Rhetorica ad Alexandrum,* vol. XI of *The Works of Aristotle Translated,* ed. W. D. Ross. Oxford: Clarendon Press, 1924.

Fraenkel, E. *Elementi Plautini in Plauto.* Florence: La Nuova Italia, 1960.

Fuhrmann, M. *Anaximenis Ars Rhetorica.* Leipzig: B. G. Teubner, 1966.

Goold, G. P. "A Greek Professorial Circle at Rome," *Transactions of the American Philological Association* 92 (1961) 168–192.

Grube, G. M. A. *A Greek Critic: Demetrius on Style.* Toronto: University of Toronto Press, 1961.

———— *The Greek and Roman Critics.* Toronto: University of Toronto Press, 1965.

Gummere, R. M. "De variis similitudinum generibus apud poetas Latinos ante aetatem Augusteam," unpub. diss. Harvard University, 1907.

———— *Seneca, Moral Epistles.* 3 vols. Loeb Classical Library. London: William Heinemann, 1917–1925.

Hackforth, R. *Plato's Phaedrus.* Cambridge: Cambridge University Press, 1952.

Haines, C. R. *Marcus Cornelius Fronto.* 2 vols. Loeb Classical Library. London: William Heinemann, 1919–1920.

Halm, C. *Rhetores Latini Minores.* Leipzig: B. G. Teubner, 1863.

Hendrickson, G. L., and H. M. Hubbell. *Cicero, Brutus and Orator.* Loeb Classical Library. Cambridge, Mass.: Harvard University Press, 1939.

Henn, T. R. *Longinus and English Criticism.* Cambridge: Cambridge University Press, 1934.

Select Bibliography

Herrick, M. T. "The Place of Rhetoric in Poetic Theory," *Quarterly Journal of Speech* 34 (1948) 1–22.

Hubbell, H. M. *The Rhetorica of Philodemus*. New Haven: Connecticut Academy of Arts and Sciences, 1920.

—— *Cicero, De Inventione, De Optimo Genere Oratorum, Topica*. Loeb Classical Library. Cambridge, Mass.: Harvard University Press, 1949.

Hudson, H. H. "Rhetoric and Poetry," *Quarterly Journal of Speech* 10 (1924) 143–154.

Jebb, R. C. *The Rhetoric of Aristotle*, ed. J. E. Sandys. Cambridge: Cambridge University Press, 1909.

Jowett, B. *The Dialogues of Plato*. 5 vols., 3rd rev. ed. Oxford: Oxford University Press, 1892.

Kennedy, G. A. *The Art of Persuasion in Greece*. Princeton: Princeton University Press, 1963.

Kroll, W. "Rhetorik," *RE* supp. bd. 7 (1940) cols. 1039–1138.

Lausberg, H. *Elemente der literarischen Rhetorik*. Munich: M. Hueber, 1949.

Leeman, A. D. *Orationis Ratio: The Stylistic Theories and Practice of the Roman Orators, Historians, and Philosophers*. 2 vols. Amsterdam: A. Hakkert, 1963,

McCall, M. "Aristotle, *Rhetoric* III.4.1407a15 and 11.1413a5," *Rheinisches Museum für Philologie* 111 (1968) 159–165.

—— "Cicero, *de Oratore* 3.39.157," *American Journal of Philology* 90 (1969) 215–219.

Matthes, D. *Hermagoras Fragmenta*. Leipzig: B. G. Teubner, 1962.

Merguet, H. *Lexikon zu den philosophischen Schriften Cicero's*. 3 vols., reprint of the Jena ed. of 1887–1894. Hildesheim: Georg Olms, 1961.

Monaco, G. "Un particolare tipo di facezia nel *de Oratore*," *Atti del 9 Congresso Internazionale di Studi Ciceroniani* (Rome 1961) I 61–64.

Naber, S. A. *M. Cornelii Frontonis et M. Aurelii Imperatoris Epistulae*. Leipzig: B. G. Teubner, 1867.

Nestle, W. "Polos," no. 3, *RE* 21 (1952) cols. 1424–1425.

Norden, E. *Die antike Kunstprosa*. 2 vols., 2nd ed. Leipzig: B. G. Teubner, 1909.

North, H. "The Use of Poetry in the Training of the Ancient Orator," *Traditio* 8 (1952) 1–33.

Oldfather, W. A., H. V. Canter, and K. M. Abbott. *Index Verborum Ciceronis Epistularum*. Urbana: University of Illinois Press, 1938.

Organ, T. W. *An Index to Aristotle*. Princeton: Princeton University Press. 1949.

Pease, A. S. *M. Tulli Ciceronis De Natura Deorum*. 2 vols. Cambridge, Mass.: Harvard University Press, 1958.

Philippson, R. "Philodemos," no. 5, *RE* 19 (1938) cols. 2442–2482.

Pickard-Cambridge, W. A. *Topica*, vol. I of *The Works of Aristotle Translated*, ed. W. D. Ross. Oxford: Clarendon Press, 1928.

Pittet, A. *Vocabulaire philosophique de Sénèque*. Paris: Société d'édition "Les Belles-lettres," 1937.

Powell, J. E. *A Lexicon to Herodotus*. Cambridge: Cambridge University Press, 1938.

Preuss, S. *Index Demosthenicus*. Leipzig: B. G. Teubner, 1892.

——— *Index Isocrateus*. Leipzig: B. G. Teubner, 1904.

——— *Index Aeschineus*. Leipzig: B. G. Teubner, 1926.

Rackham, H. *Cicero, De Finibus Bonorum et Malorum*. Loeb Classical Library. London: William Heinemann, 1914.

——— *Cicero, De Natura Deorum, Academica*. Loeb Classical Library. London: William Heinemann, 1933.

——— *Cicero, De Oratore Book III, De Fato, Paradoxa Stoicorum, De Partitione Oratoria*. Loeb Classical Library. Cambridge, Mass.: Harvard University Press, 1949.

Radermacher, L. *Demetrii Phalerei qui dicitur De Elocutione libellus*. Leipzig: B. G. Teubner, 1901.

——— *M. Fabii Quintiliani Institutionis Oratoriae Libri XII*. 2 vols., 2nd ed. Addn. and corr. V. Buchheit. Leipzig: B. G. Teubner, 1959.

——— *Artium Scriptores*, vol. 227.3 of Osterreichische Akademie der Wissenschaften, Philosophisch-historische Klasse. Vienna: Rudolf M. Rohrer, 1951.

Roberts, W. Rhys. *Dionysius of Halicarnassus, The Three Literary Letters*. Cambridge: Cambridge University Press, 1901.

——— *Demetrius On Style*. Cambridge: Cambridge University Press, 1902.

——— *Longinus On the Sublime*. Cambridge: Cambridge University Press, 1907.

——— *Dionysius of Halicarnassus On Literary Composition*. London: Macmillan, 1910.

——— *Rhetorica*, vol. XI of *The Works of Aristotle Translated*, ed. W. D. Ross. Oxford: Clarendon Press, 1924.

——— *Greek Rhetoric and Literary Criticism*. New York: Longmans, Green, 1928.

Russell, D. A. *"Longinus" On the Sublime*. Oxford: Clarendon Press, 1964.

Rutherford, W. G. *Scholia Aristophanica*. 3 vols. London and New York: Macmillan, 1896–1905.

Schenkeveld, D. M. *Studies in Demetrius On Style*. Amsterdam: Hakkert, 1964.

Schlunk, R. "Vergil and the Homeric Scholia," *American Journal of Philology* 88 (1967) 33–45.

Simeterre, R. "La chronologie des oeuvres de Platon," *Revue des études grecques* 58 (1945) 146–162.

Solmsen, F. "Theodoros," no. 38, *RE* 5A (1934) cols. 1839–1847.

—— "The Aristotelian Tradition in Ancient Rhetoric," *American Journal of Philology* 62 (1941) 35–50, 169–190.

Spalding, G. L. M. *Fabii Quintiliani De Institutione Oratoria Libri Duodecim.* 6 vols. Leipzig: S. L. Crusius and F. C. G. Vogelius, 1798–1834.

Spengel, L. Συναγωγὴ τεχνῶν *sive Artium Scriptores.* Stuttgart: J. G. Cotta, 1828.

—— *Aristotelis Ars Rhetorica.* 2 vols. Leipzig: B. G. Teubner, 1867.

—— *Rhetores Graeci.* 3 vols. Leipzig: B. G. Teubner, 1853–1856.

Spengel, L., and C. Hammer. *Rhetores Graeci.* Leipzig: B. G. Teubner, 1894.

Stanford, W. B. *Greek Metaphor.* Oxford: Basil Blackwell, 1936.

Stegemann, W. "Theramenes," no. 2, *RE* 5A (1934) col. 2320.

Steyns, D. *Etude sur les metaphores et les comparisons dans les oeuvres en prose de Sénèque le Philosophe.* Gand: J. Vuylsteke, 1907.

Sturz, F. W. *Lexicon Xenophonteum.* 4 vols. Leipzig: Libraria Gleditschia, 1801–1804.

Sudhaus, S. *Philodemi Volumina Rhetorica.* 2 vols. and supp. Leipzig: B. G. Teubner, 1892–1896.

Süss, W. "Theramenes der Rhetor und Verwandtes," *Rheinisches Museum für Philologie* 66 (1911) 183–189.

Sutton, E. W., and H. Rackham. *Cicero, De Oratore,* Books I and II. Loeb Classical Library. Cambridge, Mass.: Harvard University Press, 1942.

Teichert, P. *De Fontibus Quintiliani Rhetoricis.* Brunsberg: J. A. Wichert, 1884.

Thompson, W. H. *The Phaedrus of Plato.* London: Whittaker, 1868.

Todd, O. J. *Index Aristophaneus.* Cambridge, Mass.: Harvard University Press, 1932.

Uhlig, G. *Dionysii Thracis Ars Grammatica.* Leipzig: B. G. Teubner, 1883.

Van Den Hout, M. P. J. *M. Cornelii Frontonis Epistulae.* Leiden: E. J. Brill, 1954.

Van Hook, L. *The Metaphorical Terminology of Greek Rhetoric and Literary Criticism.* Chicago: University of Chicago Press, 1905.

Volkmann, R. *Die Rhetorik der Griechen und Römer,* 2nd rev. ed. Leipzig: B. G. Teubner, 1885.

Vooijs, C. J., and D. A. Van Krevelen. *Lexicon Philodemeum.* 2 vols. Purmerend: J. Muusses, and Amsterdam: N. V. Swets, 1934–1941.

Watson, J. S. *Quintilian's Institutes of Oratory.* 2 vols. London: Henry G. Bohn, 1856.

—— *Cicero on Oratory and Orators.* New York: Harper, 1860.

Wehrli, F. "Der erhabene und der schlichte Stil in der poetisch-rhetorischen Theorie der Antike," *Phyllobolia für Peter Von der Mühll*. Basel: B. Schwabe, 1946. Pages 9–34.

Wendel, C. "Tryphon," no. 25, *RE* 7A (1939) cols. 726–744.

Wilkins, A. S. *M. Tulli Ciceronis De Oratore Libri III*. 3 vols. Oxford: Clarendon Press, 1879–1892.

Wyttenbach, D. *Lexicon Plutarcheum*. 2 vols. Leipzig: Libraria Kuehniana, 1843.

INDEX

Where entries under terms of comparison are divided into two groups, the second group lists occurrences in which the terms do not necessarily imply strict "comparison," but "similarity," or "likeness," for example.

Index